"Based upon my interactions with Jim Gordon, author Joel Selvin accurately portrays Jim's genius as well as his development into the living hell he gradually occupied. Jim was always soft-spoken, and the first one to arrive at a session. His drums spoke for him, and he had a subtle but commanding presence. Years later, when he was scheduled for a session where I was producing a commercial, he arrived forty-five minutes late, was surly, and uninvolved. Someone else had taken over the Jim we knew and loved, and that was the last time I saw him."

—MARK LINDSAY,
Paul Revere & The Raiders

"I loved Jim Gordon like a brother and am grateful for Joel Selvin's unstinting notice of Gordon's luminescence, which adds great leavening to this heartbreaking work of staggering genius."

—VAN DYKE PARKS

"Selvin delivers a sensitive account of the life and legacy of Derek and the Dominos drummer Jim Gordon, who suffered from schizophrenia . . . [and was] once deemed the 'greatest drummer' in rock and roll by Eric Clapton and Ringo Starr. . . . Without downplaying the gruesome details of Gordon's crime, Selvin gracefully portrays the musician as 'more than his disease.' . . . This affecting account sheds new light on one of rock's most complicated figures."

—PUBLISHERS WEEKLY

"Joel Selvin is one of the Big Beasts of American music writing. He presents Jim Gordon's complex, tragic story fully in the round, as only he can. Biography of the Year!"

—MICK WALL,
author of *Life in the Fast Lane*
and *When Giants Walked the Earth*

ALSO BY JOEL SELVIN

Altamont: The Rolling Stones, the Hells Angels, and the Inside Story of Rock's Darkest Day

Fare Thee Well: The Final Chapter of the Grateful Dead's Long, Strange Trip

Here Comes the Night: The Dark Soul of Bert Berns and the Dirty Business of Rhythm and Blues

Hollywood Eden: Electric Guitars, Fast Cars, and the Myth of the California Paradise

Monterey Pop, photos by Jim Marshall

Peppermint Twist: The Mob, the Music, and the Most Famous Dance Club of the '60s

Red: My Uncensored Life in Rock by Sammy Hagar with Joel Selvin

Ricky Nelson: Idol for a Generation

Rust in Peace: The Inside Story of the Megadeth Masterpiece by Dave Mustaine with Joel Selvin

Sing to Me: My Story of Making Music, Finding Magic, and Searching for Who's Next by L.A. Reid and Joel Selvin

Sly & the Family Stone: An Oral History

Smartass: The Music Journalism of Joel Selvin (California Rock & Roll)

Summer of Love: The Inside Story of LSD, Rock & Roll, Free Love and High Times in the Wild West

Treasures of the Hard Rock Cafe: The Official Guide to the Hard Rock Cafe Memorabilia Collection by Joel Selvin and Paul Grushkin

Wear Your Dreams: My Life in Tattoos by Ed Hardy with Joel Selvin

DRUMS&
DEMONS

THE TRAGIC JOURNEY
OF JIM GORDON

JOEL SELVIN

**DIVERSION
BOOKS**

Diversion Books
A division of Diversion Publishing Corp.
www.diversionbooks.com

For more information, email info@diversionbooks.com

First Diversion Books Edition: February 2024
Hardcover ISBN: 978-1-6357-6899-2
e-ISBN: 978-1-6357-6979-1

Book design by Aubrey Khan, Neuwirth & Associates, Inc.
Cover design by Jonathan Sainsbury

Printed in the United States of America
1   2   3   4   5   6   7   8   9   10

Diversion books are available at special discounts for bulk purchases in the US by corporations, institutions, and other organizations. For more information, please contact admin@diversionbooks.com

TO SCOTT MATHEWS

Friends (and drummers) don't come better

One need not be a Chamber—to be Haunted—
One need not be a House—
The Brain has Corridors—surpassing
Material Place—

—EMILY DICKINSON

CONTENTS

PART ONE

PART TWO

PART ONE

I.
BLUE MONKEYS
AND THE BIG FILL

SANTA MONICA, 1983

J im Gordon looked nothing like the swashbuckling, rock star drummer who laid the mighty backbeat behind Eric Clapton in Derek and the Dominos. He sported an additional forty or fifty pounds now. His curly blond locks had been cut short and had lost their golden luster. His piercing blue cat eyes had dulled, no longer sparkling. His face was pasty and puffy. Few people in the desultory Monday night crowd knew Jim's distinguished background.

They would have been astonished to learn that the tall, pudgy drummer squeezed behind his kit on the tiny stage had walked with kings.

Gordon had not been playing music for several years when he fell in with the fellows who called themselves the Blue Monkeys. They were aspiring young musicians, and they knew who Gordon was when he asked to sit in with the band at some unlikely weeknight gig at a Pico Boulevard club. They were beyond astonished when he offered to take the place of the band's regular drummer, who was quitting.

Their weekly date was Monday night at O'Mahony's, an Irish bar on Main Street in Santa Monica, a few blocks from the Pacific Ocean. Opened in 1941 by a professional wrestler named Danno O'Mahony—known as the Irish Whip—who died in a 1950 car crash in his native Ireland, the bar long outlived O'Mahony. Cheap beer, free pool, live music every night, and no cover. A horseshoe bar served the room; grouchy, older Johnny tending bar on one side and a more genial Irish gal named Gracie on the other. The pool tables were on the right side of the room and the small stage on the left with about a dozen tables in front. On a good night, as many as forty or fifty people crowded in to hear the music.

As he bounced in and out of mental hospitals, struggling with demons and fighting for his life, Jim had spent endless days and nights holed up in his North Hollywood apartment, unable to venture out farther than the neighborhood liquor store. He was in the grip of terrifying madness. His bandmates knew nothing of his condition. They knew his professional reputation. They heard his playing. That was all they needed to know. They thought he was unusually quiet and reserved, and though some saw him gulping down vodka tonics between sets or snorting a little bit of cocaine on the side, nobody suspected anything was out of order with Jim.

He coiled himself behind a small, regulation, four-piece drum kit on a stage so crowded that bassist Roly Salley had to thread the neck of his bass between Jim's cymbal stands. Night after night, Roly would stand over Jim's drums while he played and lose himself in Jim's mastery of his kit. He never bashed his drums. In fact, he rarely lifted his arms. Everything was in the wrist, brain-to-wrist direct. He never raised the volume, but his playing would grow wider and lift the whole band. He could orchestrate the sound from the drum stool. In the center of his snare, his sticks left marks in a circle no bigger than a quarter.

Pete Anderson played guitar, sang, and told bad jokes. He was from Detroit, but he had been kicking around Los Angeles for ten years, scuffling, trying to make something happen. Bassist Roly Salley came to town four years earlier from Woodstock, New York, where he had played with old folkies like Happy and Artie Traum. Keyboardist John Herron was a prickly character and accomplished musician who had been on the scene since his brief stint with the Electric Prunes almost fifteen years before. He lived off a trust fund and never worked much, although he always had good gear, nice clothes, and a house in the Valley. The band did raucous old rock 'n' roll—Little Richard, Fats Domino, New Orleans R&B—nothing too trendy or fancy. When Jim slipped behind the drum kit, they began to take themselves more seriously.

Jim was all business. He showed up for work with his drums in the back of his car. His kit was nothing special; an ordinary four-piece Camco set. He came alone, no girlfriends. He wore flannel shirts, jeans, and tennis shoes and played four sets a night for $30. Triple-scale session dates were long in the past. On breaks, he was remote, almost standoffish. He didn't talk about the past. But he elevated everybody's chops in the band. His timekeeping was magical and he never, ever overplayed. He was punctual for gigs and rehearsals, pitched in loading equipment, acted like another band member. He didn't display any signs of the cocktails that he furtively slurped down between sets until the end of the night when sometimes his eyes showed the fatigue. His playing never faltered.

His bandmates didn't know about the residential treatment programs, the pharmaceutical carpet-bombing, his desperate battle for control of his life, and his tenuous grip on reality. They hadn't heard any of the rumors floating around Hollywood from years before. Nobody suspected anything. Jim put on a mask and went to work. He needed the music. It was not only what he had done all his life. It was what it did for him. With sticks in his hands, feet on the pedals, the drums transported Jim somewhere he was safe and secure, somewhere the demons couldn't follow.

There were occasional odd moments the other guys couldn't understand, like the night some of them went to dinner after rehearsing at John Herron's house in Van Nuys. Unlike the struggling musicians at the table with him, Jim felt comfortable ordering a nice, juicy steak for himself. When it arrived, he cut a bite and raised it to his mouth on the fork, only to hold it there, his hand wavering, before throwing the fork down on the plate. He hurriedly stood, tossed a twenty-dollar bill on the table, blurting out "I've got to go." He rushed out of the restaurant, leaving his bandmates slack-jawed and speechless, wondering what had just happened.

The Blue Monkeys began to attract a modest following at O'Mahony's; not the in-crowd or hip scene—Santa Monica was a million miles from Hollywood—but a nice neighborhood bunch that showed up week after week. They were beach bums and English expats, a heavy beer-drinking crew, and not a lot of pretty girls: a serious dive bar crowd that spilled out on the sidewalk smoking and drinking in the warm Southern California nights.

The Monkeys started to add original material to their bar band covers. Nobody in the band was a gifted writer. Herron had a few original songs and picked up "She Loves My Car" from his pal, songwriter Moon Martin. A songwriter named Michael Smotherman, who had written some songs Glen Campbell recorded, gave them a few tunes, including "Baby Talkin'," which Roly sang. Pete did the old Otis Clay soul song "Tryin' to Live My Life Without You."

They had no management. There was no business strategy or career direction. Pete made the phone calls and handled the details. They were serious about playing music, learning their instruments, practicing, and rehearsing, but they were not driven by professional ambition. Having Jim in the band had only made them concentrate on honing their skills even more. Still, they went into The Annex Studios in Hollywood, the former Radio Recorders where Elvis cut "Jailhouse Rock," and knocked out a four-song demo live in the studio, no overdubs. It wasn't lost on Pete and Roly that they were tracking with Jim Gordon.

The music hardly challenged Jim. His playing was relaxed, restrained, unobtrusively embedded in the band. It wasn't like the demanding symphonic work he did with Frank Zappa, or the poly-rhythmic New Orleans grooves he laid down for Johnny Rivers, or the high drama of Beach Boys records, let alone the monumental thunder of George Harrison or Derek and the Dominos sessions. It was more like the work that teenage Jim did with the Everly Brothers: Set the groove and hold it, keeping decorations to a min-imum. Drive the band, shape the sound, pump the pulse. It was not simply less is more, but something more zen—the exact right stroke at the exact right time. That was Jim's gift. He heard the music in the drums.

The drums anchored Jim's world. The rackety report resounding through his body, the fire bell clanging of the cymbals, the hypnotic, rhythmic entrainment of the all-powerful groove—they silenced his unquiet mind, focusing his entire being on driving the big beat, sub-merging him in the world the rhythm opened. The drums had been at the center of his life since he was a child, and through the drums Jim could speak freely without interference from the chatter inside his head. He knew the many languages of the drum, and he spoke them all fluently. When he was playing, he was on his own, fully alive, centered, and assured. It was a different story when he stopped playing.

Nobody knew the dread of the hours when he was not playing drums. He had few friends. He stayed home alone and spent long, lonely times in his two-bedroom apartment drinking and playing piano into the endless night. For Jim to take the bandstand again and sit behind his drum kit was a miraculous act of rebellion against powerful evil forces that were, quite literally, driving him insane. Every day was a battle.

He didn't like taking medication. He preferred to self-medicate. He liked to eat, but he would be forced to starve himself for days. There were no more recording sessions. His phone had stopped ringing a long time before. But he *had* to play drums. To Jim, the drums were the breath of life. They were his only chance.

Pete Anderson wrangled Jim to play a casual at Knott's Berry Farm and was quietly astonished when they heard a Merle Haggard record and Jim mentioned that was him playing the drums. Pete really had no idea how deep Jim's career went. He put together Jim, Roly, and John Herron to back a singer-songwriter named Teresa Tate on her showcase. There was a little money involved, and Jim went along to help the other guys make a couple bucks. The music was nothing special, something Jim could have handled in his sleep, but he seemed especially distracted on this afternoon, on the edge of agitated. The band took a break and Jim made Pete go out in the front yard to talk. Now fully worked up, Jim was huffing and puffing through his nose, his cheeks flaring.

"I've got to go see my doctor," he told Pete breathlessly. "Right now."

Pete knew nothing about any doctor. Before he could unshrug his shoulders, Jim was gone. In a flash. He disappeared in an instant.

That was the last time they laid eyes on him. A few weeks later, he was in jail.

■   ■   ■

Everybody knows how this story ends.

He was rock's greatest drummer. Nobody could play like Jim Gordon. Until a wave of obituaries followed his March 2023 death, he had been a forgotten figure, his contributions smothered by the dark cloud of his unspeakable deed. This one grotesque act has come to define his life and bury his legitimate place in rock history. The genius drummer from San Fernando Valley walked in the golden California sunshine, headed into glory, then got lost in the shadows and never found his way out.

No less expert observers than Ringo Starr and Eric Clapton agreed that Jim was the greatest drummer in rock. They both played with him enough to know. Clapton was fond of what he called "the big fill"—Jim's brilliant ability to decorate the beat with mathematically precise clatter going off like detonating fireworks. But that is not what most people remember.

Even Keith Richards, someone you might think would be a little more sensitive to the vagaries of mental illness, couldn't resist citing the lurid event in his autobiography, recalling having met Jim when he played with the Everly Brothers and the young Rolling Stones were opening the show on their first tour of England ("Eventually he hacked his mother to death in a schizophrenic haze . . .").

No drummer had a greater career than Jim Gordon, who started as a teenage prodigy with rock and roll immortals the Everly Brothers and proceeded to play on many of the best records of the day during his time as a Hollywood session player. That's Jim on the Beach Boys' *Good Vibrations,* possibly the greatest pop record ever made. With Derek and the Dominos, Jim laid down the intricate, incredibly nuanced underpinnings to one of classic rock's defining works, "Layla," a song for which he shares cowriting credit with Eric Clapton.

Drums are, by nature, an instrument of accompaniment, and drummers are rarely heroes (was poor Ringo anyone's favorite Beatle?). They sit at the back of the stage out of the limelight, keeping the beat and driving the rhythm. The great drummers are collaborators, artisans building the foundation that other musicians elaborate. They are the engine room of the rock band. Without the drums, it wouldn't be rock and roll.

When Jim played on a record, he made his presence felt. Whether it was driving home the choruses of Carly Simon's "You're So Vain" or tying together the different passages on Mike Post's "The Rockford Files" TV theme, wrapping around the supple acoustic interplay on Gordon Lightfoot's "Sundown," or pounding out the cascading rolls that drove John Lennon's "Power to the People," Jim always brought something extra to his music, some ineffable element that was the gift of his imagination. As scientific and surgical as he could be, Jim also filled his playing with surprising, luminous bursts of creativity that were his alone.

The details of his brilliance may not be obvious to many music fans, but drummers all know about Jim. He rewrote the book of drums, expanded the vocabulary, created a personal approach to the instrument that has since been adopted by many. Drummers understand how deeply instinctual his playing was. Jim never simply kept time; he drove his drums into the heart of the music. As technically accomplished as he was, his playing was touched by some nearly supernatural force. One of his colleagues said that Jim Gordon put the roll in rock and roll. Whatever, drumming was never the same after the other drummers heard Jim. His intuitive style was so obvious and attractive, he was almost impossible not to copy. "I had to learn to play like Jim in order to *not* play like Jim," drummer Jim Keltner told me.

Of course, the same electrochemical system in his brain that gave him this extraordinary gift also made him ill. The very thing that makes you rich makes you poor.

Our society turns a blind eye on mental illness, but it is among us every day. Schizophrenia is ridiculously common; the disease affects one in one hundred of the general population. By comparison, multiple sclerosis is one in ten thousand. But these aren't Jerry's Kids. There are no celebrity spokesmen and no fundraising telethons. Schizophrenics tend not to represent themselves well. The syndrome is shrouded in mystery. Nobody knows what causes it—the current thinking leans toward genetic disposition—and only half of the diagnosed schizophrenics respond to treatment at all. Still, on the other end of the spectrum, there are many schizophrenics who lead quiet, productive lives on the graveyard shift sorting mail at the post office or working in bakeries.

Mostly, they are viewed as a burden to society, given the most minimal treatment possible and sent out to deal with their confusing, conflicted lives on their own. The streets of our cities are littered with cases. Jim, who was in the fortunate position of being able to afford the best care available, experienced little benefit from treatment.

The auditory hallucinations that Jim suffered are among the most common symptoms, although Jim's symptoms were severe and extreme, which helps account for why medical professionals were so hard pressed to diagnose him. His excessive drug and alcohol use further complicated his situation, but did not cause his schizophrenia. Few schizophrenics are violent toward others (although it is not uncommon to hurt themselves to quell the voices). Even fewer can manage to navigate a profession as demanding as the one Jim followed. They are largely lost souls, trapped in a world they can't escape, unable to march in step with the rest of society through no fault of their own.

Of course, matricide is one of the most reviled crimes in human history, an act that hearkens back to ancient Greek drama. It horrifies all of humankind who hold sacred the love of a mother. Something deep in all of us recoils in primal horror at the deed. It is the unthinkable made real.

But Jim Gordon was more than his disease, even though his life and disease were intertwined all along his path. The world of rhythm that Jim inhabited held special meaning to him. When he went there, he was safe. He was somewhere that made sense to him, working with something he could master. The world outside rhythm—what we glibly call the "real world"—was more complex and vexing. Jim knew the shimmering mystery and transformative power of the drums.

But Jim had an unnatural advantage over other drummers. Like Oskar Matzerath, the unreliable narrator from the German novel *The Tin Drum* by Günther Grass, who pounds his drum to shut out the madness that surrounds him, Jim sought sanctuary in the drums. Other people played the drums; Jim lived the drums.

After his crime, Jim instantly became a pariah. Nobody visited him in jail. Nobody came to his trial. His traumatized daughter cut off all communication. All around him, eyes averted. In a music community incredibly forgiving of and accommodating to drug casualties and alcoholics, these people had no idea what to do with someone who was genuinely crazy. Nobody looked beyond the deadly assault to the years of torment and intense struggles fighting the disease. The whole thing was too traumatic, even for the casual observer. Jim simply went away and nobody looked back.

Many famous musicians heard voices. Brian Wilson of the Beach Boys would have been institutionalized if he hadn't been wealthy. The brilliant Skip Spence of Moby Grape died in a mental hospital. British blues visionary Peter Green of Fleetwood Mac, psychedelic avatar Syd Barrett of Pink Floyd—life didn't turn out well for either of them. Not only rock musicians suffer. Hans Rott, a nineteenth-century Austrian composer much admired by Gustav Mahler, died in an asylum suffering from persecutory visions. He pulled a revolver on a fellow traveler, claiming that the train they were riding had been filled with dynamite by Brahms, and away he went.

The voices may be imaginary, but the pain these people felt was as real as a gunshot wound.

When Jim died on March 13, 2023, at age seventy-seven in the California Medical Facility in Vacaville, California, he had served thirty-nine years in prison. Half a life before, he had been thirty-eight years old when he was arrested for killing his mother. He never set foot again out of jail. His professional musical career lasted only fifteen years, but he left his indelible mark on dozens of records that will last lifetimes.

Frank Zappa knew Jim. He played on some of Zappa's most demanding, complex music, attacking the dense, intricate charts with an almost inhuman ease. Zappa spoke about Jim in a 1990 interview.

"If a mental illness strikes somebody and they wind up doing something like this, there's chemistry involved and that kind of gets lost in the shuffle in a lot of these situations," he said. "I'm not defending anybody who decides to go out and commit a murder, but if a chemical reaction in the human brain can cause such a thing to happen, it could happen to anybody."

II.
RADIO KING

CHICAGO, 1927

T ommy Rockwell may have been tone deaf, but he knew what sold records. He had served as sales manager in San Francisco for OKeh Records before transferring to Chicago, where he worked as branch manager before taking over the duties of recording director in early 1927. He had already supervised successful recordings by trumpeter Louis Armstrong and his Hot Seven and many others. As he prepared for the December 6 session with Kansas City disc jockey Red McKenzie and young Chicago banjo player Eddie Condon with a bunch of his South Side jazz associates, Rockwell watched in shock and quiet horror at the two young fellows dragging a giant drum set into the studio.

The drafty, barnlike building at Washington and Wells Streets that housed the OKeh studio kept the cold out, but little more. The good-looking eighteen-year-old drummer with the silken shock of black hair had his hands full of drums and cymbals. His lanky buddy, also laden down with equipment, was helping him set up his kit. With twenty-two-year-old Condon the oldest member of the band, Rockwell realized these kids didn't know what they were doing. "What do you think you're going to do with those?" he asked the drummer, a young man named Gene Krupa.

"Play them," said Krupa.

"You can't do that," said Rockwell. "You'll ruin our equipment. All we ever use on records is snare drums and cymbals."

The electrical microphone was a recent technological advancement in recording, and musicians were still adapting to the sensitive equipment. Krupa and his friend Milton Mesirow, who went by Mezz Mezzrow, had spent many hours modifying his drum kit. To tune the Chinese tom-tom with its head tacked down, they used an icepick. They had conducted endless experiments on drumming techniques—the difference between starting a roll with the right hand or the left, getting cymbals pitched in certain keys to ring in tune, adjusting the cowbell and woodblocks just right—and they found the sound they wanted in the kit they devised.

Krupa was crushed. Rockwell was leery. He was convinced the booming bass drum would knock the needle out of the wax and ruin the recording. The other musicians prevailed on Rockwell to at least let them try, and he reluctantly agreed. The bass drum did need to be muffled and, after throwing the cover over the drum proved insufficient, the musicians started piling their overcoats on top until the drum kit looked like Admiral Byrd at the South Pole. The cymbals weren't loud enough, so Mezz held them closer to the microphone and Krupa leaned over his drums to hit them.

Rockwell liked what he heard. He invited the boys back to finish recording the next week. Krupa asked about the drums. "Didn't bother the equipment at all," said Rockwell. "I think we may have something here."

This was the big bang of the big beat. The session would change American music for the rest of the century and into the future. In the tom-tom ripples that drove the final chorus, Krupa forecast not only the entire history of swing, but the robust sound of rhythm and blues and the invention of rock and roll. These young, white, rebel musicians were disciples of subversive black New Orleans jazz, and their record would introduce one of the music's first great wrinkles, Chicago-style jazz. When the record was released, the thunderous drum sound rocked the jazz world and teenage Krupa vaulted to the forefront of jazz drummers. He would become the first star of the instrument.

Drums are as old as time. Although the first drums were probably little more than a hollow tree trunk struck with a stick, man-made drums likely entered the picture around 6000 BC in the Paleolithic Era. There are representations of membrane-headed drums in Assyrian, Egyptian, Persian, and Indian art from as far back as these things go. The Romans and Greeks shook the ancestor of tambourines. But in twentieth-century America, drums took fresh shape in the modern day. In the can-do industrial spirit of the New World, Chicago drum salesman William F. Ludwig invented the first effective bass drum pedal before World War I, a breakthrough in drum design that led to the development of something that came to be called the contraption drum set—a kitchen-sink collection of drums, cymbals, bells, claxons, ratchets, wood blocks, and whistles, often held on a tray—instantly adopted by vaudeville pit band musicians. The hi-hat entered the hardware shortly after the war, although initially it was a low-hat, only a few inches off the floor; it wasn't until the late twenties that manufacturers raised the cymbals to striking distance. The name *contraption* was soon shortened to "trap set." This product of Yankee ingenuity took man's most primal musical instrument firmly into the great American century.

More than simply the first famous drummer, Krupa, who presided over the inauguration of the swing era from the drum stool in the Benny Goodman band during the famed August 1935 engagement at the Palomar Ballroom in Los Angeles, took a direct hand in designing the modern drum set. He stripped the kit down to essentials—snare, tom-tom, bass drum, hi-hat, cymbals. After the ancient Turkish cymbal manufacturers, Zildjian, opened an American factory in Quincy, Massachusetts, in 1929, Krupa went to work with Avedis Zildjian III, the male heir in the Zildjian family line who received the secret recipe for the special blend of metals the company had used since 1623, handed down father-to-son for generations. Krupa helped design the new American cymbal—thinner, larger, flatter, with a more pronounced bell.

Krupa also signed an all-important endorsement deal with the Slingerland Drum Company and developed the Radio King, which took over as the standard drum kit. Krupa insisted on tunable tom-toms with adjustable heads on top and bottom. Cymbals were mounted on the bass drum rims. He advised the cymbal makers to create splash, crash, and ride cymbals. With that equipment, he powered the swing era itself to a stunning pinnacle with his epic drum solo on "Sing, Sing, Sing" in the 1939 Carnegie Hall concert by Goodman. Gene Krupa brought the drums into the modern world.

Of course, drums beat rhythm, which is the biological base of life—neurons firing billions of times per minute. As Grateful Dead drummer Mickey Hart is fond of saying, we live in a vibratory universe. Through the ages, drums have been called upon to play roles in rituals, rites, and all kinds of spiritual exercises. A lot of the history of drums involved the military and the call to arms. In tribal cultures, drums were used for communication. They can induce trances or make people dance or march in time. They have been thought to ward off evil spirits. The drum can tap the inner being deeper and more directly than any other instrument. The mystical properties loom over drums every time someone puts a stick to skin. To strike a drum is to shake hands with the ancestors.

Incredible drums come from every culture. The African talking drum varies pitch by stretching leather thongs strung from the drumhead. The *berimbau* is a Brazilian device shaped like a bow attached to a gourd that is held against the chest for resonance. Some Japanese *taiko* drums measure more than six feet across. Voodoo rites are conducted by the bata drums. The Incas of Peru were said to celebrate victories in battle by skinning dead enemies, inflating their empty bodies, and beating on the stomach with a stick. Drums come from everywhere and serve many purposes. But today around the world, from dance bands in Singapore to Latin jazz in Havana, the standard drum set is some variation on the model designed by Gene Krupa in the thirties. One world / one drum.

Keep in mind the shaman used the drum to induce a kind of hypnotic state, to put himself—or others—in a trance, to enter a different consciousness. The shaman knew the drum not as an instrument of communication, but as a vehicle for transformation and a beacon for his out-of-body journey to guide him home. To play the drums is to know the mysterious, intoxicating realm of rhythm, the sweeping, overwhelming sensation of the groove. If you see drums as vehicles, there is no end to the places they can take you.

This twentieth-century American iteration of the ancient drums speaks of the hurly-burly tempo of the era and the sense of limitless possibilities in the country after the turn of the century—a deeply, uniquely American instrument. While classical composers had judiciously, often dramatically, employed timpani and more specific symphonic percussion instruments—think of the side drum in Ravel's *Boléro*—the trap set made every sole drummer a whole percussion corps. The bing-bang-boom captured the cacophony of a rapidly growing country. The conglomeration of clatter suited the times and the mood of the ragtime nation. The development of the set over the early years was erratic, haphazard until Krupa streamlined the vision and turned on the power of drumming virtuosity, taking the kit and showing what could be done with it. With his matinee-idol good looks, flashy drumming style, and showman's flair, Krupa made his case persuasively.

The mastery of the four-piece drum kit slowly evolved, as drummers developed the vocabulary and established the parameters, whether it was Broadway pit orchestras or small combo jazz bands. Every drummer adjusted the set to his own preferences and then learned to speak the language. The jazz world produced an array of brilliant stylists who used the drum set in a rainbow of previously unimagined ways. They switched cymbal sizes, added more drums, different sizes, different hardware, but there was no escaping comparisons to Krupa. His shadow loomed over the drums for a generation.

As drummers grew in proficiency and experience, they began to expand the base of knowledge from which they operated. These musicians and their drums powered a historic explosion of musical creativity, starting with the world of jazz and eventually spreading across the full musical panorama and, ultimately, giving birth to the biggest beat of them all, rock and roll. Bill Haley & His Comets' 1955 number one hit, "(We're Gonna) Rock Around the Clock," was truly the rim shot heard 'round the world.

While the great jazz drummers who came after him were still compared to Krupa, the art of the trap set would be passed along to a younger generation, who would take the drums beyond Krupa.

It would be in their hands—or the sticks in their hands—to define and refine the instrument, to expand the limited and crude vocabulary that had been established, to not only elevate the instrument in the role of art but drive a worldwide revolution in how music should sound. These young drummers had not yet been born when Benny Goodman played Carnegie Hall, but they would be soon.

III.
THE VALLEY

There were so many dirt roads in the San Fernando Valley in the fifties that every time it rained the gutters filled with mud. The Valley was only beginning to wake up as a bedroom community for Hollywood and beyond. The lush, tree-covered hills of Sherman Oaks were crisscrossed by narrow, curving streets dotted with ranch-style houses sporting their pleasant front yards and closely cropped lawns—modest homes for returning veterans on the GI Bill. The neighborhood teemed with families. Farms still surrounded the area, which was also horse country. Hollywood stars like Clark Gable kept hideaway ranches in the hills. Liberace built a piano-shaped swimming pool in his Valley Vista backyard. On the Valley side of Ventura Boulevard, citrus and persimmon groves stretched for acres.

California was the land of opportunity when Jack Gordon headed west after mustering out of the Army with the rank of major at the end of World War II, taking his wife and their two sons to settle in a small, recently built, Spanish-style house in Dixie Canyon, a few blocks south of Ventura Boulevard.

Gordon wanted to escape a checkered past. He met his wife, Osa Marie Beck, when he was in the Army and was a patient in the hospital where she worked as a nurse in Washington, DC. He had two previous marriages and a daughter from one. He joined the Army in 1940 at the strong recommendation of a judge after being charged with embezzlement at a bookkeeping job. He was also a problem drinker and, at age thirty-two, he had already left plenty of wreckage behind.

Their first child, John Jr., was born in 1942 while Jack was stationed overseas. He was overseas again when their second son, James Beck Gordon, was born on July 14, 1945. Osa kept the home fires burning in Elizabeth, New Jersey, until her husband returned from the war, having turned down a promotion to reenlist, to take his family to California for a fresh start.

Despite the sylvan setting and the apparent prosperity of the transplanted family, life was buttoned down at the Gordon home. The house was spotless. Children were to be seen and not heard, speak when spoken to. They were expected to say "please" and "thank you." Belongings needed to be picked up, the phone answered with "Gordon residence." Mom and Pop were not affectionate parents; there weren't a lot of hugs and kisses. Austere Jack Gordon was a stickler, not above speaking harshly to the boys, and Osa backed him up. He was a man of strong opinions—a stern Republican who didn't like Jews or Catholics. Of course, his drinking invariably got in the way of his parenting. There were frequent absences, long hours spent in bars, and sullen, drunken moods at home.

After leaving the service, where it was automatically deducted from his pay, he refused to pay child support to his ex-wife until the courts forced him. Even then, it was Osa who wrote the monthly checks. She also purchased and sent the birthday and Christmas presents to Jack's daughter, Mary. If Jack was the unquestioned chief executive of the family, his wife served as chief of staff, making sure that policy was carried out. Both parents worked; Jack as an accountant and Osa as a maternity nurse at a nearby hospital. She did what she could to cover her husband's shortcomings.

Young Jim was a lonely, withdrawn, chubby boy with few friends. He took comfort in food but felt self-conscious about his weight. His outgoing, athletic older brother—elected president of his class—had plenty of friends and outshined his shy, lost, and tubby little brother in every way. Despite the family's apparent closeness, Jim saw himself as separate from their circle, a lonesome outsider in his own home. Jim always feared people were talking about him. He developed a rich inner life early. Lots of young boys have imaginary friends like Jim did, voices in their heads that can be comforting, a bulwark against the loneliness. Such thoughts can come well within a child's grasp of reality. They are usually outgrown harmlessly.

When he was eight years old, Jim turned over a wastebasket and some pots and pans to create a makeshift drum set in the room he shared with his brother. The report of the drum sent an immediate electric shock wave through his body. In the rhythm, he found soothing relief. He did not know this or understand it in any conscious way, but he followed the bliss of the rhythm and the report. That, he intuited instantly.

Jim grew fevered with the drums. He spent long hours playing along with records. His parents understood enough to encourage him. His father somehow recognized that when Jim picked up the drumsticks, he found his key to the world. The drums gave young Jim a safe harbor, a refuge from the tension and anxiety of family life. Lessons were arranged. He learned to read music. He performed at his Dixie Canyon Avenue Elementary School. By age twelve, Jim had acquired a full set of his own drums, piece by piece, and the house had been remodeled so that he had a room to play them in. The drums brought Jim out of his shell. His confidence improved. He was growing into a tall and handsome young man and his increasing prowess at drumming gave him the self-esteem he needed to make friends and be popular. It was his turn to shine. He was even elected class president at Van Nuys Junior High School.

In 1958, when Jim was on the cusp of adolescence, Jack Gordon went into Alcoholics Anonymous and got sober. The boys finally had the father they always wanted. He coached John's Little League team. He drove the boys when they needed rides. He was present for meals. He was no less exacting in his demands for proper behavior and still imposed strict regimens on the boys, but he was there for his sons in ways he had never been before.

Jim was exploding with talent. Barely in his teens, he marched in nearby Pasadena's Tournament of Roses Parade with the Los Angeles County Sheriff's Boys Band. He joined a prestigious youth orchestra operated by the International Order of Foresters called the Robin Hood Band, which also regularly joined the annual Pasadena parade. They wore green tights, tunics, and pointy hats and played John Philip Sousa marches and typical marching band fare. This experience cemented Jim's ambition to become a professional musician. He traveled to Europe in summer 1961 with the seventy-five-member troupe at age fifteen and, under the Eiffel Tower, kissed one of the band's drum majorettes. Jill Barabe would be his steady girlfriend from then on. She was a gorgeous blonde with a beautiful smile, raised Catholic by a single mother, two years older than Jim, and wanted to become a professional dancer. Soon they were a couple, spending hours together or talking on the phone.

Jim flourished in high school. He took music classes, played in the school band, and received private lessons from the school's music teacher, Bob Winslow, himself a tympanist, as well as playing in Winslow's after-school percussion group. Jim also studied with Hack O'Brien, a former swing band drummer who settled in Burbank, took the drum chair in the Horace Heidt Orchestra, Hollywood's leading dance band, and taught drums (his most prominent student was his son, the nine-year-old drumming phenomenon of TV's *The Mickey Mouse Club*, Cubby O'Brien). As he advanced, Jim took lessons from UCLA percussion professor Earl Hatz, an austere and stern instructor who sent him home with four-mallet Bach homework for the marimba. The Burbank Symphony Junior Philharmonic invited him to play. He also served as his high school's drum major—he cut quite a dashing figure on game days, striding down the field, his six-foot-four frame topped with the tall drum major's hat.

Ulysses S. Grant High School was plunked down in the midst of fields and meadows on the edge of Van Nuys. The student body was half Jewish and all white. While the barest beginnings of a world beyond the Eisenhower era could be glimpsed in the folk song club or the Young Democrats, Grant High was as all-American as California got. Interest ran high in automobiles, football, and girls—practically in that order. They were confident they lived in the promised land. Optimism was their birthright. These young Californians boasted a future as limitless and bright as the blue skies above them. None more so than Jim.

Grant High School freshman Mike Post was working as manager of the Putt Putt Golf Course on Ventura Boulevard in Studio City when he saw a tall, blond boy whacking the light standard with his putter. He slammed the kid up against the wall and severely admonished him. He recognized him as the younger brother of

John Gordon, whom Post had known since elementary school. When he saw John Gordon at school, he apologized for roughing up his little brother.

"Why didn't you punch him?" Gordon the elder said. "You have my permission. He's annoying. Just hit him next time."

When Gordon the younger entered Grant High School the next fall, every time he saw Post on campus, he looked away and scurried off. He remembered. At high school, Post was leading a kind of double life—high school football player by day, playing in a band in Hollywood at night. He had nothing to do with the high school music department and had his tough guy act down on campus. Post had wangled his way into playing keyboards with a nightclub band called Frankie Knight and the Jesters; he bought a Wurlitzer keyboard to take the job. Vocalist Knight had a version of "Unchained Melody" that made a few Southern California radio stations a couple years earlier, and his band was holding down three nights a week at Mama Alvoturno's on Pico and Genesee.

Post found himself at a party where a few guys were playing music and Jim Gordon was on the drums. Post took over the guitar chair in the band and, within a few bars, was locked into a deathless groove with the drummer. They played three or four numbers together, and Post couldn't believe how good Jim was. When they finished, Post told Jim he thought he played great.

"You're not still mad at me?" said Jim.

"Not at all," said Post. "You're a great drummer. In fact, I have a gig three nights a week in Hollywood, and we need a drummer."

In December 1962, with the help of fake IDs, Jim and Mike Post went with Frankie Knight and the Jesters for a two-week residency at the Condor, a go-go club on Broadway in San Francisco. The band bunked up in the Mission District at a place owned by the bass player's uncle, Jim and Mike sharing a bed until the comely blonde go-go dancer at the club, Carol Doda, took pity on young Mike Post and dragged him back to her place. As the Condor house band, they joined the New Year's Day bill headlined by Johnny Cash at San Quentin State Prison across the Golden Gate Bridge. High times for teens from the Valley.

Post met his future wife the night he and Jim spotted a pair of attractive blondes in the crowd at a Frankie Knight gig. They debated over who would take which one. Jim ended up with the long-haired blonde, an aspiring actress named Marta Kristen, and Post went with the one with the shorter hair, Darla Eyer, whom he would eventually marry. Post and Jim grew to be best friends. Post called him Gordo and kidded him about being a little flabby. They learned the music business together.

A fire burned in Jim. On Saturday nights, after leading the football team onto the field in the Valley, he would jump into his white '54 Ford convertible with the side pipes and roar down to Mama Alvoturno's for a gig. After the club closed, he would head back into the Valley and pick up another five bucks bundling the Sunday *Los Angeles Times*, heading home at dawn. In addition to Frankie Knight and the Jesters, Jim took any wedding, bar mitzvah, or casual job that came his way. He and Post began doing occasional nonunion recording sessions, cutting song demos at Metric Music, the publishing arm of Liberty Records, for $25 a side ($10 for over-dubs) with neophyte producer Lenny Waronker, whose father owned Liberty and was about the same age as Jim and Post.

There were dates with Jill—movies, ice cream sodas at Blum's in Beverly Hills, long drives. They were never at a loss for things to talk about; they could chatter for hours. Sometimes they would simply sit and stare into each other's faces, with Jill growing more beautiful to Jim as they did. They spoke on the phone nightly and wrote each other letters. They were the upright products of a conservative upbringing. Jim, Jill, and their friend Mike Post pledged to one another never to use drugs. With her strict Catholic upbringing and the general mores of those pre-pill days, they made out a lot, did some heavy petting, but they did not have sex. These two beautiful young people seemed like a perfect couple.

His head still secretly hummed with voices, but they were friendly, comforting, even helpful in daily life, like picking out what clothes to wear. Once, while getting ready to go out with Jim, his date for the evening thought it strange to overhear him sitting in the living room holding an animated, whispered conversation when nobody else was there. But the music overrode everything else.

Senior year was busy for Jim. In addition to playing and studying music, dating Jill, and taking as many jobs as came his way, he did all his homework and kept the B average his parents required. He considered pursuing a career as a music teacher and made plans for college. He was offered scholarships to study music at both UCLA and Valley State. Jill was already out of school, working with the George Moro Landis Dance Company, waiting for her big break in Las Vegas. Their relationship was on-and-off as she took lengthy out-of-town engagements dancing in chorus lines in Reno and Vegas. Big decisions lay ahead.

Joey Paige was the bass player and musical director for the Everly Brothers. He was a street-smart Philly kid who had wormed his way into the road edition of Dickie Doo and the Don'ts, one of the many fleeting fifties rock and roll acts sparked by the hometown cottage industry of Dick Clark's *American Bandstand*, but Paige had migrated to Los Angeles to pursue his rock and roll dreams and joined the Everly Brothers in time for the duo's disastrous 1962 British tour. The brothers were gearing up for their annual summer tour, and Paige hit the Hollywood nightclubs scouting talent.

Frankie Knight and the Jesters were playing Pandora's box, when Paige stopped by the Sunset Strip teen nightclub and coffeehouse owned by KRLA disc jockey Jimmy O'Neill that served no liquor. He watched carefully as the band outperformed the slightly shop-worn lead vocalist and front man. Keyboardist Mike Post was impressive, but it was the drummer who kept pulling Paige's attention. The tall, boyish figure behind the kit kept a steady rock drive going but with a distinct difference—a bounce, a lilt, a boiling undercurrent, and an instinct for when to drop bombs and when to hold back that couldn't be learned. The timing was impeccable but there was much more going on than simply keeping time.

Paige hung back until the band took a break and then introduced himself to Jim as the musical director of the Everlys. The name was magic to Jim, who had fallen for rock and roll the first time he heard "Hound Dog" by Elvis Presley on the radio while mopping his parents' kitchen floor. Seven years later, the Everlys were practically the last fifties rockers still standing. They were past their chart-topping days, but they were still undeniably one of the few rock and roll greats in existence.

"We're looking for a drummer," Paige told Jim.

IV.
THE EVERLYS

At a rehearsal space on Ventura Boulevard, Jim picked up the Everlys' music book from guitarist Don Peake and bassist Joey Paige. He studied the book front to back and didn't get nervous until the audition at the Everlys' office on Barham Boulevard in Burbank a few days later. He need not have worried. As soon as he started to play, he got lost in the groove. Don and Phil Everly saw clearly that this young man had talent. He got the job. They had no idea how old he was.

Back home, there was considerable debate about the prospect. Jim's accountant father thought the $125 a week salary was insufficient. His mother worried about young Jim traveling across the country. The issue of college loomed, and only after Jim agreed to enroll that fall at Valley State did his parents relent. He left the day after he graduated high school.

With Everlys rehearsals crowding his schedule, Jim's last few weeks of high school were a tense, stressful time. He and Jill went through one of their occasional breakups before the senior prom.

Jim invited another girl, and they danced the evening away to the Tex Beneke orchestra in the Grant High School all-purpose room before climbing aboard a bus for Disneyland, where high school seniors from all over the area were taking over the park. As the bus pulled into the main gates, Jim looked out the bus window and saw Jill and her best friend following in her car. Jim celebrated his graduation roaming the Magic Kingdom with a girl on each arm, looking forward to the start of his brilliant career.

He spent the summer of 1963 touring the Midwest with the Everly Brothers on their Greyhound bus, the stars sitting in the front of the bus and the band in the back. Welcome to show business. Don Everly caught Jim unpacking his bags the first night and putting his clothes away in drawers and the closet before explaining to him that it might be easier to leave his things in the suitcase because they would be out of there first thing in the morning. When Jim took the stage that first night at Spring Lake Park in Salt Lake City in his silver sharkskin suit and settled behind the blue Sparkletone Ludwig drum kit, electricity coursed through his body.

These were not the best of times for the Everlys. They had only mustered out of the Marines in May, and Don was already having problems with drugs again. He had married his second wife, starlet Venetia Stevenson, in February 1962, the day after he and Phil graduated from Marines basic training—appearing five days later on *The Ed Sullivan Show* to sing their latest single, "Crying in the Rain," and unveil their buzz-cut haircuts. Don and Venetia's daughter Stacey was born in May 1963.

The Everly Brothers had left Nashville in 1960 for Hollywood, where they signed with Warner Brothers Records, although the promised film roles failed to materialize. They split with their Nashville manager, music publisher Wesley Rose, who cut off their supply of hit songs. Although they still qualified as an attraction on the road, they had not seen anything remotely like a hit record in more than a year, and their latest releases didn't even make the charts. They didn't get along well—at their best, they were cool with each other—and they would occasionally stop the bus and settle matters by the side of the road.

They were disparate personalities—Don was outgoing, boisterous, even volatile, and Phil was quiet, subdued, almost brooding. They were friendly but didn't fraternize with the help. They left running the band to Joey Paige, although they were professional enough to know what they wanted. They were gone so long that summer that Don's wife in a postpartum pique filed for divorce while they were on the road, although those problems were soon resolved. While Jim didn't hurt for female companionship on the tour, he dropped a small fortune on long-distance calls to Jill back home at night in the hotel rooms.

Jim marveled at the endless hours of cornfields outside the bus window. The Everlys stopped at every A&W stand for root beer. He was adrift across America in a dream. To a young fellow straight out of San Fernando Valley, it was a big country. As he was fresh and green, an unsophisticated teenager out in the world for the first time, he listened quietly and took care not to draw attention to himself. Jim accustomed himself to changing into his stage clothes in the back of the bus. Don Peake gave him a few guitar lessons while they were tooling down the highway, and he picked it up quickly. In Minneapolis, on Jim's eighteenth birthday, Peake rented a car to take Jim to register for the draft. The Everlys still didn't know exactly how old he was.

He was such an innocent, the older guys in the band couldn't help themselves. Don Everly, in particular, loved a good prank. Although the band didn't go for hard liquor, everyone except Phil enjoyed a cold beer after the show. Don arranged with a local cop to wait for underage Jim to take his first swig and pretend to arrest him. The cop did a great job; pulled his gun and barked at Jim, "You're coming with me, son—you're spending the night in jail." Jim was so terrified that they dropped the gag instantly. The cop threw his arm over Jim's shoulder and told him it was only a joke, but Jim believed he was going to jail there for a bad minute.

Though none were as young as Jim, they were all kids. Don was twenty-six years old and Phil twenty-four. Don Peake, twenty-one, was only starting out himself, and he fumbled guitar parts almost nightly. Don Everly was continually firing him after shows, only to have Phil convince him to hire him back the next morning. On the Fourth of July, they pulled the bus over and chased each other through a cornfield, shooting bottle rockets at one another.

In September, shortly after Jim started classes at Valley State (where he also signed up for the school band), he went to England with the Everlys. This was a crucial tour after the duo's catastrophic showing the previous year. In October 1962, at rehearsal at the Prince of Wales Theatre in London the night before the twenty-two-date tour was to start, a distraught Don Everly had thrown his guitar to the floor and ran weeping into the arms of his wife. She took him back to the hotel, where he gobbled a handful of pills and was rushed to Charing Cross Hospital to have his stomach pumped. Back at his hotel room, he made a second suicide attempt. He, his wife, and his daughter left the next day for New York, where he was admitted to a mental hospital and treated with electroshock. The news was kept from the public. Phil Everly, who had never been the duo's lead vocalist, stepped up with some help from Joey Paige, and they completed most of the dates.

For the next year's tour, with Jim at the drums, the promoters booked Bo Diddley to support the Everlys. Union rules would only allow him to bring his salaciously dressed rhythm guitarist,

Norma-Jean Wofford—known as the Duchess—in her skintight cat suit, and his maracas player, Jerome Green. Opening the show was a new band that had never played outside of London; their first single, a version of the Chuck Berry song "Come On," had spent the previous month hovering around the middle of the charts. They were the Rolling Stones.

England was a different country than it had been only the year before. The Beatles had their second number one hit, "She Loves You," on top of the charts, and Don Everly had to admit to the press gathered to greet them at the airport that he had not heard their music yet. Bo Diddley knew; he told the fellows in the Rolling Stones they were going to outlast The Beatles, because they "played like black dudes." The Everlys even appeared on the BBC's *Saturday Club* with The Beatles. Don and Phil were cordial but remote and the Stones were left to hang out backstage with their backup musicians. Stones drummer Charlie Watts even arranged an afternoon drum circle with Jim and the other drummers on the tour.

The tour started in Hamburg, Germany, where the Everlys recorded four songs in German for their label there. On September 23, they played the Olympia Theatre in Paris with Peter, Paul and Mary and returned to Hamburg for two nights at the Star Club, before the British tour began September 29 at the New Victoria Theatre in London. Opening with the Little Richard song "Lucille," the Everlys sang their hits—"Wake Up Little Susie," "Walk Right Back," "Cathy's Clown," "All I Have to Do Is Dream," "Bye Bye Love"—and Joey Paige joined them, clowning around on "So Sad." They did two more Little Richard songs, "Rip It Up" and "Keep A-Knockin'," and came back for an encore with "Be-Bop-a-Lula," including a brief drum feature by Jim.

To boost sales on the tour's second half, promoters flew in Little Richard, who took over closing the show's first half. Uncontrollable and unrestrained, Richard ripped up audiences nightly, invariably going far past his allotted time, rampaging through the crowd as they tore the clothes off his back. As the tour progressed, with more and more teenage girls rushing the stage and screaming at the Rolling Stones, the band moved to opening the second half. The staid Everly Brothers in their tuxedos didn't stand a chance. Their idea of stagecraft was to play their fast songs faster and their slow songs slower. They dispensed with the Little Richard songs but often found it difficult to maintain the delirium, frequently rushing through their set because Little Richard had taken up so much time.

British audiences behaved much differently than Americans. It was not uncommon to find more than a hundred teenage girls waiting outside the stage door after shows. A few even managed to get backstage (and beyond). Jim was astonished to be asked for his autograph; after all, he was only playing drums.

But the Everlys were suddenly old news. The Beatles meant much more to England than a mere pop success. The group had refreshed England's sense of self. Bombed-out buildings could still be seen on most blocks in London, and British youth had long made do with ration stamps, war widows, and Woodbine cigarettes. After the long, gray days following World War II, The Beatles spearheaded a vivid, colorful rebirth of British culture—film, fashion, literature, and all the fabulous beat groups popping up seemingly out of nowhere. The Beatles may have modeled their vocal sound on the Everlys, but Don and Phil themselves stood on the brink of pop obsolescence, courting irrelevance.

After the final show at London's Hammersmith Odeon, fans mobbed the Rolling Stones and, in a cruel twist, threw paper cups at the Everlys.

On a night out on the town in London during the tour, Jim had his own close encounter with the nascent British rock royalty. He was visiting the Scotch of St. James, an exclusive hideaway on the cobbled Mason's Yard behind Fortnum and Mason in elegant Mayfair, where swinging London hung and swung, when Paul McCartney approached Jim and introduced himself. He had seen the show and told Jim what a great drummer he thought Jim was. McCartney would be the only Beatle that Jim never made music with, but Jim left England with his eyes open to a wider world than he had known before.

When he returned home, Jim Gordon dropped out of Valley State.

V.
SESSION
MUSICIAN

The session musician emerged as a highly skilled, technique-specific, and well-paid underclass of musicians after World War II. As big bands disappeared and radio orchestras became a thing of the past, bandstand jobs evaporated. But as the recording industry grew through the fifties, highly skilled musicians found themselves making a good living at union jobs in recording studios around New York City and sleeping in their own beds at night.

Drawing largely from the ranks of former big band musicians, the journeymen technicians made their livings providing music for other people's records. The job did not reward the mythic virtuoso with highly individualized style, but rather the versatile player who could find a place for himself in anyone's music.

Saxophonist King Curtis was the classic New York sideman. While the Texas-born tenor man could blow hard bop with the best of them—his 1960 Prestige Records solo dates matched a fiery

Curtis with Miles Davis's rhythm section—it was his whimsical musical commentary that tangled with Jerry Leiber's witty lyrics on records by The Coasters or his honking blasts that lit the choruses of dozens of twist records. He found comfortable space to play on records by Buddy Holly, Bobby Darin, and Sam Cooke.

Former swing musicians like drummer Panama Francis from the Lucky Millinder band helped shape the sound of New York rhythm and blues, until Gene Krupa protégé Gary Chester hit the scene. Chester, whose signature trademarks included a tambourine on his hi-hat or a sand ashtray on his snare drum, took over the sessions by leading producers like Leiber and Stoller, Ahmet Ertegun, and Bert Berns. Producer-arranger Burt Bacharach wouldn't schedule a session without Chester or pianist Paul Griffin, a troubled musical genius who started booking sessions while he was playing in King Curtis's nightclub band. Guitarists Vince Bell, Trade Martin, Eric Gale, and others were regular first-chair players. Everybody wore coats and ties.

In 1958, engineer Phil Ramone opened A & R Recording on West 48th Street, giving the independent labels for the first time the kind of high-fidelity recording facilities previously only available to majors like RCA Victor's Webster Hall (home of the "Living Stereo" series), Decca's Pythian Temple, or Columbia's massive 30th Street Studio. The record business had shifted gears into heretofore unexplored realms of productivity and prosperity.

After World War II, a cottage recording industry developed in Nashville around the weekly radio broadcast Grand Ole Opry, and the sound of modern country music was developed essentially under the supervision of three main record producers, Don Law of Columbia Records, Owen Bradley of Decca, and Chet Atkins at RCA Victor, using the same dozen or so session musicians on all their records. The anonymous artisans became the architects of the music; the singers were largely interchangeable figureheads.

Los Angeles was far from the center of the music business in the fifties. The movie studios employed house orchestras for sound-tracks, and Capitol Records put gorgeous recording studios in the basement of its new Hollywood headquarters built in the shape of a stack of records, but concentrated on old-fashioned pop music by the likes of Frank Sinatra, Dean Martin, and Nat King Cole. The city boasted a thriving regional rhythm and blues scene, but the sleepy, sunny West Coast was a long way from Times Square in those pre-jet travel days.

In 1957, engineer Bill Putnam moved from Chicago and opened United Recording on Sunset Boulevard (acquiring Western Studios a half block down the street three years later). With the rock and roll crowd favoring Dave Gold and Stan Ross's Gold Star Studios on Santa Monica Boulevard and the R&B folks gravitating toward Bunny Robyn's Master Recorders, Putnam opened up his facilities just as the recording business in Hollywood was blowing up.

The new world order first came together at an emergency recording session ordered by producer Phil Spector, back in Los Angeles from New York, where he had become the enfant terrible of the record business. Spector learned that another producer was planning to cut the song he had picked for the next single by his girl group The Crystals and decided to rush-record the song with another set of singers in Hollywood to beat the competition to the market. Since he owned the name of the group, he could have anyone he wanted sing the song. He called his high school friend, saxophonist Steve Douglas, who had been playing sessions—largely section work on R&B dates with Maxwell Davis's studio orchestra—for the year and a half he had been back in town since leaving the touring band of twangy guitarist Duane Eddy.

Douglas pulled together a group that assembled July 13, 1962, at Gold Star Studios. On drums was a character Douglas knew from jamming at clubs in the Valley named Hal Blaine, who had been on the road with Patti Page and Tommy Sands. Douglas assembled a crew of young renegade musicians around Blaine. None of them were part of the studio orchestra system. Spector found a new temporary set of Crystals from Los Angeles R&B session vocalists, and they cut the number one hit "He's a Rebel."

The session brought together a new generation of studio musicians who showed up in T-shirts and jeans and happily played rock and roll, unlike the New York session players who looked down their noses at this vulgar music for kids. These musicians came together like a gaseous cloud just as the Los Angeles music scene began to catch fire. They would enable a cast of new musical visionaries and assist them in running their experiments in the laboratories that the Los Angeles recording studios became. In short order, the musicians would be playing behind hit records by the Beach Boys, Herb Alpert & the Tijuana Brass, Nancy Sinatra, Johnny Rivers, former session player Glen Campbell, and others in a creative and commercial explosion of West Coast pop that would sweep the world and establish Hollywood as one of the centers of the pop music universe.

The general public never knew their names—or even that they existed—but in the music business, these men were the silent assassins. Their skills were legend, and the more they played, the better they got. It may not have been a route to fame, but fortune was definitely possible. Guitarist Glen Campbell came from Phoenix to Los Angeles to work as a studio musician and booked $100,000 in studio dates the next year. Other guitarists on sessions might include swing era big band veteran Barney Kessel; or the lovable Italian clown from Niagara Falls, New York, who could have been the best gut-string guitar player in the country, Tommy Tedesco; or Louisiana Telecaster master James Burton moonlighting from his day job with Rick Nelson's band.

Pianists might include Russell Bridges, who rode out of Oklahoma in the Jerry Lee Lewis band and also went by the name Leon Russell, or Al DeLory from the "He's a Rebel" session who had been a fixture on Hollywood sessions since he wrote the 1960 number one novelty hit "Mr. Custer." The ridiculously talented Larry Knechtel, fresh out of the Duane Eddy band, could handle any piano part, although he also recorded on bass, guitar, and harmonica. Lyle Ritz or Ray Pohlman played stand-up bass, but Fender bass was frequently handled by Carol Kaye, the lone female in this boys' club who started out as a guitarist but may have realized the bass would get her more work.

But the twin giants of this new breed of session players were drummers Earl Palmer and Hal Blaine. Earl Palmer was a widely experienced thirty-three-year-old drummer when he arrived in Los Angeles in 1957 from New Orleans, where he started out in the forties playing in the Dave Bartholomew big band and supplied the widely admired backbeat to classic rock and roll records by Little Richard, Fats Domino, and others. He immediately assumed the premier position behind the drum kits at L.A. rhythm and blues sessions. Hal Blaine grew up in Chicago, where he had taken lessons from Gene Krupa's drum teacher and bounced around the country with a bunch of nowhere bands after getting out of the Korean War before landing a job with rock and roll star Tommy Sands.

They were the anchors to this burgeoning West Coast sound that could not be found in recording studios in New York or Nashville or anywhere. Both Palmer and Blaine laid down rock solid foundations to any track they played like the crack professionals they were. They may have come to the music through jazz and dance band music, but they did not think of any music as beneath them.

Of course, Palmer and Blaine were rooted in the drum style of Gene Krupa. He was the gold standard when they were coming up and the indomitable defining figure of the modern drum kit. Both of their professional careers predated the emergence of rock and roll. Palmer cut his teeth on the rough and ready rhythm and blues sound of New Orleans, but his heart always belonged to jazz—Art Blakey–style bebop. Blaine, too, grew up listening to the big bands of the day in Chicago and idolizing Krupa. He did all kinds of work, but he thought of himself as a jazz musician. The more he played rock and roll, the better he liked it.

All these folks were studio musicians, first and foremost. They took pride in their professional skills, and they liked to encourage and support the creative efforts of the young producers and acts they worked with. That was their job, and they were good at it. Inside the music business, these brilliant session players were like knights of the realm, glorious young swordsmen at the peak of their powers ready to do battle on the field of honor. They walked the halls of the studios with their own special swagger.

The work simply exploded on the Hollywood recording scene. Surf and car songs became a productive enterprise for Hollywood session musicians, who pretty much invented the genre. In 1963, guitarist Glen Campbell reckoned he played on more than five hundred records that year alone. Even so, the record industry was only waking up on the remote California coast, slipping into the collective consciousness behind an unprecedented string of landmark hit records from the Beach Boys, Jan and Dean, and others. Phil Spector stopped making his records in New York, preferring to erect his Wall of Sound with these Hollywood sidemen. Herb Alpert & the Tijuana Brass were turning out hit after hit with the same musicians.

Enterprising engineers had learned how to mike drums by using several microphones and spreading the recording across different tracks, which gave producers much greater flexibility in featuring the big beat in detail. The drums were a keystone part of the recording, and it became standard practice to layer the tracks with an assortment of percussion instruments—tambourines, shakers, bells, xylophones—the better to build a rich, tinkling floor to the record. The Los Angeles cats were inventing rock and roll drums.

At a Frankie Knight and the Jesters gig in the Valley, Jim Gordon didn't expect to encounter some unexpected fork in his career path, but that was where he met saxophonist Jim Horn. Jim knew his work from the screaming solos on the Duane Eddy records, and Horn had only recently left Eddy's band to concentrate on sessions. Horn told Jim that his playing was so good, he should think about session work. Horn advised Jim to concentrate on playing the incidental percussion parts as a route into working recording sessions. Jim had been schooled on all the mallet instruments, played them well enough to get by, and had excellent sight-reading skills. Horn's comments stayed with him. He started to think about grooming his abilities for recording session work.

He was in the right place at the right time. Without knowing it, Jim had trained for the position since he started with the drums. He took music seriously and studied hard. He practiced, took lessons, and played and played and played. In addition, Jim had an advantage over the older drummers—Jim was born to play rock and roll. He was eleven years old when Elvis broke, and he caught the fever immediately. And while his studious nature led him to explore all realms of the percussion world and every kind of music he could play with his drums, rock and roll was in his heart. Jim would take the drums beyond Gene Krupa.

VI.
DRUMMER BOY

J im still lived at home when he wasn't on the road with the Everly Brothers, a circumstance rife with anxiety and tension. His parents did not approve of his musical career. They would have preferred he studied to become a lawyer or doctor. His mother didn't like the lifestyle and his father still ruled the home with an iron hand, not above screaming at Jim in front of guests to hang up a sweater he had left folded on the living room couch. Jim was making money, but his father worried that it was too much and too soon for his teenaged son.

Jill had landed a job dancing in Las Vegas and rented an apartment there. When he could get the time, Jim would sneak away and stay with her in Nevada, but his time was at a premium. He was burning with ambition. His entire energies were devoted to establishing himself as a professional musician. He took every opportunity he could find.

He was tucked into the bosom of the Everlys. After the British tour, Joey Paige left the band to pursue his career as a solo artist.

Don Peake was also gone, but the next time the Everlys went into
Western Recorders in February 1964, they brought Jim to play
drums in a large session featuring top sidemen like guitarists James
Burton, Billy Strange, and arranger Jimmie Haskell. More than
keeping time, Jim drove the song with little rolls and tasty fills that
perfectly teed up the lyric, giving the drums more of a part on the
record than a simple backbeat. Of course, with the first hot flush of
Beatlemania sweeping the country, the new Everlys single, "Hello
Amy," disappeared without a trace.

With Sonny Curtis of Buddy Holly's backup band, The Crickets,
on guitar and Dale Hallcom on bass, the Everlys took Jim out for
the summer tour, running through Midwest and East Coast ball-
rooms and roller rinks, stopping along the way whenever they
passed a track to chase each other around on go-karts. It was
beginning to occur to Jim that playing the same songs night after
night was tedious. He yearned for the creativity of the recording
studio, where every session was a new challenge. In November, they
all went out again through the chilly Midwest and Canada with
newcomer Roger Miller ("Dang Me") on the bill. Jim was surprised to find Miller awake at all hours, often visiting his hotel
room in the middle of the night, but Jim didn't know about diet
pills. Not yet.

Jim liked to go to the Mexican Doll House on La Cienega or the
Roaring Twenties in the Valley to catch the Page Cavanaugh band
with drummer Jack Sperling, a big band veteran who had belonged
to the Glenn Miller outfit with Henry Mancini and played on
Mancini's soundtracks. Pianist Cavanaugh was the gray eminence
of the Los Angeles jazz scene, an elegant, dignified, swinging fixture
in the clubs since the war. He came out of the Army and started the
Page Cavanaugh Trio—modeled after the hip Nat King Cole Trio—
with guitarist Al Viola, who eventually spent most of his career

playing for Frank Sinatra. Cavanaugh owned his own club in Studio City for many years, but in 1964 he was leading a seven-piece band that featured the phenomenal guitarist Joe Pass, at the time still a closely guarded secret confined to Hollywood recording studios. Sperling played a double bass drum and was one of Jim's favorites. When Sperling had to leave the band, Jim worked up his nerve and auditioned for the job. He did not get the position, but when he returned for a second audition, he did.

Cavanaugh adored the eager, sweet, young drummer. He featured Jim on Duke Ellington's "Cottontail" and let him try his hand at writing arrangements. Jim wrote a version of The Beatles' song "And I Love Her," complicated enough to throw off his buddy Don Peake when Peake substituted for Pass for a couple weeks.

Meanwhile, Jim was knocking on every door, making all the phone calls, doing whatever he could to work his way into the recording studio scene. He wanted to do this. He was obsessed with clawing his way in. Jim spent mornings at A&B Corned Beef, the session musicians' hangout, drinking in the atmosphere and expanding his contacts. He was constantly looking for work. He took any date he could book, and there was a lot of work beyond record dates—commercials, soundtracks, jingles, TV shows.

People began paying attention; it was hard not to notice the gangly, tall blond with the curly locks and shy smile. His pal Mike Post, who had ambitions of his own as an arranger or producer, brought Jim into a soundtrack for a surf 'n' sand epic titled *Swingin' Summer* to play some percussion with all the top Hollywood players including Hal Blaine behind the drum set. Lee Hazelwood noticed him. The grizzled producer had moved to Hollywood from Phoenix five years earlier after launching the career of guitarist Duane Eddy, and he brought Jim into the sessions for his third album as an artist, *Friday's Child.*

Hazelwood had also been assigned production duties on a trio of elite Hollywood spawn, the sons of Dean Martin, Desi Arnaz and Lucille Ball, and a Filipino friend of theirs. No less a figure than Frank Sinatra himself, owner of the Reprise record label, had auditioned the group and approved the signing. Hazelwood did not love working with the semi-amateur teenage rock and roll singers Dino, Desi & Billy, but he understood the show business implications of the deal. He surrounded the Beverly Hills teens in the studio with the most formidable professional musicians he could find with Jim on the drums.

On the group's hit single "I'm a Fool," Jim found a cooking groove he punctuated with fills and stop breaks to give the arrangement extra momentum. He skipped across the track like he was dancing on the drums, rolling into the choruses, and punching up the rhythm parts with little controlled explosions. Prodded by a supple bass part from Larry Knechtel, Jim led the record where it went, instinctively elevating the role of the drums. His first hit record, it was an altogether auspicious chart debut by Jim.

As he started making headway on his professional aspirations, Jim was surrounded by outside pressures beyond the uncomfortable living situation with his parents at the Ventura Canyon place. Like all young men in the Vietnam era, Jim faced an escalating draft call. The Vietnam War made no sense to Jim—he had seen the madness up close the year before when he went with the Everlys on a USO tour of Vietnam—but he was determined not to interrupt his path.

Jim knew some musicians from the Grant High School band who had signed up with the Air Force Reserve to play in the band at the Van Nuys Airport. It was a matter of locating the right recruiter, and Mike Post helped Jim make the connection. By the time he received his call from the draft board, he had already submitted his application.

Jim joined the 562nd Air National Guard Band. They practiced once a month in street clothes at an upstairs room on the base, sitting on metal chairs with rubber tips on linoleum floors. He knew some of the other band members from high school like fellow drummer Alan Estes, whose father played recording sessions, and saxophonist Tom Scott, a couple years behind Jim at Grant who had joined the reserves while still in high school. People were getting shipped to Vietnam from the base—Jim's older brother, John Jr., had joined the Marines and was headed overseas—but the Air National Guard band was strictly public relations. There was both a marching band and a concert band that played on weekends at Busch Gardens in Van Nuys. The band was led by Captain Robert Brunner, who worked as a composer at Disney Studios, a straight arrow with a good sense of humor.

Jim did not take his military duties seriously. He showed up wearing a bandage around his head to hide the sideburns he didn't want to shave. Captain Brunner pretended not to notice, but Jim marched in parades wearing the bandage like he had a head wound. He eventually stopped showing up and managed to get an honorable discharge anyway.

He was also being pressed by Jill to get married. They finally had sex one furtive afternoon at her home while her mother was out, but Jim was reluctant to take the big step. It wasn't that he wasn't in love with Jill—he definitely was—but his future seemed uncertain still, and he was filled with the desire for accomplishment more than any relationship. For the immediate future, the Everlys were keeping him busy.

In May 1965, the Everlys took Jim, guitarist Sonny Curtis of The Crickets, and bassist Marshall Leib of the Teddy Bears to a whirlwind promotion tour of England, where the band did seven television shows in eight days in support of their fine new single, "The

Price of Love." The effort was successful as the single went all the way to number two on the British hit parade—it never touched the US charts—the first Top Ten appearance by the brothers over there in more than three years.

On their return, the Everlys took over United Recording for three long nights in June to cut a new album with an all-star crew of session players. With Jim on drums, Sonny Curtis joined James Burton and Glen Campbell on guitars with Larry Knechtel on bass and Billy Preston from the Ray Charles band on organ (Leon Russell added a second keyboard on the last night of the sessions). Fresh from the British scene, the Everlys were adopting a can't-beat-'em-join-'em strategy to break the English logjam on the US charts, modeling the guitar-heavy sound on the British beat groups that had swept the country in the wake of The Beatles. The sound was brilliant, but the Everlys gravitated toward well-known fifties rock and roll songs like "The Girl Can't Help It," "Money," "Lonely Avenue," and others. *Billboard* noted that the single—a cover of the 1957 Mickey and Sylvia hit "Love Is Strange"—had an "English-Nashville feel," but the record utterly failed to launch when it was released in November.

At the same time, Jim was beginning to find other session work. Their pal Mike Rubini slipped Jim and Mike Post into a Gold Star session by Phil Spector go-fer Sonny Bono and his wife, the former Cher LaPiere, in June. Post found himself holding his electric twelve-string guitar in a murderer's row of killer guitarists—Barney Kessel, Howard Roberts, Don Peake, and Steve Mann. Jim joined a percussion squad anchored on the kit by the dean, Hal Blaine, and they cut Sonny and Cher's "I Got You Babe."

As Jim rolled across the Midwest again on the Everly Brothers summer tour, he thought long and hard about Jill back home. He still had his flings on the road, but he was increasingly convinced that Jill was the one. What he was not so certain about was whether he was mature enough for marriage. Jim racked up serious long-distance phone bills talking to Jill from his hotel rooms. The long rides between shows gave him time to think over everything thoroughly. By the time Jill showed up to join the tour for a few dates in Wisconsin, he had reached a conclusion. Sitting on a bench in the warm summer sun, Jim asked her to marry him.

"I'd love to," she said.

That night, Jill was sitting next to Phil Everly's wife, Jackie, when the brothers announced their drummer's engagement from the stage. The date was set, the church had been hired, and invitations to the wedding had already been mailed when Jim and Jill whooshed off to Las Vegas to quickly marry on August 26 to beat a deadline for Jim's draft deferment. They went through the subsequent lavish Catholic church wedding as if that never happened. Several hundred people attended the wedding and reception that followed at the home of one of Jill's mother's friends. Page Cavanaugh took over the piano for the occasion. Jim's employers Don and Phil Everly attended, as did Jill's boss, TV host Dick Clark. They planned to honeymoon in Santa Barbara, but Jim neglected to make any reservations, so they wound up spending the night in distinctly less glamorous Santa Maria and coming home the next day. They had already rented an apartment off Ventura Boulevard in Sherman Oaks but did not move in before they were married.

They soon moved from their small apartment into another place only a couple blocks from Jim's parents' house, where the couple dined regularly. Sometimes they joined Mike Post and his wife, Darla, at their house for dinner—Jim and Post both married their childhood sweethearts. They spent time with Phil and Jackie Everly, who introduced the young couple to the joys of antique furniture.

These were happy, exciting days for the newlyweds, frolicking with other musicians and their wives at the second Renaissance Pleasure Faire, living their dreams, watching their life together bloom. Jim was starting to book session work and Jill won a spot on the dance squad for the new Dick Clark weekday after-school TV show, *Where the Action Is,* where rock groups lip-synched their hits in outdoor locations around Los Angeles while the Action Kids wiggled and wobbled in and out of the frame. She was pert blonde Action Gal Jill. Sundays were their only time together.

With the Sonny and Cher record "I Got You Babe" that they recorded in June shooting up to the top of the charts, the suddenly white-hot duo needed a band for a weeklong engagement in September at the former Ciro's on Sunset Strip, so they simply hired their studio musicians with arranger Harold Battiste serving as musical director, his New Orleans pal Mac Rebennack, recently relocated to Hollywood, on guitar, and the usual crew, guitarist Don Peake, keyboardist Mike Rubini, percussionist Gary Coleman, and Jim. At the end of the week, the troupe took over the entire first-class cabin on a red-eye flight to New York, where they checked in to the Essex House on 59th Street to play an exclusive private party the next night.

Hosted by high society industrialist Charles Engelhard at his elegant Waldorf Towers apartment, the party was held to welcome back into society presidential widow Jackie Kennedy after a year in mourning. It was a small, elite gathering, and she had specifically requested her favorite new pop group, Sonny and Cher. When the musicians were introduced to the former First Lady, Rebennack charmed her by speaking Creole French. Mike Post confessed that it was his twenty-first birthday. Jackie kissed his cheeks. *Vogue* editor Diana Vreeland took one look at Cher and declared she needed to be photographed by Richard Avedon, which was quickly arranged.

After the party, the musicians all adjourned to the Peppermint Lounge and took over that place. Rarified air for these young Hollywood studio musicians to be breathing.

After some more recording sessions in September, the Everlys and Jim spent October back in England on an eighteen-date sweep through the country, where the "Love Is Strange" single was showing signs of life. The Everlys were headliners on "Star Scene '65" alongside Cilla Black and Billy J. Kramer and the Dakotas—they were paid a monumental £7,000 a week—on a tour promoted by Beatles manager Brian Epstein in conjunction with the pirate radio station Radio London, who mercilessly flogged the shows, which promptly sold out. Phil showed up in more fashionably long hair than brother Don. Jim, tired of doing the same numbers every night, playing the songs so fast he broke dozens of drumsticks, wanted to work sessions.

Jim came back to prospects of more studio work, a new home, and new wife. They both had their show business jobs—Jim, a studio drummer and Jill, a TV dancer. They were young, beautiful, and blond, a golden couple. They had some money and nice cars. The sunny dream of California life was coming true for Jim. He was twenty years old.

VII.
THE BEAT
GOES ON

Hal Blaine took a liking to Jim. Who didn't like the enormous cherub? He was tall, natural, polite, a sponge around the other session players, soaking up everything he could. And everybody who heard him play went away amazed.

His technical ability had been polished to a fare-thee-well by all the training and practice, but that wasn't what knocked everybody out. It was his complete command of the drum kit, his unerring instinct for punctuation, decoration, percussive commentary. Jim knew things about drums that no amount of training could teach him. He knew when to leave space and when to fill it. He understood the drums in some cosmic way; he knew exactly what to put exactly where. In Jim's hands, the drums bloomed into a fully musical instrument, not a glorified metronome. To the seasoned professionals, Jim's gifts were obvious and astounding.

They played on sessions together, Jim and Hal Blaine, Earl Palmer, all the standing percussionists. In another world, the appearance of a talent as glowing as Jim's might be cause for envy and competitive angst, but in Los Angeles at the time, work was everywhere, more than anybody could handle, and a cooperative, collegial attitude prevailed. Jim was embraced as a kind of new, younger brother.

In January 1966, when the Everlys brought a large session into United Recording, arranger Jack Nitzsche heard Jim play. Blaine was on the same session. Nitzsche was white hot at the moment with producer Phil Spector; they were in the midst of a string of smash hits that were changing the sound of pop music. Nitzsche was also coproducing great records with Sonny Bono with singer Jackie DeShannon at Liberty, playing keyboards on Rolling Stones sessions, producing Bob Lind's "Elusive Butterfly," and cutting hit instrumentals like "The Lonely Surfer" on Reprise under his own name. Nitzsche would be Jim's ticket into Spector sessions.

But it was Hal Blaine who recommended Jim to Brian Wilson of the Beach Boys. At this point in his work schedule, Blaine had more than he could do; he was making three sessions a day, six days a week. He had a cartage company schlepping three sets of drums around town, breaking down the last session and setting up the next, while Blaine whizzed back and forth on a motorcycle in case he got caught in traffic. Blaine was an extrovert's extrovert, always ready with a bad joke and wise quip, and he sensed in Jim a protégé who could do him proud. He started handing off to Jim jobs he couldn't take, and he knew that Jim and Brian shared the childlike enthusiasm that marked both musicians' work.

Brian Wilson was the key figure on the Hollywood recording scene. His series of Beach Boys hits had put the Los Angeles recording scene—if not all of Southern California—on the map. He started working with Blaine and the other studio musicians from the earliest days of his producing the Beach Boys records for Capitol.

Brian found these musicians to be willing collaborators in his imaginative excursions into new realms of pop music. Unindicted coconspirators. He was a delicate personality who had separated himself from the rest of the Beach Boys, staying behind in the studio to write and produce their records while the rest of the group took the show on the road. As long as he came up with hit after hit, there was no problem, even as his grand musical aspirations often eluded the rest of the group. But locked into an unspoken drive to keep pushing his boundaries and moving forward, Brian's commercial certainty had finally faltered and, as he was creating his next masterpiece, the rest of the group was looking over his shoulder with some skepticism.

He had found a new lyricist named Tony Asher, whose previous experience was mostly relegated to writing jingles for an advertising agency, and they were deep into experimental sessions for the next album, and Brian was madly trying fresh ideas and fanciful notions to come up with new sounds. The session musicians, loving the creative atmosphere, encouraged him at every turn. In March 1966, Jim found himself sitting behind the kit at Western Recorders for his first Beach Boys session. While fellow session musician Gary Coleman handled the tympani for "I Am Waiting for the Day," Jim exploded on his snares and toms behind the tympani, dropping bombs of pure thunder to slam the song to its start.

The next day, Jim joined the percussion section for the epic "River Deep—Mountain High" sessions with Ike and Tina Turner, Phil Spector and Jack Nitzsche's ultimate masterpiece. With two dozen musicians crammed ass-to-elbow into Gold Star Studios (and another couple dozen guests observing from the control room, including Mick Jagger and Brian Wilson), Jim added some shakers and bells to the massive orchestral sound while Earl Palmer sat behind the kit.

The day after that, Jim joined another giant session call at Western Recorders to track another Brian Wilson song for the Beach Boys, "God Only Knows." Hal Blaine was playing drums, and Jim was set to add percussion. On a break, Brian saw Jim fooling around with a plastic orange juice bottle, and the two of them lit on the idea of turning the bottle into a percussion instrument. Jim took a razor blade to four bottles and cut them each to a different pitch. He was able to make the clip-clop of the bottles follow Blaine's drum pattern. It was the kind of innocent, playful touch guaranteed to hit Brian's sweet spot, and the click-clack of the empty bottles illuminated the track. Two days later, they finished the recording in a long post-midnight session, Jim on orange juice bottles.

In a few short years, Los Angeles had moved from a quiet, sleepy backwater in the world of pop music to one of its global centers. Television's Dick Clark had relocated his *American Bandstand* to Hollywood, and Phil Spector closed his New York office and returned to Los Angeles. The brilliant Hollywood studio musicians had first invented and perpetrated surf and hot rod records, and then the folk-rock of The Byrds, Barry McGuire, and others. Hit records by new groups like The Mamas and The Papas, The Turtles, and more were streaming every day out of Hollywood recording studios. Los Angeles was the glamorous, glorious home of the new sound of West Coast pop, and studios were operating practically around the clock.

Jim's name was on everybody's lips. He was the phenomenal young drummer who had to be heard. He signed up with an answering service and started spreading out. Jim was booking sessions at a breakneck pace—like Blaine, soon working three sessions a day, six days a week, a cartage company hauling his drum sets from studio to studio. Having grown up with an accountant father, Jim carefully marshaled his money; he was making more than both his parents combined. Jim was driven by powerful desires he kept under wraps. Beneath the timid smile lay secret, private ambitions, lofty, grand, and silent.

Work came flooding at Jim. If back-to-back Beach Boys / Phil Spector sessions were not enough, the next two weeks in March found him in a variety of different, creative circumstances: alone in the studio with bassist and songwriter James Guercio adding rhythm tracks to already recorded vocals by Chad and Jeremy— Guercio's "Distant Shores," with Jim's supple, rolling undercurrent, would be the last chart record for the soft-pop Brit duo of "A Summer Song" fame; working with young producer Lenny Waronker, who used to pay Jim $25 a song to cut demos at Metric Music, trying to revive the sagging fortunes of teen pop star Bobby Vee, who knew Jim from his work with the Everlys; backing former Blues Project vocalist Tommy Flanders with guitarist Frank Zappa, who arranged the track; adding percussion to another brilliant Phil Spector session, "I Wish I Never Saw the Sunshine," an absolutely gorgeous record by The Ronettes, featuring Spector's wife, Ronnie, on lead vocals, that Spector could never bring himself to release, even though it could have been his most sublime creation with his wife's fabled girl group.

In May, Jim did four more Beach Boys sessions with Brian, who was about to release the *Pet Sounds* album, but had already moved on to an obsessive, self-conscious masterpiece that he first started recording in February, "Good Vibrations." Realizing the track did not fit comfortably with the other material he was developing for *Pet Sounds*, Brian put the ambitious mini-suite on the shelf, picking it up again at the beginning of May. Jim added shakers, tambourine, bells, and sat behind the kit. By the time Brian finished the record in September, he had gone through twenty-two sessions, more than ninety hours of magnetic tape, a historic $50,000 budget. It was the pinnacle of the West Coast pop music movement, arguably the greatest pop record ever made, and, without doubt, the biggest hit ever for the Beach Boys. Jim was all over the finished record. He shared the composite master track with Hal Blaine; Jim's drumming drove the second and third bridges, the final chorus, and outro.

In June, Jim was back in United Recording with the Everly Brothers, who were completing an album titled *Two Yanks in England* that they had started with songs and accompaniment from British pop group The Hollies in London, but only finished half. The second half of their British album would be done in Hollywood. The same week, Jim was in Columbia Studios backing up jazz singer Mel Tormé on his *Right Now* album, squeezing in a quick Lee Hazelwood session in between Tormé dates. He was as busy and in-demand a session musician as there was.

Sometimes Hollywood could still seem like a small town. When Action Gal Jill, Jim's wife, mentioned her husband's work as a session musician to the house band on her TV show, *Where the Action Is,* Jim landed another new client, Paul Revere & the Raiders. He went into Columbia Studios in July to track the group's next single, "The Great Airplane Strike," which was exciting since it was a certain hit with the Raiders coming off two consecutive Top Tens already that year.

Of course, Jim joined the sessions for the upcoming television program starring those prefab four, The Monkees, that started in June. Songwriters Tommy Boyce and Bobby Hart were not considered experienced enough to produce the sessions, but after trying out Snuff Garrett and Leon Russell, who made The Monkees' theme song sound like a Gary Lewis and the Playboys record, and songwriters Gerry Goffin and his wife, Carole King, who left the session in tears after a beef with the band, Boyce and Hart were allowed to go ahead. They brought their own band, the Candy Store Prophets, to form the basic studio unit but augmented the lineup with plenty of Hollywood gunslingers like Jim.

But even a prolific songwriting team like Boyce and Hart couldn't supply the material necessary for a season's worth of episodes featuring three songs per show, so music publisher Don Kirshner was summoned. Kirshner had recently sold his company to Columbia Pictures, which was producing the television series, and was one of the kingpins of the Manhattan teen pop business with top writers under contract like Goffin and King, Barry Mann and Cynthia Weil, and Neil Sedaka and Howard Greenfield.

In a flurry at RCA Studios that July, the crew punched out enough songs for a debut album, part of a second album, and the first season of the TV show. The show was already in production, lending extra pressure and chaos to the sessions. Jim joined Hal Blaine on drums, James Burton, Glen Campbell, and Mike Deasy on guitars, Larry Knechtel on keyboards, and other stalwart session players rounding out the band on The Monkees sessions. Don Peake arranged some of the tracks. There was a minor scandal in teenybopperland when it was revealed that The Monkees didn't play all the instruments on their records, but the tracks sounded great, and it didn't stop the records from becoming hits.

At the same time, Ken Nelson, the cagey veteran who had been running the country music division of Capitol Records since 1951, wanted to punch up the sessions by one of his recent signings, a twenty-eight-year-old singer out of Bakersfield named Merle Haggard. His 1965 single "(My Friends Are Gonna Be) Strangers" was his first Top Ten country hit, followed by "Swinging Doors." Haggard was verging on the stardom Nelson had envisioned for him, but Nelson wanted to bring in extra artillery for his next session at Capitol Studios and hired guitarists James Burton and Glen Campbell to round out Haggard's band. Burton suggested bringing in Jim Gordon.

"The Bottle Let Me Down," recorded at Capitol Studios in June at those first sessions with the Hollywood sidemen, was Haggard's third Top Ten, but it was "I'm a Lonesome Fugitive"—cut in five productive sessions with all the guys over three days that August at Capitol—that made Merle Haggard a star, Jim's insistent drumming haunting the paranoid lyrics.

That August, the week after the Haggard sessions, Jim joined a massive midnight call at Gold Star Studios for Bobby Darin, who was about to make an unexpected major pivot in his career. His latest album, *In a Broadway Bag*, had been more Vegas showroom big band pop, but Darin was ready to try something different. New York music publisher Charles Koppelman and Don Rubin had been pitching songs to Darin that had been written by their client John Sebastian of the Lovin' Spoonful, which Darin turned down.

The third time they visited Darin at his office, he joked with them. "I'll record anything you tell me to record," he said. They played him Tim Hardin's "If I Were a Carpenter."

"This is the song," said Darin. "I'm not letting this one get away."

Darin had seen songwriter Tim Hardin years before at a Greenwich Village nightclub, but he had not considered recording his material. He told Koppelman and Rubin that he wanted them to produce the session, a task they customarily farmed out to people who worked for them, like Erik Jacobsen or John Boylan. The former songwriters had little actual studio experience, but Darin insisted, so on a late August night at Gold Star, Koppelman and Rubin were behind the board with Gold Star engineer Stan Ross. Don Peake did the arrangements and contracted the session.

Darin's wife, actress Sandra Dee, had filed for divorce three days earlier, but Darin the perfectionist was supremely focused through those wee hours, making take after take, until he had finally wrestled to the ground "If I Were a Carpenter" and a second Tim Hardin song, "Misty Roses," adjourning just before dawn.

Darin's record label did not know what to make of his sudden transformation into sincere folk-rock singer with his subdued, earnest vocal performance. They put the single out with a leftover from the Broadway album on the other side and were caught by surprise when "Carpenter" slowly caught fire and burned up the charts. Darin hadn't seen the sunny side of the Top Forty in more than three years and, with this record, he was back. For Darin, it was more than a hit record, as he slipped out of his tuxedo into a pair of jeans and started letting his hair grow.

Jim's dance card remained full. There were more sessions with the Beach Boys, as Brian Wilson leaped headfirst into yet another extravagant, creative work, an album called *Smile* that he never really finished; Jim cut "Heroes and Villains," pretty much Brian's last cogent Beach Boys single. Merle Haggard used him on more sessions with him and his wife, Bonnie Owens. Bobby Vee brought him back on a cover of the Beach Boys' "Here Today" from the *Pet Sounds* album. He did some stellar Everly Brothers sessions with James Burton and Glen Campbell on guitars, Larry Knechtel on bass, and Billy Preston on organ.

Life was good. Jim and Jill bought a bigger house on Hartsook Street in North Hollywood, a cozy two-bedroom, one-bath Spanish number built in 1928 with a big shady tree in front. They furnished the place by shopping for antiques. They purchased a beautiful vintage Knabe piano. They loved cars and owned a few (including a '39 Cadillac with a rumble seat). When Jill fell in love with the Mercedes

280SL, they canceled their order for a new Cadillac and went shopping at a German car operation in Encino, where the snooty salesman didn't believe the young couple could afford the $9,000 price tag. They bought the car instead from a dealer in Hollywood. She was still Action Gal Jill on television. Jim may have been marginally more interested in his work than their relationship, and Jill might not have been paying all that much attention to what Jim was doing, but show business was their life.

In December, Jim found himself behind the drum chair—not the percussion section—one night at Gold Star for a Sonny and Cher session. Mike Post was on the session, as was Michel Rubini, who'd brought Jim and Post into the Sonny and Cher circle the year before. "I Got You Babe" had been a worldwide, number one hit, a huge smash that saved bankruptcy-bound Atlantic Records and launched the unlikely duo as the Louis Prima and Keely Smith of the hippie set. They were there to make a hit record called "The Beat Goes On." *Drums keep pounding rhythm to the brain.* At this point, that was Jim's life story.

VIII.
SPRINGTIME

The record business in Hollywood was booming beyond anyone's imagination. Los Angeles was a burbling stew of young talent rising to the surface. Jim was part of a new generation of musicians infiltrating the industry.

After several years of playing as much as he did, Jim had sharpened his skills to extraordinary heights. He could bring his unique bounce, his intuitive musical touch, to any style of music he tried. Playing drums is the art of accompaniment, and Jim studied his craft like a scholar, but his skills went far beyond his training. Some ineffable touch, some gift from the gods, some supernatural power made Jim a better drummer than anyone else. He brought to each record that he cut a significant contribution to the success, like a character actor whose job is to make the star look good, but whom you can't imagine the film without.

Making hit records was the hot new game in town. Over the hill from Hollywood in Burbank, quietly tucked into the massive film studio, Warner Brothers Records was a sleeping giant ready to wake. With the Everly Brothers on the label, Jim quickly came to the attention of the folks at Burbank. Staff producers like Lee Hazelwood and Jimmy Bowen tumbled to Jim's skills right off, and Warners was on the verge of becoming a major force in Hollywood pop with Jim at the center of their studio cadre.

In April 1966, about the same time studio work was exploding for Jim, Lenny Waronker went to work at Warner Brothers Records. There had never been any doubt that he would go into the record business. His father founded Liberty Records—Si Waronker was the namesake for one of his label's best-selling artists, Simon of The Chipmunks—and his son grew up around the office. Lenny's first job at Warners was to sort out the acts that came with the purchase of San Francisco's Autumn Records, a small, independent label run by KYA disc jockeys Tom "Big Daddy" Donahue and Bobby Mitchell.

The Beau Brummels were Autumn's big hit act; their "Laugh Laugh" probably would have been a number one hit on a label with better distribution. The Tikis were a Santa Cruz rock group with a polished vocal sound, and the Mojo Men had a minor regional hit on the label with "Dance with Me."

Waronker was young and inexperienced, naturally conservative and deliberate, wearing suits to work, but with definite ideas about how records should sound. He began to assemble around him a repertory company of songwriters and musicians that included Jim. Warner Brothers was not exactly a hit factory yet. The label's best sellers were comedy albums by Bob Newhart and Bill Cosby, along with their Frank Sinatra and Peter, Paul and Mary albums. Twenty-five-year-old Waronker was about the same age as the young musicians, and he understood the contemporary pop scene in ways the other Warner Brothers executives did not.

He first made the charts with the Mojo Men's "Sit Down I Think I Love You," a song written by Stephen Stills of Buffalo Springfield, a group Waronker dearly loved but could not convince Warners to sign. The brilliant Van Dyke Parks, fresh from collaborating with Brian Wilson on his lost masterpiece *Smile*, provided the baroque arrangement and played harpsichord on the track, backed by a crew of Hollywood session players including Jim, who well remembered Waronker from cutting demos with him for the publishing arm of his dad's label. It would be a long time before Waronker went into the studio without Jim. He thought Jim and his wife were as clean-cut and all-American as high school cheerleaders.

Under the spell of the Beach Boys' "Good Vibrations," Waronker heard a snippet of the Simon and Garfunkel song "Feelin' Groovy" on a radio commercial and envisioned an elaborate vocal arrangement. He brought in Leon Russell, who fleshed out the vocal parts and added strings and woodwinds. Since the official members of the group Waronker tapped for the song wouldn't be playing the instruments, only the two vocalists—Ted Templeman and Dick Scoppettone of The Tikis—came to the session, where Jim, Glen Campbell, and others played the tracks. The group was reluctant to use the name The Tikis because they thought it might hurt their following back in Santa Cruz, and at the last minute the group was named Harpers Bizarre. When it was released in January 1967, the record almost made its way into the Top Ten, a strong showing for Warners.

Waronker also tapped his childhood friend and next-door neighbor, songwriter Randy Newman, a Metric Music writer who studied music at UCLA when he could find parking, to provide material for the Harpers Bizarre album and play piano on the sessions. They covered the Van Dyke Parks song "Come to the Sunshine." Waronker was beginning to pull together his little Motown of California pop—these early experiments were only the start.

The Beau Brummels were a different matter. The group already had a national profile and boasted the evocative, reflective vocals of Sal Valentino and superb songwriting from guitarist Ron Elliott. Their Warner Brothers debut, *Beau Brummels '66,* had been a waste of time, a collection of uninspired covers of currently popular songs from other better-known artists. The Brummels had higher aspirations. When vocalist Sal Valentino came to the studio and first saw Jim sitting behind a drum kit, he flew into a rage. Ron Elliott had already recorded delicate, intricate acoustic guitars for the song, and Valentino couldn't see how overdubbed drums could do anything but ruin the piece. He couldn't watch. He stormed out of the studio. When he returned an hour later, Jim had laid drums beautifully into the track, lifting and separating the tangle of guitars and voices in a way Valentino hadn't thought possible.

After that, Jim joined the group. Brummels drummer John Peterson had defected to Harpers Bizarre—although Waronker also used Jim in the studio on those tracks—and the group was down to three members, four with Jim. That was the band that recorded *Triangle,* a little recognized 1967 gem from the Brummels. They also covered Randy Newman. Van Dyke Parks was around. Waronker started using Ron Elliott on sessions. Waronker's troupe was coming together.

When Waronker went into the studio to cut a single with a folk-rock quartet featuring former members of the Back Porch Majority called MC Squared, of course he brought Jim. When MC Squared's drummer Jim Keltner walked into the cavernous TTG Studios that afternoon and saw the blue Sparkletone Ludwig set, he realized that he was going to be watching—not playing—and pulled up a piece of the wooden floor next to Jim's kick drum.

Jim Keltner had been a jazz drummer working for $85 a week in a drum store. When Gary Lewis of Gary Lewis and the Playboys offered him $250 a week to play in his group, Keltner decided to give rock and roll a try. Hal Blaine had watched like an understudy at Keltner's first Gary Lewis session when they cut "She's Just My Style." Keltner knew Hal, but Jim took his breath away. To Keltner, Jim was Hal on steroids. He had the Hal Blaine confidence in his sound, only he hit harder and played louder. His snare was pitched lower, not as tight. He had Hal's command, but he played more modern and had a better vocabulary. Keltner found Jim friendly but quiet, confident but distant. Keltner bought his own blue Sparkletone kit after that. He and Jim would meet again.

Among the many projects Waronker was overseeing in Burbank was an ambitious artistic endeavor by Van Dyke Parks, a sprawling vision of words and music from the extravagantly verbal and abundantly musical Southerner seven months in production, an album eventually titled *Song Cycle*. He signed his pal Randy Newman as an artist and produced a little-heard, lavish, orchestral debut album, although nobody noticed the crunching Rolling Stones–style follow-up single that Waronker and Parks produced, "Last Night I Had a Dream." Jim worked all his sessions. Waronker was trying to build a team and encourage their collaborative and artistic instincts, a relatively untested strategy in the record business.

Jim's life was like a river in spring, filled to the brim and rushing along at top speed. He had accomplished his goals so swiftly that his career consumed him. As he reaped the rewards of his rapidly advancing status, the attention started to go to his head. His parents worried about his ability to handle his success. He was making plenty of money, enough to lose a bundle on a dubious investment in a Canadian amusement park that was supposed to include the largest swimming pool in the country. Along with Larry Knechtel,

Hal Blaine, Joe Osborn, James Burton, Don Randi, and some other session players under the influence of a shady investment manager, Jim and a few of the other investors flew up to Banff to inspect the project. Jim was unnervingly quiet on the trip, in a contemplative mood, and clearly unhappy with the investment, which went bankrupt shortly after.

He began to feel constricted at home. He lost common ground with Jill. He no longer had much to talk about with her. She was a lighthearted, cheerful woman who laughed and hung out with friends. Jim was more serious, something of a loner. He had grown bored with his marriage. His interests lay elsewhere, not necessarily other women, but not necessarily not. They were not happy. Jill didn't feel Jim was there for her, and he didn't see her as an important part of what was going on with him. They had been madly in love, but now they were growing apart.

Jim moved out of Hartsook into a small Hollywood apartment, but would get lonely and go back to Jill for a day or two. He was not interested in making the marriage work. Jill was. Jim was growing remote, living inside his own head.

At the same time, the public appetite for new sounds, new groups, new records seemed insatiable. The whole pop music world was in full bloom, and Los Angeles suddenly sat at the sonic center of the universe. Jim would be involved in several important projects in the coming months with the growing creative community. A fresh crew of visionaries were vying for attention, but behind the scenes, the same characters were pulling the strings.

Jim sat behind the kit for the beginning of the illustrious solo career of Neil Young, thanks to Jack Nitzsche. Young and Nitzsche fell in together as friends after a crazy, drunken night when Nitzsche followed Young from the Whisky a Go Go to his log cabin in the Hollywood Hills and crashed his Cadillac convertible head-on into another car before getting hauled off to jail. It was the beginning of a beautiful friendship. Eventually, Nitzsche made his way to Young's house. Aware that Nitzsche knew the Everly Brothers, Young took out a twelve-string guitar and played him a song he had written that Young thought would be perfect for the Everlys.

Halfway through the song, Nitzsche blurted, "Fuck—what a great song."

"Shhh, just listen," Young told him.

Young had left Buffalo Springfield, and Nitzsche had grand ambitions to produce the piece, "Expecting to Fly," as the debut of Neil Young's solo career. In May 1967, Jim joined Carol Kaye on bass, Don Randi on piano and harpsichord, and on guitar, songwriter Russ Titelman—who had been at Young's place when he and Nitzsche mapped out the arrangement—along with a full string section and a mini-choir of background vocalists at Sunset Sound to cut the hallucinogenic track a month before *Sgt. Pepper's Lonely Hearts Club Band*. If anything, the swirling soundscape was inspired by Brian Wilson's pastoral *Pet Sounds* inventions. Nitzsche and Young spent weeks on the track. Young was so insecure about his vocals in the studio, he practically needed to record them line by line. They spent endless hours perfecting the dreamy mix, all in service of a potential Neil Young solo project.

Young and Nitzsche were living together by this point with Nitzsche's amusing buddy, Denny Bruce, and the three talked about moving to England, where the tapes of the session caused something of a stir. Graham Nash called to say it was the greatest record he'd ever heard. With Young unable to loose himself from his recording deal with Springfield to make a solo album, he, Nitzsche, and Denny Bruce made plans to move to England. Young was titillated by Nitzsche's connection to the Rolling Stones. By August, however, the mercurial Young had rejoined Buffalo Springfield, dropped the solo project, and contributed the track to that group's next album.

Jim was also on the date when Glen Campbell finally cut his breakthrough. After five years signed to Capitol Records and making tracks with five different producers, Campbell informed Capitol country chief Ken Nelson he was ready to pick the songs he would record. Campbell figured he couldn't do any worse than the knuckleheads who had him trying everything from bluegrass to protest folk-rock. One week after the Neil Young session, Jim joined a handful of Campbell's closest associates—guitarist James Burton, bassist Joe Osborn, pianist Leon Russell, and Doug Dillard on banjo—for an informal demo session at Capitol Studios. It took only a half-hour overtime for these pros to knock out five tracks. Campbell had collected the songs—a couple he wrote himself, one from a young, unknown Hollywood writer named Harry Nilsson, one from the Everly Brothers' British bass player, and one from a record he heard on the radio and bought a copy to learn, "Gentle on My Mind" by Nashville recording artist John Hartford.

Campbell had big plans for the Hartford song—strings, polished vocal, elegant production—but Nelson was so taken with the relaxed, impromptu performance he heard on the demo tape, he lopped off the instructions Campbell gave the musicians over the introduction and put the darn thing out. In retrospect, Campbell wondered if his casual vocal performance didn't serve to enhance the song's emotional center, but there it was, almost by accident— the record that kick-started his immense solo career. These guys were that good.

The Los Angeles recording machine was cranking out hits daily, records of every kind. The brilliant cadre of skilled studio musicians provided a corps of accomplished sidemen who could play any style of music required. The more they worked together, the better they got. They were the cutting edge of the recording industry, the advance guard of new sounds, and masters of the studio.

In August, Jim found himself in the middle of a huge, twenty-six-musician call at Columbia Studios with producer Jerry Fuller for sessions with a new rock group from San Diego called the Union Gap, featuring vocalist Gary Puckett. The group's five members were given minimal chores—their sax player sat in with the horn section, their bass player plugged in next to session player Larry Knechtel, the keyboardist sat at the organ, and the drummer played tambourine. The string section and horns all crowded into the room. This was big band rock and roll recorded live.

From an isolation booth in the center of the room, Puckett soared over the mammoth sound with Jim slamming the drums, playing loud enough and hitting hard enough to drive the giant sound. Puckett was so overwhelmed by the massive sound coming through his headphones, he could barely manage to sing and wound up over-dubbing his final vocals. Fuller, who broke on the scene writing the Ricky Nelson hit "Travelin' Man," was an exacting producer. He knew in detail how he wanted the song sung, and he trusted the studio musicians to deliver the widescreen sound he needed. "Woman, Woman" was a smash hit out of the first session, and Jim was behind the kit for the rest of the Gary Puckett and the Union Gap sessions.

Substituting or augmenting existing rock groups at recording sessions was nothing new for the Hollywood session players. The studio musicians did not receive credit on the album jacket, preserving the delicious image that the characters pictured on the cover actually made all the music on the record, but the confidence that came from packing sessions with ringers like Jim and his associates proved irresistible to producers. Hired guns were only a phone call away, and who played what on the record mattered mostly to the band members themselves, who frequently didn't have a say in the decision.

Like when The Byrds went into Columbia Studios to record the band's first record, "Mr. Tambourine Man." Only guitarist Jim McGuinn played on the track, and there had been some discussion about bringing Glen Campbell in to do his twelve-string part. Hal Blaine provided the drive, and Larry Knechtel's booming bass tied everything together. Leon Russell also played piano at the session, but his part was taken out in the mix. The three Byrds at the session only sang. The other two members did not even attend.

Of course, that was more than simply a number one hit for The Byrds, it was a key record in igniting the whole folk-rock boom, establishing songwriter Bob Dylan as a major force, and it turned The Byrds into the American Beatles. They immediately followed "Mr. Tambourine Man" with a second number one hit, "Turn! Turn! Turn!" By the time, two years later, when the fractious group entered the studio to make the band's fifth album, *The Notorious Byrd Brothers*, there were four members. The album's production turned out to be a protracted affair over many months, as the band battled over creative and personal issues. In August, after a screaming match during sessions at Columbia Studios between David Crosby and drummer Michael Clark, who had played on every Byrds record since "Mr. Tambourine Man," band members threatened to bring in Hal Blaine. Three days later, the band reconvened at Columbia Studios with Jim on drums and Michael Clark nowhere to be seen.

Two weeks after that, Crosby blew his top over the Goffin and King song "Goin' Back," which producer Gary Usher had found for the group. Crosby wanted the album to include his song "Triad," a risqué hippie ballad about a ménage à trois, and he did not want to cover some other writer's song. He stomped out of the session and his Byrds partners Chris Hillman and Roger McGuinn visited him at his Laurel Canyon home a few days later to tell him he was fired.

In October, Hillman and McGuinn regrouped at Columbia with Jim and an assortment of other session musicians—guitarist James Burton, Moog synthesizer specialist Paul Beaver, Red Rhodes on pedal steel guitar, a string section, a harpist, and others. Half the album was in the can and another six songs in various stages of completion. Work focused on finishing "Goin' Back," which the record company had already announced would be the next single, with Jim's grand flourish boldly announcing the final chorus. While Jim finished key tracks like "Wasn't Born to Follow," because of his heavy work schedule, they did have to call Hal Blaine for a session after all. The album, patched together by session musicians with the group on its last legs, would be one of their best sellers.

Yes, the record business in Hollywood was on fire. Talent was everywhere and record companies were getting hipper by the day. Jim bounced from one fascinating double-scale date to another. He went to work with neophyte producer John Boylan, who was trying to resurrect the moribund career of faded teen idol Ricky Nelson. Although Nelson was roughly the same age as the members of Buffalo Springfield and The Byrds, he was widely considered old and in the way, a leftover from rock's embarrassing recent past and a former cast member from one of the most square television shows in history.

Working for Koppelman and Rubin in New York, Boylan, fresh out of Bard College and one year younger than Nelson, came west to see if he could pump some life into Nelson's recording career. The former teen idol had been making efforts at relevance since falling off the charts—earnest country music albums, a record with Burt Bacharach—and pairing him with a producer his own age who was hip and understood the changing music scene made sense.

Boylan also knew the West Coast session players by reputation and was excited to work with them.

Guitarist James Burton, of course, had worked in Nelson's band since his fifties rock and roll hits, and he made the sessions, along with a tight circle of familiar faces. Boylan passed out carefully written lead sheets to all the musicians. He watched Jim barely notice the sheet music while he was making small talk with the bass player and then play the score perfectly on the first rundown.

Jim spent the fall bouncing in and out of town while he played some college concerts with Chad and Jeremy, his first bandstand dates since the Everly Brothers. He still found time to knock out an album of Beatles songs in country and western style by singer Jerry Inman and producer Jerry Fuller, alongside guitarists Campbell and Burton. He did the Ricky Nelson album, plus some Byrds and Beach Boys sessions.

In November, Jim joined a rhythm section of bassist Larry Knechtel, pianist Mike Melvoin, and guitarist Al Casey with a full string section at RCA Studios for the second album by a promising young songwriter and vocalist named Harry Nilsson, whose first album had been recorded with a small, unobtrusive jazz combo. Producer Rick Jarrard decided to bring in the A-Team session players this time.

Nilsson had been trying to break into the business for years, working nights at a bank and haunting recording studios during the day. He wrote some songs for Phil Spector that Spector never released. Glen Campbell cut his "Without Her," but when The Monkees recorded his "Cuddly Toy," his music publisher told him he could quit the bank. Paul McCartney studied his demos and there had been some talk of The Beatles hijacking him from RCA for their record label, but nothing came of that.

His second album, *Aerial Ballet,* with Jim on drums, led off with his song "One" as the first single, which would be a hit for Three Dog Night but not Nilsson. Then, when film director John Schlesinger used Nilsson's recording of the Fred Neil song "Everybody's Talking" as the theme to his 1969 Oscar-winner *Midnight Cowboy,* Nilsson was a made man. Jim would be an important part of his music for years.

IX.
AMY

When Jill told Jim in fall 1967 that she was pregnant, he worried that he was too young to have children. He wanted out of the marriage, but he couldn't let go entirely of Jill. He thought she should consider having an abortion, but Catholic girl that she was, Jill wasn't letting that happen. Reluctantly, Jim moved back into Hartsook with his pregnant wife.

Where the Action Is went off the air, but Jill had landed on her feet with the new variety show *The Carol Burnett Show*. Once she was pregnant, she withdrew from the cast. But financially, the couple would be just fine. Jim had become one of the most in-demand session players in town, routinely booking two or three sessions a day, six days a week, working around the clock. He was pulling down big money, $2,000 or more a week, and living like a lord.

He had attained all his professional goals and accomplished what he set out to do. Every day, he went to the studio to solve a new set of creative problems and surgically bring drums and percussion into somebody else's music. He felt invincible, a young Athenian who undertook heroic deeds every day. He saw himself emerging in a new powerful character and no longer felt comfortable being married. Instead of being a joyous time for the expectant parents, it was a sad period for Jim. A dark conflict brewed inside him as he struggled to come to terms with his life and his marriage.

It was not something he discussed with his wife. She felt completely supported in her pregnancy by Jim. He was kind, sweet, accommodating. She knew nothing about his reservations. He kept those thoughts to himself. Jim did look forward to being a father. He was more at home handling his infant nephew born about six months before their daughter than his nephew's father, Jill's brother. Jill went with Jim to Brian Wilson's house in Bel Air, where Jim and Brian worked together in Brian's home studio while pregnant Jill sat drinking tea and petting Banana, the dog, with Brian's wife, Marilyn, who was also pregnant.

If his studio work enveloped Jim, his best friend, Mike Post, had understood early in his career that playing sessions would never be enough for him; he wanted to be the one who decided how the music would sound. Post was a scrappy hustler who took a job with producer Jimmy Bowen, who warned him not to arrange the records he produced, advice Post completely ignored.

Post found some disgruntled members of the New Christy Minstrels and put together a group they called the First Edition, even though Post was not especially keen on the baritone vocalist. Post thought the focal point of the group's music would be lead vocalist Mike Settle, but when the baritone sang the group's second single—the psychedelicized "Just Dropped In (To See What Condition My Condition Was In)," featuring backward guitar by Glen Campbell, fuzztone solo by session man Mike Deasy, and double drums from Hal Blaine and Earl Palmer—and it hit the Top Five in early 1968, Post started to see the beauty of Kenny Rogers.

Assigned to produce Mason Williams, chief writer for *The Smothers Brothers Comedy Hour* who played flamboyant folk guitar, Post took Williams's simple guitar instrumental, wrote a middle section he cribbed from Richard Wagner, built a massive orchestration (with co-arranger Al Capps, who did all the big band Gary Puckett sessions), and created a genuine pop epic out of Williams's slight guitar number. At the center of the giant, twenty-four-piece orchestra assembled at United Recorders that day was Post's longtime close associate Jim Gordon, who provided one of his finest performances.

"It's a motherfucker," Jim shouted at the end of the master take.

But when Williams's roommate and benefactor Tommy Smothers stopped by the studio during post-production and heard the playbacks, he lost his mind. "That's the most over-arranged piece of shit I've ever heard in my life," he snapped at Post.

Post, who didn't lack for self-confidence, summarily threw Smothers out of the studio. The next day, Smothers called Post to admit he was wrong—the radical departure from the original composition had been too rude a shock to his system, he said. Indeed, "Classical Gas" sounded like nothing else on the radio when it hit in April 1968 and soared to the top of the charts. With that, Mike Post was on the scene, another blooming creative figure in whose music Jim would play an important role.

Richard Perry was next. The fledgling record producer who had only recently moved from New York and landed a job as staff producer at Warner Brothers Records was assigned to record the eccentric song stylist Tiny Tim. Perry had already recorded the one-of-a-kind oddball on the cheap in New York, but this would be a full, major label budget and Perry's introduction to Jim Gordon, who would become a key weapon in Perry's arsenal as he evolved into one of Hollywood's top producers. Tiny Tim's "Tiptoe

Through the Tulips" would be one of the strangest, most unlikely hit records of the year.

Working constantly with all the other great musicians, Jim's skills developed to another level. He could see around corners on the drums and forecast the path of the arrangement intuitively. He seemed to instinctively understand what the song needed and worked his way into the heart of every arrangement. Because the drums invariably sat at the bottom of the orchestrations, his subtleties might often be obscured, but they were unquestionably crucial to the record. The other musicians all noticed.

In May 1968, Jim was in Capitol Studio A with Glen Campbell to record his follow-up to the mid-chart hit "By the Time I Get to Phoenix," a song from writer Jimmy Webb that Campbell learned from a Johnny Rivers album. To capitalize on the modest success, Campbell went to Webb and asked if Webb had any more "place" songs like "Phoenix." He came up with "Wichita Lineman."

In the studio, bassist Carol Kaye thought up a clever six-note introduction on her Danelectro bass and Campbell tuned down his guitar into Duane Eddy range for a trembly solo that carefully followed the song's melody on the middle part that Webb never finished. On a break between sessions, while producer Al DeLory wrote the string arrangement, Webb played Campbell the creaky Gulbranson church organ he kept in his silent-film-star mansion down the block from Ozzie and Harriet's Hollywood home. Campbell insisted he add the organ to the track and the unwieldy instrument was broken down and carted to the studio where Webb played a repeated four-note figure over the final chorus, which Jim lit up by stealthily switching from brushes to sticks to kick the track into overdrive on the outro. "Wichita Lineman" was the record that put Glen Campbell over.

Eighteen-year-old Jim poses for his first publicity portrait, looking into his brilliant future, 1964. *Courtesy of Amy Gordon.*

Robin Hood Band; where Jim first cemented his ambition to be a professional musician, standing in the rear left, drumsticks in his hand, age sixteen, performing "Musical Americana" in Berlin, Germany, July 1961. *Photo by Stan Wayman/The LIFE Picture Collection/Shutterstock.*

Frankie Knight & The Jesters, Jim on drums (left), Mike Post on keyboard (right), at Mama Altvoturno's in Hollywood, 1962. The restaurant owner's daughter was singer Timi Yuro. *Courtesy of Mike Post.*

Everly Brothers, Phil and Don, with Jim on drums, Sonny Curtis on guitar, Dale Hallcom on bass, 1964. *Photo by Chuck Boyd,* from the book *Riot on Sunset Strip: Rock 'n' Roll's Last Stand in Hollywood* (Domenic Priore, Jawbone Press).

Big Band jazz bandstand date with Page Cavanaugh (guitarist Joe Pass barely visible over Jim's shoulder), 1966. *Courtesy of Amy Gordon.*

Jim on tympani with trumpeter Roy Catan (left) and percussionist Julius Wechter (right) in studio. *Photo by Hal Blaine.*

Beach Boys mastermind Brian Wilson passed out toy firemen's hats for the "Fire" portion of his "Elements" suite planned for the aborted *Smile* album at Gold Star Studio, November 1966. *Photo by Jasper Daily, Courtesy of the David Leaf Collection, All Rights Reserved.*

Jim outside Western Recorders on Sunset Blvd., with keyboardist Don Randi and guitarist Don Peake, 1965. *Photo by Hal Blaine.*

Producer Brian Wilson, bassist Lyle Ritz, and Jim at *Pet Sounds* sessions, 1966. *Photo by Jasper Daily, Courtesy of the David Leaf Collection, All Rights Reserved.*

Jim and Jill's wedding day, September 1965. *Courtesy of Amy Gordon.*

Mr. and Mrs. Jim Gordon. *Courtesy of Amy Gordon.*

Action gal Jill on the Dick Clark TV show *Where the Action Is*, 1965. *Courtesy of Jill Gordon.*

The Gordon family: Jim, Jill, and Amy, in the drive-way of their Hartsook Street place, May 1969. *Courtesy of Amy Gordon.*

Jim and Amy Gordon on his twenty-fourth birthday, July 1969. *Courtesy of Amy Gordon.*

"His Two," Jill, Amy, photo by Jim Gordon, 1969. *Courtesy of Amy Gordon.*

Jim at the Hollywood Professional Drum Shop, 1968. *Courtesy of Pro Drum Shop, Hollywood.*

Delaney & Bonnie and Friends, Birmingham Town Hall, December 4, 1969. Left to right: Jim Price on trumpet, Jim on drums, Carl Radle on bass, Bobby Keys on saxophone, Bonnie Bramlett on vocals, George Harrison (rear) on guitar, Delaney Bramlett on guitar, Eric Clapton on guitar. *Daily Mirror/Mirrorpix.*

Jim with Bonnie Bramlett, George Harrison, Delaney Bramlett (playing Harrison's rosewood Telecaster), and Eric Clapton in Copenhagen, Denmark, December 1969. *Photo by Jan Perssen/Redferns/Getty Images.*

Mad Dogs & Englishmen film still; Joe Cocker, Jim, Leon Russell, 1970. *Getty Images.*

Jim with Joe Cocker on the "Mad Dogs & Englishmen" tour, Philadelphia Academy of Music, April 1970. *Photo by Linda Wolf.*

Jim and Rita Coolidge, 1970. *Photo by Andee Nathanson.*

The debut performance by Derek and The Dominos at the Lyceum Theatre, June 14, 1970. Left to right: Bobby Whitlock on organ, Eric Clapton on guitar, Carl Radle on bass, Jim Gordon on drums, and Dave Mason on guitar. *Photo by Koh Hasebe/Shinko Music/Getty Images.*

With Carl Perkins, Johnny Cash, Derek and The Dominos on *The Johnny Cash Show* filmed at Ryman Auditorium, Nashville, November 1970. *Photo by Disney General Entertainment/Getty Images.*

Jim at sound check for Derek and The Dominos, Berkeley Community Theater, November 1970. *Photo by Arthur Rosato.*

Traffic, the "Low Spark of the High-Heeled Boys" edition (left to right): Steve Winwood, Rebop Kwaku Baah, Jim Capaldi, Ric Grech, Chris Wood, Jim Gordon, July 1971. *Photo by Dick Polak.*

On June 13, Jim's daughter, Amy, was born by cesarean at St. Joseph's Hospital in Burbank, where his mother, Osa, was a nurse and attended the birth, although she stayed outside the delivery room, pacing the halls with Jim. If his parents had been disappointed by their separation, they were greatly encouraged by Jim's return home and the pending blessed event. In Jim's mind, he was acting out of a sense of duty rather than some renewed emotional commitment to his marriage. His feelings for Jill had gone numb. At the same time, he was also in the middle of recording one of the finest albums he had ever done, and he excitedly showed Jill the box of cigars he bought to distribute at the recording session that night. He had already enthused to her about the girl singer who he said played piano like a man.

For the eighth album by folk singer Judy Collins, producer David Anderle, fresh from running the Beach Boys' record label but with limited experience actually making records, carefully put together an exquisite ensemble to back her new record. In addition to Jim on drums and Chris Ethridge of the Flying Burrito Brothers on bass, he brought James Burton on guitar and Van Dyke Parks on piano. Burton recommended Nashville pedal steel guitar player Buddy Emmons, who had moved to Los Angeles to play in Roger Miller's band. Also, knowing he needed the help, Anderle brought one of his closest friends, Stephen Stills of Buffalo Springfield, to play guitar. The sparks between Collins and Stills started the first time they met at a welcome to Los Angeles party the recording engineer threw for her at his Laurel Canyon home the night before the sessions started.

Recording took place at the ultra-modern Elektra Studios in the Beverly Hills company complex with a garden in the center and a bridge over the stream running through the middle where Stills and Collins first shared a kiss while the playback of her freshly recorded song "My Father" wafted through the air. At night, they repaired to Stills's Malibu hideaway in his Bentley. They were falling rapturously in love.

Collins—who was coming off the first Top Ten hit of her lengthy career, "Both Sides Now," by an unknown writer named Joni Mitchell—had been surrounded by classically trained musicians on previous albums and had never recorded with a band like this. Material came from some obvious sources—Bob Dylan, Leonard Cohen, Collins's own song about her recently deceased father—but she had never heard Sandy Denny of Fairport Convention when Anderle played her "Who Knows Where the Time Goes?" which would become the cornerstone piece and title track of the album.

The extensive sessions ran all through June. The players grew both tight and loose, happy to jam for fifteen minutes behind Collins's nine-year-old son, Clark, as he sang his song that went "I am flying . . . don't you know." Stills and Collins were riding back to Malibu one night toward the end of the sessions, with the album one song short of being done, when Stills started singing the old Ian Tyson song "Someday Soon." As Collins fell right in harmony with him, she realized she knew every word. Buddy Emmons whipped his steel guitar on the track, Jim gave it his Merle Haggard touch, and the new album had its first single.

Jim always thought of this as some of his finest work, which offers considerable insight into how Jim viewed his music. The band on the sessions played a kind of folk-rock-chamber-pop, elevating Collins out of her typical folk music context into a unique realm that the musicians specifically created for her. Stills especially brought filigreed touches to practically every track. Jim's work was enmeshed in the ensemble playing—no fancy stunts, no showy fills, no obvious Jim Gordon riffs. He didn't even play on some selections, and some that he did, including the title track, he doesn't come in until the track is well underway. But when he does play, every step of the way his sure hand supports, lifts, and defines this crystalline sound. The album is the ultimate product of dedicated session musicians, playing at the highest level of ability, customizing their work to suit the artist and songs they are backing. This was Jim's highest aspiration for his art. This was what he did.

In July, producer Lou Adler booked Jim to play drums with a trio he signed called The City, which featured songwriter Carole King. With her husband, Gerry Goffin, she had been the queen of teen pop in New York, writing big hits for The Shirelles, Drifters, Bobby Vee, Aretha Franklin, and many more. They also worked on Monkees records. After she and Goffin split, she moved to Los Angeles with her boyfriend and started to record under Adler's supervision. By the end of the year, the group experiment was over, and Jim was playing on demos for Carole King solo sessions.

At Warners, Lenny Waronker had launched an ambitious project with the Everly Brothers and was conducting sessions whenever their hectic road schedule allowed. He pulled together his repertory company around the vocalists—including a new member introduced to Waronker by Jack Nitzsche, slide guitarist Ry Cooder. Waronker saw the Everlys as a wasted resource at Warners, having watched their record career deteriorate to almost nothing through the indifferent, practically incompetent direction they received from the label. He wanted to frame the Everlys as the fathers of the emerging Hollywood country-rock sound, at the same time establishing their credentials on the current scene (Byrds, Burrito Brothers, Poco, etc.). The Everlys themselves were skeptical and kept their distance from the project.

From April to October, Waronker mixed old-fashioned country fare from Jimmie Rodgers, Merle Haggard, and Ray Price with contemporary writers like Randy Newman, Ron Elliott of the Beau

Brummels (who did many of the album's arrangements), and a fuzztone remake of "I Wonder If I Care as Much," the original B side to the Everlys' first hit, "Bye Bye Love." Waronker used his tight team of seasoned professionals, of course including Jim. Waronker was less nervous going into sessions when he knew Jim was going to be there.

They salted the tracks with excerpts from a 1952 recording of Phil and Don singing on their parents' radio show. The resulting album, *Roots,* was a tidy little masterpiece from the creative cabal that Waronker had built. Although the commercial reception of the album may have proved to be less than hoped for, Phil and Don eventually came around. They took Waronker aside at the company playback party at United Studio B and thanked him.

At the top of his form, in December, Jim laid down an explosive and demanding rhythm on a vocal version of the Hugh Masekela song "Grazin' in the Grass," lyrics written by one of the members of the Los Angeles vocal group Friends of Distinction, a record Jim ruthlessly drives from the first downbeat. John Florez was a twenty-two-year-old freshman record producer out of Phoenix with a job at RCA Victor who happened across the group, managed by football star Jim Brown, at the trendy Hollywood discotheque the Daisy. He took them into the studio for his first sessions as a producer. He had watched Jim work out on a José Feliciano session helmed by his boss at RCA, producer Rick Jarrard, and knew that Jim was his drummer. In fact, Jim was the only player Florez picked for the session.

Florez brought arranger Ray Cork Jr. from Phoenix, another neophyte who had scored every note of music to be played on the session. Jim was frustrated to find that his bass drum part as written duplicated the bass part, something he always tried to avoid. But he found a Latin boogaloo beat that fit the rhythm like a glove.

Joining him on the session was the charismatic conga player King Errisson, who had vaulted out of Nassau after filming a scene in the James Bond film *Thunderball* and had only recently relocated to Los Angeles. On the drum break after the chorus, Jim went off like a cluster bomb and Errisson jumped aboard as the record caught fire on the percussion volley and burned to the close.

Although he was at the height of his skills, Jim was growing tired of the challenges of the studio. He had been locked in rooms without windows playing music for four years, and he had done everything from television pre-records and movie soundtracks to radio jingles and TV commercials. Chasing hit records was the only truly exciting game in town, but most work lay elsewhere. Jim had found a way to make himself integral to virtually everything that he played, laying down beats that were crucial to the sound. It was no accident that all these hit records featured his drumming.

But the music scene had changed drastically in those four years. The heroes of Woodstock were not only crowding the top of the charts, they were leading a vast musical movement. British rock groups like Led Zeppelin and The Who had brought powerful, dynamic music to the concert stage that made their records seem like mere blueprints for live performances. The Hollywood hit factory was no longer the center of the pop music universe, and the fabulous new rock stars were the same age as Jim. He and Jill attended the concert by Cream the year before at the Shrine Auditorium, and Jim had marveled at the expansive prowess of drummer Ginger Baker, although that was also the first time he saw guitarist Eric Clapton, who would wind up playing a crucial role in Jim's career.

Important and provocative projects still called Jim. He cut a double-record tribute to Jimmie Rodgers with Merle Haggard and did sessions with producer Richard Perry, who was trying to bring

Theodore Bikel and Ella Fitzgerald into the contemporary scene, having them sing Beatles and Motown songs. He did some spectacular work on the Mike Post album *Fused*, a collaboration between rock generation Post and big band arranger Pete Carpenter, a deliciously eclectic, sumptuous production that showcased Jim holding down the big sound in the center of the massive orchestra on tracks like "The Briarwood Express."

Jim and Jill went with Post and his wife to the eleventh annual Grammy Awards in March 1969 at the Century Plaza Hotel where Post was up for several awards for "Classical Gas." Glen Campbell, who was hosting the show with vocalist Bobby Gentry, had already told Post he thought Post would win the Best Arrangement award, and when he opened the envelope onstage, Campbell looked down at Post sitting in the front row next to his boss Jimmy Bowen and Bowen's wife, Keely Smith, and spoke off-mike to him. "I told you so," Campbell said before announcing Post's victory for "Classical Gas." The tables in the back of the room full of his rowdy fellow session players, unaccustomed to this kind of industry recognition, went wild.

That March, Jim performed in the studio essentially as a member of the new group Bread, a soft-rock group composed of Hollywood music business veterans determined to find a place on the charts. Although he appeared with the group at the record company showcase at the Aquarius Theatre, he declined the invitation to tour. In April, he cut an instrumental solo album in two sessions for producer Bob Thiele's Flying Dutchman label, *Hog Fat* by Jimmy Gordon and his Jazznpops Band, with a handful of his session associates like Don Peake, Gary Coleman, Jim Horn, and Tom Scott. He was called in to put drums on the Graham Nash song "Marrakesh Express" on the debut album by Crosby, Stills & Nash. He told his wife they were going to be huge.

But Jim was feeling uncomfortable. He wanted out of his marriage. The only thing he and Jill had in common now, he thought, was having a baby. Jim liked being a father. He played with her, gave her bottles, put her to bed. But it wasn't enough. He wanted to start over. He had been married for five years, almost a quarter of his young life, and he was ready to move on. There was a whole new world out there for him. Jim had not tasted all the fruits of his success, and he was hungry to see what there was for him. Jill was no longer part of what mattered to him. He talked it over with his friend Mike Post. Although neither of the two young husbands had been faultlessly faithful in their marriages, Post never heard Jim say a cross word about Jill. He wanted freedom, he told Post. He was too young to be married. It was too confining.

Quiet, private thoughts guided him. The still waters beneath his smile ran deep and dark. He had been working on the Andy Williams television show, where Mike Post served as musical director, and when Williams offered him a bandstand job for his June run at Caesars Palace in Las Vegas, Jim took the gig. He packed his bags, threw them and his drums in the car, and left his wife and daughter for a new life and a Las Vegas engagement with Andy Williams. When he came home from the lengthy run, he fled his home in a mad dash for freedom, leaving behind a miserable wife and their two-year-old daughter.

It was his twenty-fourth birthday.

X.
DELANEY & BONNIE

D elaney and Bonnie got married in a fever, seven days after they met at a gig at the Carolina Lanes bowling alley out by the Los Angeles International Airport. Delaney Bramlett, son of a Mississippi sharecropper who grew up dirt poor without shoes or running water, played guitar alongside Leon Russell with The Shindogs, house band for the television show *Shindig!*. Bonnie Lynn O'Farrell was a bleached blonde soul belter from St. Louis who spent a hot moment as one of the Ikettes with the Ike and Tina Turner revue.

Memphis musician Don Nix brought Russell into the fall 1968 sessions for Delaney & Bonnie at Stax Records; they were the first white act signed to the Memphis soul label. Both Russell and the Bramletts took hostages when they left Memphis to return to California in November. Delaney and Bonnie brought twenty-year-old Bobby Whitlock, a preacher's kid from Memphis who had never been past the Arkansas state line but who could sing like an angel and play his ass off on organ. Russell took Rita Coolidge, his new girlfriend, a stunning Southern belle with Cherokee cheekbones and a voice that blended with the Bramletts like colors in a sunset.

Back in Los Angeles, Russell lived in a split-level, four-bedroom home in the hills above Universal City on Skyhill Drive, where engineer Bones Howe had installed a studio in the summer of 1965. Cables snaked along the floor through every room. Drums were in the den, keyboards in the living room, a bathroom served as echo chamber, and a spare bedroom was the control booth. Musicians lounged around night and day. A drummer slept in the upstairs closet. The place came stocked with hot and cold running women.

Russell also kept a dozen more musicians stashed in a complex in San Fernando Valley dubbed The Plantation. After a brief stay stuffed into a small house in Hawthorne with Delaney, Bonnie, their two kids, and extended family, Bobby Whitlock settled in The Plantation. Living a few blocks away, Carl Radle was a quiet, rock-solid bass player Russell had brought out from their hometown of Tulsa, Oklahoma, and placed in the Gary Lewis and the Playboys band.

Jim knew Russell from hundreds of hours in recording studios together and, freshly single, he started spending time at Skyhill. He was staying in the Hollywood Hills with Don Peake, sometimes sleeping in the Volkswagen camper he bought. He had left the house and the Mercedes to Jill and Amy and was on his own. Jill didn't ask for alimony, but Jim ponied up a modest $100 monthly in child support. There was a lot of anger and resentment over finances between the divorcing couple. They battled in court, and when Jim prevailed, he felt bad enough to visit Jill and apologize (but not bad enough to adjust the settlement).

Jim was living the bachelor life. Jack Nitzsche sent Denny Bruce to introduce Jim to marijuana. He had long before broken his pact with Post about not using drugs. He was letting his hair grow long. Russell's place was turning into a bustling hive, and Jim was attracted to the free-flowing energy and the prospects of the possibilities. Compared to the rigid discipline of the studios, this was unbridled creativity in keeping with the wild, keening spirit sweeping through the music world of the day. Jim was fascinated.

Leon Russell was the ringmaster. He always had something to do, somewhere to be, and someone to do it with. His romance with Coolidge settled quickly into a kind of chaotic domesticity, Coolidge assuming household and kitchen duties while Russell oversaw a three-ring circus with an abundance of clowns. A single that Coolidge recorded while still in Memphis, "Turn Around and Love You," had found favor on Los Angeles radio stations, and she escaped being typecast as the old lady while she made the rounds of local TV shows lip-synching her hit record. She had already inspired a couple of Russell's best songs, "Delta Lady" and "A Song for You," a starkly sentimental love letter to a relationship that was already cooling off.

Delaney & Bonnie and Friends started playing regularly at a dump on Laurel Canyon Boulevard in Studio City called Snoopy's Opera House on a stage so small that Whitlock's organ had to be set up on the floor. A shifting cast of characters took the bandstand on any given night. Johnny "J. J." Cale, one of the Tulsa Mafia who lived at The Plantation, started out on guitar, although he soon drifted off to concentrate on his own career. Texan saxophonist Bobby Keys, who had been on the rock and roll highway since he was a teenager with fifties rocker Buddy Knox ("Party Doll"), along with college-educated Texan trumpeter Jim Price, staffed the horn section. Russell brought in Jim Keltner on drums to replace Jimmy Karstein, another ex-Tulsan, who, ironically, had replaced Keltner in Gary Lewis and the Playboys four years earlier.

Delaney and Bonnie introduced real-deal Southern soul to the California rock scene. Delaney was a strict bandleader with definite ideas about what he wanted, and Bonnie could scorch the vocals. They were the white Ike & Tina, down to the abusive relationship. With Whitlock and Coolidge to fill out the harmonies, the band boasted a rich, gospel-flavored sound. Their manager was Hollywood scenester Alan Pariser, heir to the Sweetheart straw fortune, one of the brains behind the Monterey International Pop Festival, and favored pot dealer of the cognoscenti, who brought a steady stream of other musicians to the club. Guitarist Dave Mason of the British rock band Traffic had recently moved to Los Angeles and became something of a regular. Gram Parsons of Flying Burrito Brothers was around. Stephen Stills and Buddy Miles climbed onstage with the band at the Whisky a Go Go. Jim found the scene irresistible and began to show up and sit in.

The group had already signed with Elektra Records when George Harrison saw the band play and flipped. He wanted to make Delaney & Bonnie the first signing on The Beatles' new Apple Records label and took a tape back to England. Although subsequent negotiations with Apple went nowhere and only managed to infuriate the Elektra executives, Harrison played the tape incessantly for anyone who would listen, including his best friend, Eric Clapton.

On the strength of his contributions to the Delaney & Bonnie and Friends album, Russell was invited to play on Joe Cocker's second album, and he wound up also writing arrangements and coproducing the set. He gave Cocker his song about his girlfriend, "Delta Lady," and hired Bonnie Bramlett and Coolidge to sing backgrounds at the A&M Studios session, which is where Coolidge first saw tall, handsome Jim Gordon, who struck her as looking like Tony Curtis in *The Great Race*, down to the twinkly front tooth. By the time she moved out of Russell's Skyhill place into the guesthouse at the old John Garfield home on Branson Canyon Road, she and Jim had already started seeing each other surreptitiously, and Jim soon moved into the cabin with her.

Jim and Rita fell into a tight relationship. Jim had been a lone wolf since he left his wife. He still felt guilty about leaving the marriage, and he was reluctant to make new connections. He kept parts of himself deeply shielded. Rita encouraged him to spend time with his three-year-old daughter, Amy. They took her to Disneyland and the Griffith Park Zoo together, and Coolidge was struck by how precious this man was, so gentle, tender, and kind with his little daughter and immensely talented as a musician. She was falling in love.

Jim wanted in. The action in the music business had shifted from the studios to the concert stage, and Delaney & Bonnie were showing signs of becoming a Next Big Thing. The album did not strike an immediate chord with the public, but the burgeoning rock press jumped all over it, and it shot through the upper echelons of the music world like a lightning bolt. Jim craved the action. His career had long consumed his consciousness, and his ambitions ignited again as he recognized the maw of opportunity opening before him. Jim seized the moment. He negotiated his way into the drum chair by trading session dates with Keltner, who practically idolized Jim anyway. Jim joined Delaney & Bonnie in time for Eric Clapton to insist the band open the US tour by Blind Faith, the new supergroup he started with Steve Winwood of Traffic and Ginger Baker, his ex-bandmate from Cream. With Jim in the band, he was able to bring his new girlfriend, Rita, along to sing background vocals.

With one album under their belt, Blind Faith made the band's concert debut in June 1969 before a crowd of more than one hundred thousand in London's Hyde Park and headed off the next month on a six-week tour of hockey rinks and basketball arenas across America. With quarrelsome Baker back on drugs and many of the same personal problems that previously sunk Cream reappearing, the Blind Faith performances were often lifeless, leaden affairs that even the musicians in the band found uninspiring. By contrast, the Delaney & Bonnie outfit seemed to grow tighter every night and, even more important, played with an infectious joy that drew Clapton to the wings to watch, tentatively shaking a tambourine. Before long, he joined the band as a phantom guitarist onstage and was spending hours in hotel rooms jamming, playing, and writing songs with Delaney, who wanted to produce a solo album with Clapton and kept urging him to step out as a vocalist. He wanted to call the album *Eric Clapton Sings*.

Although Keltner played on the Elektra album, Jim held down the drum chair in August at Elektra Studios when Delaney & Bonnie cut the Dave Mason song "Only You Know and I Know" and a song written by Bonnie Bramlett and Rita Coolidge, but credited to Delaney Bramlett and Leon Russell, "Groupie (Superstar)." On "Only You Know and I Know," Jim's motor-driven paradiddle ties the track together like a slipknot with Russell's supercharged Jerry Lee Lewis pumping piano driving the instrumental breaks while Bonnie simply burns down the song. Clapton and Dave Mason supplied the guitars. At this moment, Delaney and Bonnie were leading one of the best bands in the world.

Rock music was reaching an effulgent pinnacle. The big new attraction on the concert circuit that fall was Led Zeppelin, a British hard rock quartet that presented a near half-hour drum solo by drummer John "Bonzo" Bonham during the band's customary two-and-a-half-hour set. The Who, featuring reckless, maniacal drummer Keith Moon, was touring the country in exhaustive performances of the band's rock opera *Tommy*. Rock bands were exploding on concert stages with new sounds and new talents. The action had shifted to the live arena. Even the regal Rolling Stones had been coaxed out of complacency and were making plans to launch the band's first US tour in a long three years.

Back to working clubs around Los Angeles in November, Delaney & Bonnie and their crew were playing one of their regular weeknights at a San Fernando Valley club called the Brass Ring when the Rolling Stones with Gram Parsons in tow stumbled into the place. The Stones were in town finishing the *Let It Bleed* album and preparing for their hotly anticipated upcoming tour. After taking in the set, they brought Bobby Keys to Elektra Studios the next night to play sax on the record. They had Bonnie try the background vocal part to "Gimme Shelter," but she blew out her voice and the Stones ended up getting vocalist Merry Clayton, pregnant, out of bed in the middle of the night to come down to the studio and sing that crucial line—"It's just a shot away."

If Clapton's top gun status had been wearing on him for some time, playing guitar in the band with Delaney & Bonnie set him free. He loved the band with its monumental rhythm section and bright, shiny horns. He wanted to belong to this band—it suited him; his overblown reputation had grown to be a burden. Weary is the head that wears the crown. Clapton accepted Delaney's suggestion that they tour England and Europe together as Delaney & Bonnie with Eric Clapton.

Clapton had only recently moved into Hurtwood Edge, his country estate in Surrey. He'd first seen the place in a magazine and plopped down a formidable £40,000 for the fourteen-acre estate with the twenty-room Italianate mansion built in 1910, ornamental gardens, swimming pool, an observatory, and a donkey in the meadow. Jim and Rita arrived ahead of the rest of the group that November and on their first day in the English countryside decided to indulge with a couple tabs of Owsley Orange Sunshine. They let Clapton's Weimaraner, named Jeep, lead them around the grounds as the chemicals took effect. It was a storybook trip, full of bright, beautiful light, and ecstatic visions.

By the time they returned to the house, the acid was peaking, and the rest of the band had arrived. Bonnie was perched on the arm of a sofa chattering amiably when psychedelic hallucinations overcame Rita. Suddenly Bonnie looked like a big, pink chicken squawking away. Rita turned to Jim to have him take her back outdoors only to see that Jim had transformed into a giant, terrifying bird of prey, flapping his wings and staring down at her. She was instantly filled with fright. She had never been afraid of Jim before. Now something seemed threatening. Jim had never worried her, although sometimes she had wondered if his easy smile was a place he went to hide when he experienced uncomfortable feelings. She had seen him rely on that smile often, but there was nothing concrete about her vague suspicions she could articulate. This scary vision was something new.

When Bonnie walked into Olympic Studios in London a few nights later, she saw Jim and Rita sitting at back-to-back grand pianos, Jim ham-fistedly clunking out a set of chords that Rita wrapped in a lacey, ethereal melody. Bonnie stopped and drank in the scene; two young, beautiful people, so obviously in love, playing this beautiful music together. It was a piece they had composed together at John Garfield's guesthouse, Rita elaborating the basic chords Jim had found. Rita had written lyrics to the song she called "Time" and sang it for Clapton and the others in the studio. She later left Clapton a tape of the piece.

The first shows on the tour in Germany did not go well. The local promoter had advertised the concert as an Eric Clapton show, so when the Southern soul singers struck up the band, the outraged, jeering German crowd made their objections loudly heard. By the fourth song, the band retreated and turned the show over to the police and their dogs to calm the riot.

It was with some trepidation, then, that the band took the stage for the first British show at the Royal Albert Hall in London, where the rhythm section alone—Clapton, Whitlock, Radle, and Jim— opened with a hard-charging blues drive, Clapton playing loose and lengthy, stretching out right at the start, Jim pounding out the big beat for all he was worth. A blitzing "Gimme Some Lovin'" with Whitlock on vocals followed. They sold everybody before Delaney & Bonnie even hit the stage. They rocked the stately old Albert Hall. Bonnie hiked up the red velvet dress that Clapton bought her and danced like James Brown in her knee-length white snakeskin boots. The concert drew many members of the British rock aristocracy, and George Harrison stood and wavered in his box seats, regretting that he wasn't up onstage in the middle of the action. The next morning, the tour bus picked him up outside his Surrey countryside home, and he joined the band.

After thirteen shows in seven nights, the tour headed to Scandinavia with Harrison still onboard and Billy Preston also coming along. In joining the band, Harrison, making his first live appearances since the end of The Beatles, was timid at first, playing rhythm guitar almost anonymously in the dark corner of the stage. By the time they got to his hometown of Liverpool, he had loosened up considerably. Alone onstage after what was supposed to have been the final encore, he stared out at the raucous, happy crowd. "This is really bringing back memories," he said before calling everybody back for an unplanned finale.

Clapton was beside himself, too. "This is the first time I've ever been really happy playing," he told *Rolling Stone* in London.

The tour bus was always full of people playing guitars and singing. It was during the Scandinavian swing that Harrison started chanting "Hare Krishna" and strumming the chords that would eventually become "My Sweet Lord." Back in London, the entire troupe joined John Lennon and Yoko Ono and others like Keith Moon of The Who and Larry "Legs" Smith of Bonzo Dog Doo-Dah Band in "Peace for Christmas," a free-for-all UNICEF benefit concert on December 15. Jim and Lennon session drummer Alan White played double drums at London's Lyceum Theatre, where this sprawling, awkward conglomeration droned on for more than an hour on only two numbers. Lennon, in his white suit period, offered extended improvisations of the latest Plastic Ono Band single, "Cold Turkey," while Yoko writhed onstage in a bag. It was the perfect crazy/wonderful end to this epic European trip. Clapton went back to the States with the band and parked himself on Delaney and Bonnie's living room couch in Sherman Oaks.

Back home in Los Angeles, Jim saw himself in a different light. He had graduated from the ranks of the studio musicians into the knights of the realm, now operating in the most elite circles in rock. With Clapton set to start recording his first solo album in January at Village Recorders with Delaney producing, Jim was busy finishing the debut album by Leon Russell in two sessions at Gold Star (Russell had recorded the bulk of the album in London with Clapton and various Stones and Beatles on the sessions), although Jim was still nervous about being around Russell since he had "stolen" his girlfriend. He also tracked three songs for the solo album by his sometimes-Delaney-and-Bonnie-associate Dave Mason. Working with bassist Radle and guitarist Mason at Elektra Studios, Jim cooked up a march time drum part that locked everything down on

Mason's song "Only You Know and I Know," entirely different from the version Delaney and Bonnie had already recorded with Jim. He completely reinvented the rhythm track of the song for Mason's version. They cut the track, did the guitar overdubs and vocals in about one hour, and finished two more songs before the session ended. Jim was out the next night with Delaney & Bonnie at the Brass Ring.

In January 1970, waiting for the Clapton sessions to begin, Jim finished an album with Friends of Distinction and overdubbed percussion for producer Lenny Waronker on new albums by guitarist Ry Cooder and Canadian songwriter Gordon Lightfoot, newly signed to Warners with an album containing his breakout hit, "If You Could Read My Mind." Although Lightfoot customarily made his records with a tight-knit group of musicians in Toronto, Waronker not only brought in Jim for the Burbank treatment, but he had Randy Newman write some arrangements.

After a couple experimental sessions in London, the Eric Clapton solo album went into serious production, taking over Village Recorders for more than a week in late January. The band functioned crisply in the studio, and Delaney guided the sessions with focus and purpose. They took one day off from the sessions at Village to cut a single at Sunset Sound with the great saxman King Curtis. They did another couple tracks during the Clapton sessions back at Village with the surviving members of Buddy Holly's band, The Crickets (Crickets J. J. Allison and Sonny Curtis sang background on some Clapton tracks). In addition to songs that Clapton and Delaney wrote, Bonnie played him an old single by J. J. Cale, "After Midnight," and Clapton made a version of his own. In February, the album largely done, Clapton joined the band for a three-week tour of the United States, highlighted by a big weekend at the Fillmore East in New York.

But the Delaney and Bonnie camp was no bed of roses. The music was great, but Delaney could be a tyrant with the band and a mean drunk. Screaming matches between him and Bonnie were commonplace; those two could fight. He was not beyond making his point with his wife by slapping her around, and more than occasionally Bonnie would show up in the morning sporting oversized sunglasses that barely hid her black eyes. Snorting as much cocaine as he did didn't help. His controlling instincts were wearing thin on the other musicians. Band members were grumbling about money. The promised all-for-one/one-for-all recompense never materialized, and the musicians made do on their $125 a week salary. And if he once courted Clapton's devotion like a suitor, even Clapton was no longer immune to Delaney's abuse. Fed up, Clapton went back to England after playing Fillmore West in San Francisco in February and didn't even stay for the Los Angeles show the next week at the Santa Monica Civic Auditorium. Dave Mason stepped up in Clapton's absence, but without the superstar guitarist, the Delaney and Bonnie juggernaut quickly lost forward momentum and settled into discontent and dissension among the band members.

XI.
MAD DOGS &
ENGLISHMEN

On Wednesday, March 11, 1970, Joe Cocker arrived in Los Angeles ready to rest, recover, and plot his next move. The twenty-five-year-old British vocalist was exhausted after nearly nine straight months on the road, starting out unknown and winding up as one of the giants of Woodstock. He left his backup band in England to their own devices and came to California, not expecting to go straight to work. The day after he arrived on Thursday, however, he learned that his agent had booked another two-month tour due to start in eight days in Detroit. His agent also explained to Cocker that if he didn't play the dates, his career would be finished. The unions and immigration officials would see that he never toured again in the United States.

Cocker's new record producer, Leon Russell, went right to work. He scrambled to put together a band and, by the end of the day Friday, he had ten musicians including Jim reporting the next day,

Saturday, March 14, to A&M Studios for rehearsal. Russell, intimately familiar with the discontent in the Delaney and Bonnie band, started by stealing their rhythm section and horn players, leaving behind only Bobby Whitlock, who was not needed with Chris Stainton on hand from Cocker's backing group, the Grease Band. The musicians left Delaney and Bonnie high and dry on a moment's notice without any apparent second thoughts. Around that core, Russell built a giant orchestra and chorus fashioned on the sessions he used to play for producer Phil Spector.

On Saturday at the sound stage where they shot the *Perry Mason* television series, Russell commanded his ten-man band and a choir of eleven vocalists for a grueling twelve-hour rehearsal with an audience of more than three hundred bystanders milling around. On the A&M lot, the circus had come to town and word spread. People wandered in off the street. The party had started.

The enormous band boasted formidable percussion capabilities. Russell matched Jim on a second set of drums with Jim Keltner, who was making a living doing sessions that Jim couldn't do. Also on hand was Chuck Blackwell, another ex-Tulsan and the drummer Jim replaced with the Everly Brothers; Sandy Konikoff, who played drums with Taj Mahal; and Bobby Torres, a Puerto Rican conga player who had talked his way into the Joe Cocker band during the last tour.

Russell had a choir of voices, including Rita; another one of Leon's former girlfriends, Donna Washburn; and songwriting brothers Matthew and Daniel Moore. Rita brought onboard Donna Weiss, who had written her hit song "Turn Around and Love You." Pamela Polland was a full-on hippie chick whom Russell picked out of the crowd at A&M, dancing and grooving. He knew her as one-half of the folk duo Gentle Soul whose one album Jim had played on, and she looked the part. Her only condition was that she be able to bring her dog. No problem. Claudia Lennear wandered into the rehearsals the second night when she was singing demos down the hall for Gram Parsons. Russell took one look at the gorgeous black gal and former Ikette who inspired Mick Jagger to write "Brown Sugar" and asked her to join the band before he heard her sing one note. She didn't know any of the material, but volunteered to sing "Let It Be," which the band barely knew but pulled off as she felt the warmth of Jim's solid backbeat wrap around her like a gentle hand as soon as the band struck up behind her.

After four days of twelve-hour rehearsals running deep in the night, the band recorded a single on the sound stage the last day—a walloping cover of the Box Tops hit "The Letter" and a rousing gospelish song from choir member Matthew Moore, "Space Captain," which had been his ticket to the show. Wearing a plumed silver top hat, Russell was the bandleader, conductor, arranger, chief cook, and bottle-washer; Cocker was only the singer—it was Russell's show. With his solo album about to hit the stores, Russell saw the opportunity for a star turn that he intended to make the most of. He was moving out from behind the scenes.

This massive orchestra made a mighty sound, at the center of which was Jim's explosive, hard-hitting drumming. It was like Gary Puckett, Beach Boys, and Phil Spector sessions all at once. Jim Keltner danced around Jim's lead, decorating the power drive with a lot of offbeat accents and hi-hat. He hit softer than Jim and had more jazzy inclinations. Jim was all about elevating the power of the groove, and the band's percussion battery could be truly awe-inspiring. It was no accident the show opened with Russell on guitar using the fanfare from Bobby Bland's R&B standard "Turn On Your Lovelight" to start with a Fourth of July fireworks display by the drums.

Over the week rehearsing at A&M, plans grew ever more grand—rent a private plane, bring a film crew and make a movie, hire a bigger private plane, bring everybody who wants to come, old ladies, kids, dogs. The day before they left, everyone showed up at The Plantation for a massive jam session. "Man, it looks like we have a band," Jim said.

By the time the Mad Dogs and Englishmen troupe staggered on the beat-up, old Lockheed Constellation four-engine propeller plane, more than forty miscreants, reprobates, and degenerates were making the trip, which quickly descended into an unrestrained bacchanal. The party took to the road. As the tour progressed, people coupled up (or tripled), swapping partners, and swinging from the chandeliers. Every person was under thirty years old; it was like a traveling summer camp with sex, drugs, and rock and roll. Cocker came down with the clap. They kept an astrologist on staff who gave daily readings. Amid this rollicking craziness, Jim and Rita kept largely to themselves.

Jim discovered an appetite for drugs on tour. He was smoking, snorting, drinking, dropping anything people gave him. His capacity proved immense. In Seattle, he came backstage with a handful of Owsley LSD tabs and offered them to Keltner, who broke off a piece of one as he watched Jim pop an entire pill. A short while later, Keltner sat behind his drum set, holding his sticks, unable to play. In his psychedelized state, he couldn't even remember what rhythm was, let alone what to do with the sticks in his hand. From behind the other drum set, while Jim pounded out the beefy beat without pause, he kept looking over at Keltner and shouting "Play!" Keltner, unable to comprehend Jim's perfect composure under a monster dose of acid, could not gather enough presence of mind to even strike his drums. Finally, he burst into tears and rushed off the stage where some of the women from the choir surrounded and comforted him in the wings. Jim carried on.

Although she and Jim shared hotel rooms and were a loving couple when they were together, Rita liked to spend time on her own or with other people during the day. After shows, she and Jim avoided the flagrant, hard-core partying in favor of quieter activities—strumming guitars and watching Johnny Carson in somebody else's room. Jim developed a touching friendship with Claudia Lennear, who frequently found herself dining with Jim, Carl Radle, and Bobby Keys; Rita never joined them, and her name never came up. Lennear found Jim, like everybody did, sweet and gentle, yet there was something about his easy smile that she didn't trust. She could never figure it out and ignored the feeling. They were wandering around Greenwich Village one afternoon when she stopped at a head shop window where she admired an Egyptian scarab ring. Jim surreptitiously purchased the ring and surprised her with it later as a gift. But they were pals, not lovers.

Jim moved through his life like a ghost. He was friendly but he had no real friends. He hid himself from any close observation. His smile served him; it kept him safe and unquestioned. He was not threatening, so he went unchallenged. Nobody really knew him. He wore his trademark crisp white shirts and black slacks like a uniform. The drums were his face to the world. As long as he could play drums, he was all right.

Jim did fool around on his girlfriend with another Southern belle choir member, Donna Washburn, who had been Russell's girlfriend before Rita. When Rita found that Washburn had slipped her room key under Jim's pillow, she was furious. She harangued Jim about it enough that other members of the troupe were aware of her beef. In the tiny world of the tour, few secrets could be kept. Of course, with the swinging level of debauchery among the troupe, Jim's dalliance barely raised an eyebrow with anyone but Rita.

The tour schedule was a killer, fifty-eight shows, twenty-nine cities, eight weeks, crisscrossing the nation twice, after slamming the band together and hitting the trail in five hectic days. The musicians' physical endurance was stretched to the limit. Between the hard work, travel, and nonstop partying, people were exhausted and depleted before the tour was halfway through. Drugs and alcohol eased the stress and strain but created problems of their own. These people, many of whom barely knew one another, had been thrown together and were working out their relationships on the road. This was a million miles from sedate, long-distance bus rides with the Everly Brothers or the college campus tour with Chad and Jeremy; this was Jim immersed in rock and roll madness like he had never seen before. The ceaseless barrage of drugs didn't help. His inner voices were getting louder, less friendly, barking. He began to feel that, off in the distance, he was being secretly watched. The more drugs he took, the worse his paranoia grew.

Then one night at New York's Warwick Hotel after the show, Jim and Rita sat around Carl Radle's room laughing, joking, and smoking with some of the others. Jim snorted a little cocaine. Quietly, so nobody else could hear, Jim leaned into Rita's ear. "Can I talk to you for just a minute?" he said. They stepped out into the hall.

Rita dreamily entertained the thought that Jim was going to ask her to marry him. They had been so cozy and warm sitting together with their friends. He had seen the error of his ways and come to the obvious conclusion. They were in love, and they should be together.

Once out in the dingy hallway, Rita's dreams were literally shattered when Jim, without a word, slammed her in the face with his fist as hard as he could. The blow lifted her off her feet and dropped her against the wall. She slid down and lay crumpled on the floor, unconscious. Jim stepped over her inert body and went back into Radle's room. "I just hit Rita," he announced blankly to the room. Nobody said anything, but the party quickly fell apart as the other musicians drifted back to their rooms.

One of the other choir members, Nikki Barclay, who heard the body hit the wall, looked out her door and found Rita slumped on the hallway floor. She dragged Rita into her room and summoned the tour manager, who took Rita to the hospital. Although she had a spectacular shiner, the hospital simply sent her back to the hotel and told her to put ice on it. With two weeks left on the tour, Rita took out a restraining order against Jim and made arrangements to avoid him at all costs. She wore sunglasses to hide the bruise. The road manager accompanied her to and from the stage and her hotel room.

Word of the assault whisked through the troupe, treating the offense with a minimum of outrage. So much drama had rifled through their scene since departing Los Angeles, this episode only seemed like more madness and chaos, conditions they had come to embrace on the Mad Dogs and Englishmen tour. There had been so much drug-riddled, music-driven drama day in, day out, Jim belting Rita just slipped into the background noise. For Jim, it was a crack in the mask he wore. His herculean self-control had failed him, letting the dark forces he had kept under tight wraps peek out, dark forces that would have shocked anyone who knew sunny Jim. There was no small irony that, amid all this depravity and debauchery, nobody could distinguish authentic psychotic behavior.

When the tour was over, Jim nevertheless got back together with Rita, who was staying with her sister Priscilla and her husband,

Booker T. Jones of Booker T. and the MGs in Beverly Hills. They went off to Palm Springs for a few days together. They talked about putting together a band, but Rita was reluctant to commit. Jim parked his VW camper on the street in front of Booker's home many nights. In the end, it was Rita who drove Jim to the airport to go to London.

XII.
DEREK AND
THE DOMINOS

J im Keltner could not take up the invitation from Eric Clapton and Bobby Whitlock to come to England and start a band. He couldn't leave for two weeks due to sessions he'd scheduled with the great Hungarian gypsy jazz guitarist Gábor Szabó. When Jim heard the news from Carl Radle, he jumped on the next Lufthansa jet to London. He didn't ask or tell anyone he was coming—he simply showed up and took Keltner's gig. He could be ruthless when it came to his career, and Jim was accustomed to getting his own way. He spent his first jet-lagged day, June 10, 1970, in the IBC Studios in London playing behind soul singer P. P. Arnold, who originally was supposed to have been produced by Barry Gibb of the Bee Gees, only to have Clapton step up to substitute after Gibb was no longer available.

Jim joined Carl Radle and Bobby Whitlock at Clapton's country estate, Hurtwood Edge, where they set up their equipment in the cavernous front room and started to rehearse. Dave Mason added rhythm guitar. They were scheduled to play a benefit concert at London's Lyceum Theatre in four days, appearing as Eric Clapton and Friends. Clapton was not comfortable with even that much billing—he was tired of being the star and wanted to be simply a member of the band—so when Tony Ashton of Ashton, Gardner and Dyke introduced the act that night, he used a nickname he had for Clapton and jokingly called the band Derek and the Dominos.

George Harrison's solo album was already underway at Abbey Road Studios with producer Phil Spector, although the sessions had been suspended temporarily while Harrison attended his mother's deathbed. Clapton's new band sat around Hurtwood Edge and jammed endlessly, marathon sessions lasting through the night, into the next day and beyond, fueled by massive amounts of drugs and alcohol, waiting for Harrison to start recording again and join him as his studio musicians. Once they got into the studio, the first thing they did was to track a new original for a Derek and the Dominos single, "Tell the Truth." After that, they turned their attention to Harrison's remaining material, starting with "What Is Life," which Jim opened with massive rolling thunderclaps, boldly announcing his own entrance to Harrison's music. With McCartney's recent announcement that he was leaving The Beatles, the sessions took on Olympian status; Jim was basking in the royal court of the rock world.

The Mad Dogs horn players Bobby Keys and Jim Price each got an airplane ticket out of Clapton's office. By the time they arrived, Clapton had settled on the four-piece band, but they did make the Harrison sessions. Ringo Starr had played on some of the early tracks, and when he returned from Nashville, where he had cut a country and western solo album of his own, and turned up at the Abbey Road sessions, Harrison insisted Ringo play tambourine while Jim held down the drum chair. Ringo didn't mind. They were playing double drums on tracks together before they were done.

They recorded eight songs for Harrison and finished the sessions with long days of more jamming. After weeks playing together in the close-up world of the recording studio, the Clapton crew could read each other's minds. They all crashed the sessions at Trident Studios by New Orleans voodoo priest Dr. John (who had done time as a Hollywood session player with Jim under his real name, Mac Rebennack), where Mick Jagger and other luminaries were also hanging out. As the drummer in Eric Clapton's band, swinging London opened all its doors to him. Yet, at the same time, Jim, even after the past year with Delaney & Bonnie and Mad Dogs and Englishmen, still knew so little about rock star style that Bobby Whitlock had to insist on lending him a fringed shirt for the band publicity photo shoot so that he would at least look like he belonged.

Meanwhile, Clapton's personal life was a mess. He had fallen in love with the wife of his best friend, George Harrison, and while he tried to convince Pattie Harrison to leave her husband, he had broken off with the seventeen-year-old blueblood daughter of Lord Harlech, Alice Ormsby-Gore, and taken up with Pattie Harrison's younger sister, Paula Boyd. Rehearsals at Hurtwood Edge ran on copious amounts of the exotic liquor from the New World called tequila, ashtrays filled with spliffs, and mounds of cocaine. The coke dealer insisted on selling packets of heroin with the cocaine, and Clapton collected a healthy stockpile of the drug, which everybody would get into soon enough. Dave Mason, appalled at the massive drug use, went back to the States and his solo career. At the same time, Clapton was at the peak of his musical skills, an eloquent and facile guitarist who played great no matter how smashed he was. To avoid dealing with his catastrophic personal life, he threw himself into work. And drugs and drink.

Jim started his affair with Chris O'Dell shortly after arriving at Hurtwood Edge. An American gal from Arizona, the comely O'Dell had worked for The Beatles at Apple Records, before flying off to Los Angeles in a romance with Leon Russell, who was still nursing a broken heart after Rita Coolidge left him for Jim. Russell wrote "Pisces Apple Lady" about O'Dell. After she and Russell broke up, she returned to London and Apple, only to lose her job when Yoko Ono identified her as too closely associated with the George Harrison camp since she had been living with George and Pattie at their Friar Park mansion. She called Clapton, who invited her to move into Hurtwood Edge, where Derek and the Dominos were ensconced rehearsing. She had met Jim briefly at a session in Los Angeles with Leon Russell, who she sensed didn't want anything to do with Jim. With Jim still carrying a torch for Rita, and Chris hurting over Russell's rejection, their attraction to each other carried an element of revenge.

O'Dell found a flat for the band above a real estate office across the street from the South Kensington tube stop in London and moved in to handle household matters. They drew straws for bedrooms, and when Whitlock set up his antique brass bed in the dining room rather than the tiny closet on the third floor next to Jim's room, Jim expressed his displeasure by throwing a television set out the window.

Clapton would stop by and moan about how he was in love with his best friend's wife. Pattie herself sometimes visited Clapton at the flat, encouraging him, hoping to make her husband jealous. George, meanwhile, was toggling between periods of heavy meditation and celibacy and cocaine binges and secret assignations.

Clapton could be drunk and volatile from cocaine. Once, over a midnight meal of beans and eggs, he interrupted his whining about Pattie by suddenly throwing his wineglass across the room, shattering it against the wall. A silence enveloped the room until Jim, a wild look piercing his eyes, threw his plate on the ceiling, where it crashed to the floor, leaving eggs and beans dripping from the chandelier, as everybody in the room burst into laughter.

In August, Derek and the Dominos embarked on a strenuous eighteen-date UK tour playing some tiny club or small hall virtually every night. They played places so small and crowded that Carl Radle's glasses fogged up onstage leaving him unable to see. Clapton really came into his own on this tour, opening up and playing loose and fiery. The rhythm section was operating on practically telepathic levels, and Jim, freed from the microscopic intensity of the recording studio, was unchained and unbound, exploding on the drums in all directions at once. His playing was compositional, winding his way into the bedrock of the song, using the drums as a complete musical instrument, not simply the flawless metronome that was always Jim.

The band traveled to France for a concert in Provence that failed to materialize. They stayed several days at the house of an artist named Émile Théodore Frandsen de Schomberg, where Clapton saw the painting that reminded him so much of Pattie Harrison that he insisted on using it for the cover of the Derek and the Dominos album. They repaid the hospitality by trashing the farmhouse, starting with a raw egg fight and ultimately ending by wrecking a piano.

Jim again found himself far from home and familiar surroundings. He would take out a photo of his daughter, Amy, to show Whitlock. He was more than a little lost, quite high, and often unruly. His frayed edges could sometimes show. Not that the other members noticed much, as drunk and high as they were. Jim grew uncharacteristically moody. He could be irritable with Clapton and get under his skin. They were traveling through England in a first-class rail car when Clapton took offense at something Jim said.

He reached up on the luggage rack, pulled down Jim's bag, threw it out the train window, and went back to reading his book.

"What the fuck did you just do?" Jim demanded while Clapton simply looked up at him and said nothing.

The day after the British tour ended, the band flew to Miami to record their album at Criteria Studios with producer Tom Dowd, who had just finished the second album by the Allman Brothers Band. As the second employee of Atlantic Records, Dowd engineered all the great records by Ray Charles, John Coltrane, Bobby Darin, and Aretha Franklin. He had also recorded Cream albums. While Dowd was a pipe-smoking straight arrow who handed out score sheets to the band on the first day of the session—paperwork they regarded quizzically—the four musicians were like a pirate crew who had more than their ration of grog. By the time the band hit Miami, they had polished their heroin habits to a high gloss. They mixed cocaine and heroin into what was called a speedball, drank large amounts of hard liquor, and gobbled Mandrax, the British cousin of Quaaludes, a kind of sedative that mixed well with alcohol. They found heroin easy to obtain from the gift shop off the lobby at the Thunderbird Motel where they were staying. Within days, the tops of amplifiers in the studio were littered with bags of powder.

The third night the band was in Florida, Dowd took them to see the Allman Brothers Band play a benefit concert. Clapton knew the band's twenty-three-year-old guitarist, Duane Allman, from his session work on the Wilson Pickett track "Hey Jude." The band was performing on a flatbed truck, and sandbags were stacked across the front of the field as a barrier to the audience. The Dominos scooted under the truck and took up positions leaning back on the sandbags while guitarist Duane Allman was playing a solo. When he opened his eyes and saw Eric Clapton staring up at him, he stopped playing, dumbfounded. The two bands repaired to the studio after the concert and jammed together through the night until dinnertime the next day. Clapton played his 1956 Fender Stratocaster, "Brownie," and Allman had his goldtop 1957 Les Paul. They traded licks, swapped instruments, talked shop, and played endless hours into the night and day. Allman promised to return.

Dowd was surprised when Clapton showed up without the giant wall of Marshall amplifiers he used with Cream, but instead a modest Fender Champ and battery-operated Pignose amp. This band would be recording at such a low volume that Jim could hear everything. Allman turned out to be the secret ingredient this well-oiled musical machine needed, a spark of inspiration. When Allman returned the next day, his daredevil slide guitar lit up the remake of "Tell the Truth." His value to the project was immediately obvious. With Allman onboard, they made quick work of the old Big Bill Broonzy blues "Key to the Highway," the Clapton-Whitlock original "Why Does Love Have to Be So Sad," and "Have You Ever Loved a Woman," the Freddy King number Clapton had cut with John Mayall & the Bluesbreakers many years before.

Allman had to miss some sessions to play Allman Brothers Band dates, while Clapton and the Dominos added overdubs and revisions to tracks in progress. Jim dumped a bunch of percussion on "Keep on Growing." On his return, Allman dreamed up a sterling three-chord riff to open their incendiary cover of Jimi Hendrix's "Little Wing," but it was on "Layla" where Allman left his most indelible mark. Although the song was originally conceived as a ballad, Allman lifted some licks off Albert King's "As the Years Go Passing By" and sped them up to create that ringing, anthemic opening. His slashing, bottleneck guitar seared the track, while Jim's supple and complex drum part kept the bottom of the track bubbling and simmering. The next day, two weeks after they started, principal recording finished with one last acoustic number from Whitlock, "Thorn Tree in the Garden," recorded on two microphones with the musicians sitting around in a circle.

The band returned to Criteria at the top of October to finish any details left undone. Clapton still felt "Layla" was incomplete. He recalled a piano piece he heard Jim play on the studio grand in September. He decided he wanted to graft the part on the end of the "Layla" track. Whitlock objected. Not only did it not sound to him like it was part of anything they were doing, but Whitlock remembered hearing Jim and Rita play the piece when they were living together at the John Garfield house. He reluctantly overdubbed a track that Jim first played somewhat stiffly on piano. Dowd made a composite of the two versions and edited the "Piano Exit" on the end of the piece. Clapton and Jim decided against adding Rita's name as a songwriter, sharing the credit between the two of them.

But Jim was still obsessed with Rita. In his room, he took out a piece of Thunderbird Motel stationery, scrawled a set of lyrics, and addressed an envelope to her:

> I am tired, I am tired, I am tired
> of waiting on you.
> I am tired, I am tired, I wish your games were through.
> There's only so much you can put me through.
> You better watch your step,
> I'll find somebody new.
> I am tired, tired, tired, of waiting on you.

When Jim came back to England, heroin was his diet. All the band members had moved from dabbling into daily habits. They had recorded their album in a pharmaceutical blur and smack had taken center stage. At the Dominos' flat with Chris O'Dell, Jim spilled a pile of powder on top of the piano and cut it into lines. He snorted one of the generous little piles and handed the straw to Chris, who knew immediately after snorting her line that it wasn't cocaine.

"What is this?" she asked.

"Heroin," said Jim.

She spent the rest of the evening throwing up.

All the drugs Jim was using were causing not too subtle changes in his behavior. He came back from Miami a different man. Circulating among the ranks of The Beatles, Rolling Stones, and the British rock aristocracy was rubbing off on the boy from Sherman Oaks. His intake of drugs and alcohol was growing downright Falstaffian, and he could no longer control himself as completely as he once could. Where he had been shy, he was now more withdrawn. He grew distrustful of the people around him. Fears and doubts began to crowd his mind. He thought he might be fired from the band because he didn't play well enough. The struggle between his inner life and outward demeanor was beginning to show.

He and Chris had been sitting around the flat drinking and sniffing coke all day when they got into a minor argument upstairs in the bedroom they shared. They were in the place alone; Clapton and the others were off somewhere else. Jim and Chris had argued before, even shouted at each other, but the relationship lacked the intense passion that could turn disagreements into fights. They sat on the bed arguing, which gave way to yelling and screaming. Chris was shocked as Jim's face transformed into an ugly caricature of the choir boy she knew. His eyes turned fierce and feral. He jumped up and pushed Chris back on the bed and held her down.

Chris managed to wriggle free and bolted down the stairs with Jim right behind her. She ran though the kitchen into the living room and Jim followed, now brandishing a butcher knife that he picked up in the kitchen. Chris used the sofa as a barricade, but Jim, his face a rictus mask flushed crimson, lunged at her over the couch with the knife.

"Stop it," she screamed. "Leave me alone."

As Jim came around the sofa, Chris ran back up the stairs. Jim came after her, taking two steps at a time, when a voice rang out below.

"Hullo? Is anyone here?"

It was Clapton's manager, Robert Stigwood, who had a key to the flat and had let himself and a friend in at this propitious moment. Jim snapped. A blank look came over his face as he turned around to walk docilely down the stairs. He gently laid the knife on the piano, careful not to scratch the surface. Stigwood and his friend explained that they happened to be in the neighborhood and stopped by on a whim. When Chris came into the room, a look of terror still frozen on her face, Jim smiled sweetly at her. She realized the storm had passed and quickly pulled herself together to greet these welcome visitors.

Later, Jim apologized to Chris, although he had no memory of a knife being involved. Chris wrote it off to stress from the upcoming American tour plus all the drinking and drugging they had been doing. She knew nothing about Rita Coolidge and the Warwick Hotel. The incident was never mentioned again.

XIII.
LONDON DAZE

The night before Derek and the Dominos left for the American tour, everybody dined at a local Indian restaurant and repaired to the flat. They had been drinking. And drinking. And drinking. Carl Radle looked up at Clapton.

"Hey, Eric, remember that night when you threw the glass and it shattered all over the place?" he said.

"Yeah, I remember that," Clapton said.

"What a crazy ass thing to do," Radle said.

Slight pause, one, two, three beats, and Radle hurled his wineglass across the room. The glass exploded and left streaks of red wine running down the wall. There was a collective intake of breath and then an outburst of laughter. Jim stood and threw his glass against the wall. Clapton went through an elaborate cricket bowler's windup and tossed a heavy glass ashtray filled with cigarette butts. Jim waltzed into the kitchen and emptied the glassware from the shelves while Clapton went to the wine cabinet and began smashing crystal stemware on the floor as fast as he could.

They were leaving the country the next morning, the lease on the flat was up, and they destroyed the place. The finale came when someone threw a glass at the television set, which exploded with a mighty poof, spraying tiny gray shards and leaving a dark, jagged hole in the center of the screen. A moment of stunned silence was followed by more belly laughs. They left it to Chris O'Dell to hand over the keys the next day to the rental agent, who took a few steps into the living room, stopped, and brought her hand to her throat. "Oh, my God," she said.

"They'll pay for everything," Chris said.

After a month of concerts at larger halls around Britain, the band opened their American tour in October, a week later rolling into New York City's Fillmore East, the album still a month away from release. The heroin in New York was decidedly less strong, more adulterated than what they had been using, and the band was running on drugs by now. Immaculate in white sport coat and clean-shaven face, Clapton was so far gone during the second night at the Fillmore, Whitlock worried whether Clapton would make it through the show. The record company threw a lavish post-concert reception attended by Crosby, Stills, Nash and Young and other luminaries. Bob Dylan caught the show, but didn't make the party, although Paul McCartney did.

In November, the band took two days off the tour to record with Chicago blues greats Junior Wells and Buddy Guy at Criteria in Miami. Clapton had flown to Paris earlier in the fall to catch Wells and Guy, where he saw Ahmet Ertegun of Atlantic Records back-stage and suggested Ertegun sign the bluesmen. He agreed, provided Clapton would produce the record. In Miami, however, Clapton was too high to handle the assignment. He and the Dominos (augmented by Dr. John on piano) managed to track one song before turning over production duties to Ertegun and Tom Dowd.

In Nashville, they appeared on the Johnny Cash television program, playing "It's Too Late" from the Dominos' album because they figured it was the closest thing to a country song in the set, before living out teenage dreams backing Cash and rock and roll pioneer Carl Perkins on a couple old rockabilly numbers. Three days later, Clapton was called back to England to attend the deathbed of his grandfather Jack Clapp, who had raised him. Clapton had already been hit hard by the death of Jimi Hendrix six weeks before and returned to the tour four days later in a sour mood.

The band hubbed for five days out of San Francisco, flying to other West Coast concerts and returning nightly to their temporary home base. They held a late-night jam session with the red-hot new San Francisco band Santana at Wally Heider Studios, where the group was recording their second album, *Abraxsas*. Neal Schon, a sixteen-year-old guitar phenom who had been hanging out with the Santana crowd, so impressed Clapton that he not only invited Schon to sit in at their Berkeley concert but asked him to join the band. Schon decided to go with Santana instead. At the Sacramento Memorial Auditorium show, Jim proudly hosted backstage his half-sister Mary Gordon, her boyfriend, and her three children, happy to introduce his family to Clapton and the band. On a rare day off in Los Angeles the next week, Jim squeezed in a Gary Puckett session. Puckett didn't know who Derek and the Dominos were.

In between dates with the Allman Brothers, Duane Allman finally managed to join the tail end of the tour for two dates in Florida and New York, and Clapton could finally include "Layla" in the set, as he was unable to sing and play the guitar part at the same time.

By the end of the tour, Clapton was exhausted, disgusted, and drug abused. Whatever fire and fury attended the first UK tour before recording the album had disappeared entirely. Drugs had

extracted a severe price from everybody. Clapton was barely speaking to Jim. Whitlock was whispering in his ear about getting Jim
Keltner in the band. Jim heard whispers himself, voices in his head
telling him this Clapton guy wasn't all he was cracked up to be, that
his other bandmates didn't have his best interests at heart. He grew
taciturn, remote, leery. As ambitious as he was, Jim did not handle
the spotlight or the realities of life on the road well, and his fragile
mental condition was starting to show.

There was no apparent end to his appetite for drugs. He was
routinely shooting speedballs. On the US tour, airport police con-
fiscated a bag containing his works and surgical tubing, although he
was not arrested. Everybody in the band had developed voracious
drug habits, but Jim was having problems holding his. Whatever
personality problems and inner conflicts Jim was suffering, his
immense intake of drugs was throwing gasoline on the fire.

Back in London, Jim leased a three-story flat in Chelsea and
bought a 1948 two-door Bristol to drive. Chris O'Dell had moved
back to Los Angeles, so Jim was leading the rock star bachelor life
on the town. Christmas at Hurtwood Edge was rife with the ten-
sions that had come to suffuse the band. Still, Clapton went all out
and decorated with a seven-foot Christmas tree and a mantel hung
with stockings stuffed with candy canes and poppers. After dinner,
the band tooled around the peaceful, snow-covered yuletide countryside in Clapton's Land Rover, swigging liquor and puffing joints.
Clapton bought everyone lavish gifts. He gave Jim an antique, red
wooden marching drum with a sash and gold braids. Jim opened his
gift and scowled.

"What the hell is this?" he said.

Clapton, stunned, offered to take it back, but the damage had
been done. Jim had grown ever more disagreeable over the course
of the US tour, so turning into the grinch didn't come as a surprise

to his bandmates, only another disappointment. Jim was suspicious of everyone; his congenial side had long evaporated.

In January 1971, with Radle back in the States working with Leon Russell, Whitlock started recording a solo album, recruiting George Harrison and Eric Clapton to play guitars with Jim on drums. Jim tried out a new custom monster drum set with twelve pieces, not dissimilar to Hal Blaine's classic fourteen-piece kit, that allowed him unprecedented musicality. It had two kick drums and a spiral of tom-toms—from the smallest to the biggest—around two floor toms, with each requiring separate tuning.

Meanwhile, Ringo Starr's vacation gave Jim another opportunity. John Lennon called him to Ascot Studios at his Surrey country mansion, Tittenhurst Park, with Klaus Voorman on bass, Billy Preston on keyboards, Bobby Keys on saxophone, and Phil Spector producing. After returning from Japan with Yoko Ono in January, Lennon had given an interview to leftist rhetoricians Tariq Ali and Robin Blackburn of the Marxist newspaper *Red Mole*. The next day, he jotted down a polemic inspired by the interview, "Power to the People," a sloganeering song that suited Lennon's political mood of the moment, a simple broadside to post on the village green. He pulled together the recording session the next day while the song was still fresh. Jim covered the rhythm like Ringo on steroids, constantly mutating rolls that folded into one another in a kind of endless cascade, his superior skills abundantly on display.

Jim was living in the middle of the vaunted British rock scene, brushing shoulders with various Beatles, Stones, and other officers of the empire. He was surrounded by creative opportunities. He had come to know drummer Jim Capaldi of Traffic and sat in on an experimental session with the band a few days after the Lennon date in February at Olympic Studios where Traffic tried out a new jazzy composition by Capaldi from a title suggested by actor

Michael J. Pollard, "The Low Spark of the High-Heeled Boys." The basic trio of Winwood, Capaldi, and Chris Wood had been augmented by Rebop Kwaku Baah, an African conga player they met in Sweden, and bassist Ric Grech, fresh from Blind Faith with Winwood, along with Jim.

In May, Jim went with Bobby Keys to Mick Jagger's wedding. Jim was producing a solo album by Keys, writing some of the material and supervising sessions with sidemen like Clapton and George Harrison playing on the tracks. They joined the party on the charter jet to Saint-Tropez alongside Peter Frampton, Ronnie Wood, Ringo Starr, and Paul McCartney (although since those two were embroiled in litigation, they were seated far apart). The wedding itself was a nightmare of provincial French laws, which rendered the ceremony problematic, and an infestation of paparazzi, who jammed the plaza outside the church, but the reception featured a jam session with Stephen Stills, Bobby Keys, Nicky Hopkins, and some of the guys from Santana. Keith Richards would have joined them, but he passed out early.

On Jim's return, the Dominos came back together at Hurtwood Edge to rehearse for the next album. They had written some new material on the road, but not much. "Got to Get Better in a Little While" and "High" had been performed live, and Whitlock and Clapton wrote a shuffle called "Snake Lake Blues," but never came up with lyrics. Jim had ambitions to write and even worked up one song on which he planned to sing. Whitlock thought he sounded lost even trying. Whitlock told Jim on numerous occasions that he and Clapton wrote the songs; Jim played the drums and should keep to that.

They went into Olympic Studios in the small room with engineer Andy Johns, but no adult authority figure like Tom Dowd. Between the growing subtext of resentments among the band members, the massive amounts of drugs everyone was using, and the lack of material as heartfelt and inspired as the songs on *Layla*, the band was in no position to repeat the masterpiece they had made in Miami. Clapton and Jim locked into a kind of musical duel of wits, each trying to top the other. The sessions were tense, and not especially productive, when Jim decided to bring in his new monster drum set and moved the sessions to Olympic's big room.

That morning, Jim assembled the band members on the street in front of his flat for a special event he would not reveal beforehand. As the musicians lolled on the sidewalk outside his building, Jim wheeled around the corner in a brand-new, all white, Ferrari Daytona Spyder. Clapton and Whitlock both owned Ferraris, but, unlike Jim, they were high-end automotive enthusiasts with experience and knowledge in the field. They gave each other a skeptical glance. They knew Jim didn't know anything about such cars. Whitlock didn't understand how Jim could afford expensive new drums and this gorgeous car. They split income evenly among the four musicians, and he and Clapton had trouble living within their means. He couldn't help wondering where Jim was getting the money.

At the studio that night, the atmosphere was tense and cold. The first order of business was Jim tuning his new, massive drum set. Each drum needed to be tuned to a different note. Whitlock hit a piano key and Jim would strike the drum while he adjusted the tuning.

Plink . . . ponk, ponk, ponk.

Plink . . . ponk, ponk, ponk, ponk.

An hour passed, and he was still tuning his drums. *Plink . . . ponk, ponk, ponk.* Clapton sat on a chair, guitar across his lap, and smoked his way through a pack of cigarettes. Whitlock lounged at the piano bench and played the single notes, over and over, while Jim kept tuning the drums. The tedious process took forever. After two hours, Jim played a lengthy drum solo and pronounced himself in tune. Clapton started to tune his guitar. It was his first chance to hear himself. He fumbled with the tuning, and Jim lost his temper.

"Do you want me to tune that damn thing for you?" he shouted at Clapton.

The air in the room turned crisp. Whitlock and Radle exchanged looks. Clapton stood and glared at Jim. "I'm never going to play with you again," he shouted back. He put his guitar down and stalked out of the room. Derek and the Dominos was over.

Jim didn't look back. He was fired up on a rock star tear, living large in London, and going for broke. With the ashes of Derek and the Dominos still smoldering, days later he went into the studio to continue working with Traffic on the band's next album. He found session work around London, doing commercials, odd bits here and there. He did an all-star session for B. B. King with Bobby Keys and others at Olympic. When producer Richard Perry brought Harry Nilsson to record at London's Trident Studios in June, Jim played an integral role in the album that would produce the number one hit "Without You" and establish Nilsson once and for all. With Klaus Voorman on bass, Gary Wright of Spooky Tooth on keyboards, British session player Chris Spedding on guitar, and Jim on drums, Perry would work through the night, take after take, filling reels of two-inch tape with different versions of the same song. He would make intensely intricate composite mixes of vocals and scrupulously edit the instrumental tracks, seeking a kind of heightened realism in sound that was about to make Perry the most sought-after producer in the business.

Jim echoed the singsong lyrics to Nilsson's "Coconut" with brilliant polyrhythmic inventions that danced around the words like a bouncing ball. The sole hard rocker on the *Nilsson Schmilsson* album was "Jump into the Fire," a near-seven-minute romp in which Nilsson unveiled his gruff, raspy bellow and Jim charged into a cacophonous, clattering drum solo that consumed the last half of the track. He went on so long, in fact, that bassist Voorman decided the track would be faded out and started fooling around with his tuning pegs, detuning the bass as he played along with Jim.

The same month, Jim started rehearsing and doing dates as a member of Traffic. Capaldi decided he wanted to get out from behind the drum kit and sing with the band. With Dave Mason back onboard for a handful of British dates, Ric Grech on bass, and Rebop on congas, this augmented edition of Traffic cut a live album in July at Fairfield Hall in Croydon, Jim powering the locomotive sound with some of his most athletic playing. The group also appeared that summer at the second Glastonbury Festival. In August, minus Mason, who returned to the States and his solo career, the band entered Olympic Studios to make the album *The Low Spark of the High-Heeled Boys*. Jim and Ric Grech collaborated on the song "Rock and Roll Stew," which was released as a single in the States. In September, the band hit the road in the United Kingdom, followed by an extensive US tour in October. Jim was happy to entertain his father, mother, and brother backstage when the band played the Anaheim Convention Center.

While the fellows in Derek and the Dominos shared the same bad habits, the Traffic musicians did not. Chris Wood may have been a serious alcoholic, but Steve Winwood and Jim Capaldi were more mild-mannered in their practices. Jim, Ric Grech, and Rebop, however, continued down the same road Jim had traveled in the Dominos—prodigious amounts of blow and smack and drunken romps in hotel rooms with low-rent groupies. The longer they stayed on the road, the worse it got. Winwood never saw the alliance as permanent—he wondered how long Jim would stay committed to their music—but chemical differences would take their toll. By the end of the tour, the Traffic fellows had had enough, and management fired all three of the new members.

Another Christmas was coming. Jim was strung out on drugs and he knew it. His London experience seemed to be coming to a conclusion; he'd grown tired of England and missed Los Angeles. No California kid likes the British winter. He missed the constancy of recording session work in Hollywood. He longed to return to the science of the studio. He was living hard, shooting dope, juggling girlfriends, nightclubbing nightly, drinking ceaselessly. His inner life was a roiling, poisonous swamp, growing ever larger. His reckless, self-destructive behavior reached a peak the night he crashed his Ferrari on a dark, rain-slick street. As his too-fast car spun out of control on the rainy road, the front end slammed into a truck that had stopped when the driver saw Jim's car spin out. The car was a loss, although Jim and his lady friend that night walked away miraculously unharmed. That was the coda.

It was time for Jim to go home.

PART TWO

XIV.
RENEE

V ocalist Renee Armand came out of the jazz world where she learned that her dialogue as a singer was with the piano. Coproducers Barry De Vorzon and arranger Perry Botkin Jr. first used her to sing their song "Lost" from the motion picture soundtrack for *Bless the Beasts and Children* and decided Armand had what it took to be a pop star. With the new album *Tapestry* shipping millions of units every week off the lot, the folks at A&M Records had no problem with the idea of packaging their new thrush as a sexualized version of Carole King.

In March 1972, the first day in A&M Studios, Armand sat among the hired hands her producers assembled and began running some of the songs she had written with her cowriter, Kerry Chater, formerly with the Union Gap. As she adjusted her headphones so that she could listen through one earpiece but keep her other ear free to hear the room, the slightly surprising realization crept into her head that the entire room was playing not to the pianist but the drummer.

The twenty-seven-year-old vocalist knew drummers. She had played with the great Sonny Payne when she toured with the Woody Herman Orchestra, and she had heard Elvin Jones, but this was something new. What she heard was a heartbeat to the music, the drums being employed as a melodic instrument. Across the room behind the drum booth, sitting at the kit, she could see the golden locks on the head of the drummer, which was the first time she laid eyes on Jim Gordon.

After returning from England in time for Christmas, the moment Jim hit town, everybody was hiring him. His reputation still preceded him with perhaps some additional gloss and glamor from his two years on the road and in England. *Layla* was not yet a hit record; the initial single, absent the lengthy piano coda, had fizzled on the charts when it was first released. But he had seamlessly slipped back into high gear on the Hollywood recording scene, routinely booking three sessions a day. He parked himself in a studio apartment in Studio City with a sleeping bag, stereo set, and little else. Mike Post reluctantly helped him move.

The record business had changed considerably since Jim left Hollywood. *Tapestry* was on its way to taking over from *Sound of Music* as the all-time best-selling album. Albums, not singles, now ruled the day. The entire music industry had risen to new levels of prosperity and prestige. Bustling Tower Records had taken over the location of the "Madman" Muntz car stereo store on Sunset Strip, where billboards now routinely advertised new albums. Jim stepped back into the scene with his elite status intact, instantly returning to his position among the top session players.

His first sessions back were incidental—England Dan and John Ford Coley, a Phil Everly solo session. Producer Toxey French booked him for an album by singer-songwriter Chi Coltrane, a good-looking lady who was Clive Davis's entry into the Carole King sweepstakes at Columbia Records. French had spent an evening on the town in London the year before with Jim and Harry Nilsson, returning to Nilsson's hotel room where Jim passed around heroin like a party favor. French took the opportunity to sample the drug but was not converted. At the Coltrane sessions, when the diva commanded Jim to slow the tempo during a certain passage, Jim grumbled that it went against all his training; he was there to keep time, which he went ahead and did.

In February 1972, Jim spent a quick afternoon with other session regulars recutting a track off the latest album by Australian vocalist Helen Reddy for a film soundtrack. The movie quickly tanked but the new version of the forgotten album track, "I Am Woman," would go on to become a massive record on its own. Jim hadn't been back in town for six weeks, and he was already cutting hits again.

Jim and Renee got together and not only began a personal relationship but started writing together. Since his England trip, Jim had been expanding his vision. He was writing music, producing sessions, and saw his role growing beyond merely playing the drums. Renee found his home stocked with guitars and a piano that Jim played. For Jim, Renee sparked a creative explosion. She fired her producers De Vorzon and Botkin and Jim took over as producer, cowriter, arranger, multi-instrumentalist, and creative collaborator.

In April, Jim took Renee with him to London where he went to reclaim his car, plus some other possessions he had left behind, and to collect some overdue royalties from Clapton. They took a hotel room in London but wheeled Jim's Ferrari into the Surrey countryside to visit, first, Bobby Keys, next George Harrison and his wife, Pattie, then staying with Clapton at Hurtwood Edge.

Clapton was deep into his heroin addiction, living alone in this dark, cold, and mostly empty mansion with a skeletal staff and a handful of large dogs who left dog shit all over his Oriental rugs. In the couple of days they were there, the three nevertheless managed to make some extraordinary music; a twelve-minute track that featured some of Clapton's most inspired guitar playing with Renee singing lyrics she wrote for the song, "Devil Road," never to be released. It was like a tree falling in the wilderness of Clapton's darkest days that nobody heard. Jim left with a pile of cash.

Renee fell violently ill at Hurtwood Edge and was simply dropped off at an ancient country hospital with metal bed frames lining the ward walls and a trench running down the middle of the floor so it could be hosed off. Hospital workers searched her clothes and found a note George Harrison had scrawled and put in her pocket with his phone number. They called Harrison, who came and took Renee to his place in London, where she recuperated for a couple days, while Jim sat around their hotel room shooting dope.

While they were in England, Jim's father, Jack, died. His youngest son did not hurry home to attend the funeral, telling his mother he couldn't get a flight, but Osa insisted the mortuary keep his father's body on ice until Jim came back and could view the remains. Their relationship had been complicated, to say the least.

His father had become virulently religious in his sobriety and Alcoholics Anonymous membership, and he moved from the relatively orthodox Congregational church where he taught Sunday school to the metaphysical Religious Science church. Jack Gordon fancied himself something of a philosopher and could be forthright in his opinions. His father told Jim he was going to burn in hell because of rock and roll. His parents worried, of course, that Jim was using drugs while he was in England. His father was also convinced that Jim showed signs of incipient alcoholism. As much as three years earlier, he had written Jim a letter urging him to seek psychiatric help. Jim didn't so much as mention his father's death to Renee.

Back in Los Angeles, they completed her album *The Rain Book*, but the label paid scant attention since Renee had deposed the original producers. Life together for Jim and Renee was work and solitude, living in Jim's new house in the Sherman Oaks hills and riding in his new Mercedes 450SLC. They had no friends or any social life, although Jim did resume seeing his daughter, Amy. He loved his little girl dearly but had no idea how to be a father. He still harbored guilt over breaking up the marriage. But Jim was drinking all day and doing drugs, so he remained cushioned from whatever emotions he might have had. None of this interfered with his exhausting work schedule or his surgical drum skills, but with Renee as his partner, Jim grew ever more private and self-contained. He could be clever and smart about things in the studio, but he had no intellectual pursuits. There were no books in the house. They didn't listen to records.

Since he left for England, the Hollywood studio scene had changed dramatically. New players had appeared, and the level of ability had risen sharply. In June, Jim anchored Johnny Rivers sessions that also fielded three key players who had emerged in his absence. Guitarist Larry Carlton came out of the jazz scene but was tearing up sessions with his searing, exact tones and fiery playing. The brilliant guitarist Dean Parks moved from Texas and landed with the Sonny and Cher road band before starting to work sessions. Michael Omartian was a gifted keyboard player out of Christian music who had only recently begun doing sessions but had already made an impression.

Rivers convened sessions for a new album at Western Studios with this utterly ferocious studio band (veteran Joe Osborn on bass). Jim and company spent most of the next month working on the *L.A. Reggae* album with Jim's snazzy, syncopated, second-line drumming driving the hit single "Rockin' Pneumonia and the Boogie Woogie Flu." The extraordinarily skillful professionals knocked out two or three incendiary tracks in each three- or three-and-a-half-hour session.

Session work was endless. But Jim and Renee continued to write songs and make demos. They went into Clover Studios with some of Jim's old associates like guitarist Mike Deasy and bassist Joe Osborn alongside hot new players like keyboardist Michael Omartian and bassist Lee Sklar, another former high school drum major from the Valley who first met Jim when he sat out his teenage rock group's recording session while studio musicians like Jim played their parts. Jim was all over town doing sessions, cutting hits like "It Never Rains in Southern California" with Albert Hammond or working with old clients like Gary Puckett or the Raiders. It didn't hurt Jim's reputation when the record label rereleased "Layla" as a single—this time including the lengthy piano passage at the close—and the record finally hit home in the Top Ten almost two years after its original release.

Rita Coolidge first heard "Layla" on the radio playing in the background during a publicity photo shoot at A&M Records for her upcoming solo album. She wasn't paying much attention, but as the piece moved into the piano part at the end, it slowly dawned on her—that was her music. It was the song "Time" that she and Jim had written at the John Garfield house and played for Clapton at Olympic Studios, only without the lyrics. When she got her hands on the album and saw the writers listed as "E. Clapton" and "J. Gordon," no mention of R. Coolidge, she felt violated. Furious, she talked it over with her record producer and the label president and finally she phoned Clapton's manager, Robert Stigwood, not especially known for his generosity.

"You're going to go up against Stiggy?" Stigwood said. "The Robert Stigwood Organization? Who do you think you are? You're a girl singer—what are you going to do?"

She knew she didn't have the money to fight her claim and realized it was a lost cause. She had already watched Delaney Bramlett and Leon Russell hijack the songwriting credit for the song she and Bonnie Bramlett wrote, "Groupie (Superstar)." Although she was clear that both Jim and Clapton knew she was the song's coauthor, she had no real recourse. The music business was a pirate ship, and she was nothing but a wench to them.

Frank Zappa knew Jim from a 1966 session with producer Tom Wilson when Jim had navigated some especially tricky arrangements from the maestro. Zappa had spent most of the past year in a wheelchair after being punched in the face and pushed off the stage in London by a crazed fan. He fell fifteen feet to the concrete orchestra pit floor below and broke many bones. With Zappa laid up, without steady work, his band had evaporated. Zappa took the opportunity to embark on an ambitious project, putting together a new twenty-piece orchestra to perform his orchestral work at a handful of US and European dates, after which the group would disband. Jim's sight-reading skills landed him the drum chair.

Rehearsals for the Grand Wazoo tour started in late summer at a downtown Los Angeles warehouse with two parking spaces in the rear where the musicians would stick their cars, unload their instruments, and then go look for parking. Jim earned the nickname "Skippy" because of his blue eyes, blond hair, and All-American good looks. Among this crowd of extroverts and colorful characters, Jim was quiet, reserved, almost shy. Zappa's demanding music called for difficult, detailed, written passages along with long sections for improvisation. Jim found the dense, businesslike rehearsals stimulating. The unwieldy expedition launched September 10 at the Hollywood Bowl before traveling to London, Denmark, Germany, Holland, and finishing with shows at the Felt Forum beneath Madison Square Garden in New York and then in Boston. The massive tour would cost $100,000 and wind up losing $2,000.

Jim remained onboard when Zappa cut the group's membership down to ten musicians and continued to tour the rest of the year through Canada and the United States as the Petite Wazoo. In Columbia, South Carolina, the local vice squad set up Jim and another band member in a sting. They sent a couple young girls backstage to offer them cocaine, and just as the drugs were produced, the cops came crashing in, beating the two musicians over the head with flashlights and dragging them off to jail before the show. Zappa borrowed a drummer from the opening act and shifted around horn players to do the concert. Jim felt certain he would be fired, as he well knew how much Zappa hated drugs, but Zappa distrusted the Southern policemen and, even though he was plenty angry, he let the episode pass.

Like everybody else Jim played with, Zappa was impressed with his ability to move around the drums and still keep rigid time. Jim's insistence on properly tuning his drums appealed to Zappa's own command of details, and he didn't mind Jim's excessive drinking, although he made note when Jim guzzled an entire bottle of gin one day in New York, where the tour paused long enough for Zappa to capture a frenzied instrumental jam at Electric Lady Studios in Greenwich Village with him, Jim, Cream bassist Jack Bruce, and Zappa rhythm guitarist Tony Duran. Zappa would edit the jam into the instrumental title track of his next album, *Apostrophe (')*, which would become the best-selling record of his career.

When the Grand Wazoo tour stopped in London, Jim, always mindful of his professional associations, put in a call to producer Richard Perry, who Jim knew was recording in town. Producer Perry needed to make a hit with Carly Simon. That was his assignment. That was his specialty. Perry, who had just completed a tortuous, drunken album project with Harry Nilsson at London's Trident Studios, was set to start sessions in the same room for Simon's crucial third album that September. Perry, who had helmed Nilsson's 1971 popular breakthrough, *Nilsson Schmillson* (with Jim on drums), brought Barbra Streisand back to the charts, brushed off and polished up Fats Domino, and discovered Tiny Tim, was the epitome of a hot record producer—arrogant, extravagant, self-absorbed. Perry lived with a Playboy model in a Hollywood Hills home built by silent-screen cowboy star Tom Mix.

In June, Perry had presided over the Nilsson follow-up, using a handful of star British rock musicians and an assortment of Beatles on the sessions, where he played symphony conductor to a debacle, as Nilsson, who had conflicting feelings about his commercial success, worked tirelessly to undermine the project. His wife and baby son had left him and, morosely depressed, he dove into a bottle. He routinely showed up for the sessions brandishing a half-empty fifth of cognac he had already drunk and which he would proceed to finish.

Meanwhile, after a promising mid-chart debut album (with the Top Ten hit "That's the Way I Always Heard It Should Be") and a modestly successful follow-up with a Top Ten near-miss ("Anticipation"), Carly Simon was poised to become a big star with the right hit album. Her record company dismissed her idea to have British arranger Paul Buckmaster produce the album and assigned Richard Perry to the project. When Perry sniffed during their first meeting that her last album could have been a big hit if the drums had been louder, she took silent offense and began to see the relationship as more adversarial than collaborative. Perry, who was accustomed to taking complete charge of his productions, found Simon resistant. Soon after transporting her band to London and starting sessions at Trident Studios, she put in an emergency phone call to the label president to ask him to take Perry off the project. He never returned the call.

From the first time she played him the song that was then called "Ballad of a Vain Man," Perry recognized the song's hit potential, picking up his bongos and beating out a rhythm as she demonstrated the number on piano. The song had various roots in lines she remembered from a lost notebook, some offhand comments by a friend ("look at those clouds in your coffee") and another friend at a party who remarked that a gentleman who entered wearing a scarf looked like he was walking onto a yacht. The song had been through the mill, revised, rewritten, scrubbed down, buffed, and revised again. Perry was prepared to lavish special attention on the track in the studio.

Perry came to London to work with Trident Studios house engineer Robin Geoffrey Cable, who had garnered quite the insider's reputation for the lush, spacious sound of his Elton John albums. The Beatles had put the studio on the map with their "Hey Jude" session. Located in a tiny alley in crowded, old Soho in the center of London, the third-story studio was reached by a rickety elevator. The control room loomed over the tall, rectangular, wood-paneled room from a window across the top of the wall and was reached through a staircase. Cable, with his meticulous, scientific ear, was an ideal counterpart to Perry, whose sensitivity to microtonal issues, slight rhythmic variations, and subtle note shadings bordered on unearthly. He commonly put Harry Nilsson through sixty, seventy, eighty, or more takes to produce the vocal performance he wanted.

From the session's first day, there was friction between Simon and Perry, who she thought was barking orders at her jet-lagged band members like a drill sergeant. She was a somewhat haughty, spoiled child, articulate and intelligent, who was seriously distracted by having fallen in love with James Taylor. They were already a celebrity couple and would soon be wed, but at this point, she was nearly distraught over their separation, even after what amounted to little more than a long weekend London visit by Taylor before he was called back to the States to attend to his own sharply ascendant career.

Perry worked his studio crew mercilessly. He brought top players to augment her band like bassist Klaus Voorman and pianist Nicky Hopkins. With his sensitive, trained ear, Perry kept going until he heard what he wanted, after hours of endless takes. With "Ballad of a Vain Man," he could not find the drum sound he knew the song needed. They spent a week on the track and everybody else thought they had it, but Perry knew better.

First, he tried Andy Newmark from Simon's band. Then he cut the track with seasoned British session player Barry Morgan, but he still didn't have the breadth of sound and impact in the arrangement he wanted. It didn't have the magic drum sound. Perry knew what the track needed was Jim Gordon and then, with playwright's timing, the phone rang and there was Jim. He had been Perry's first call drummer for the past four years, and he couldn't have turned up at a better time. They had one free night left in the studio. Perry told him to come straight over that night.

Jim walked in like the hired gunslinger he was, ambling into the room with his practiced smile. In his haste to get Jim into the studio, Perry neglected to inform Carly Simon, and when she arrived at the studio and saw Jim and Frank Zappa, who had come along for the ride, she took Perry aside for a heated private conference, where she burst into tears. Why did they need a third drummer, she wanted to know. Didn't they already finish the track? And what was Frank Zappa doing there? Perry ignored her tantrum and huddled with Jim before he arrayed himself behind the kit in the drum room, a twelve-by-twelve box at the far end of the studio from the control booth, surrounded by movable walls with windows so Jim could see out. Andy Newmark, the drummer with Carly Simon's band, introduced himself and asked if Jim would mind if he sat in the corner of the drum booth and watched him play. Jim welcomed him and, with Carly at the "Hey Jude" piano, the band started to run the track. The first run-through was all they needed to hear.

Right off, Perry knew he would get what he wanted. On the first take, Jim conquered nuances and subtleties Perry had worked hours to achieve with the other drummers. Newmark watched, astonished, as Jim turned in flawless take after flawless take over the course of five hours and sixty takes. He barely said a word. He took Perry's comments and went back to work on the next take with supreme focus but a loose, casual manner. For Perry, it was imperative to capture the basic instrumental track in one complete take, and not go back and fix parts or rebalance the instruments, and he was willing to take the time to do that.

Jim hit the snare drum in the exact same spot with every stroke, giving every take the precisely identical sound. By the end of the session, he had beaten a six-inch crater into the head of his snare drum. The tom-tom fills rolled like thunderclaps. He stopped the verse with a terse clip on the side of the snare drum, opened the pre-chorus with a booming kick drum, pounding out straight eighth notes in unison, one hand on the floor tom, the other on the high tom, building to a crescendo where he snapped off the roll on his snare, punching the track into the chorus. What Jim did was nothing short of orchestrating the entire track from the drum chair.

For Jim, this was more than a drum part; there were no written score sheets and no click track. He saw the composition as one whole piece and worked to serve the music. He strengthened, lengthened, held time suspended and brought it crashing back. He pushed the vocals in and out of the choruses and underscored the lyrics with a drum set he made sound like tympani. Throughout the course of the evening, Perry directed Jim over the talkback from the elevated control booth with minute instructions on flourishes and decorations. He carefully hand-picked the spots where he wanted Jim's fills. Perry was looking for a semi-spectacular, monster fill to set up the choruses along the lines of Motown drummer Benny Benjamin, a tall order for any drummer other than Jim. He moved the other musicians' parts around while he built the drum track. Jim drove everything with his trademark mathematical accuracy, making the minor adjustments Perry wanted like a smooth functioning machine until Perry had nothing more to say.

Newmark was amazed at how Jim committed to every note, how he owned every stroke, how he could elongate notes, leave them hanging in the air, snatching them back as the beat came around once again with his perfect time. He pounded cannon fire out of his tom-toms. He drilled staccato triplets on his snare. The drum kit was an extension of his being and he danced all over it. He made the track sound like a big, juicy hit record on the first take, and at the end of the evening, he left no doubt in the minds of everyone in the room that that was exactly what they now had.

Of course, "You're So Vain" was not done. They returned to the studio a few nights later after Jim had moved on to make some fixes, to add a guitar solo to the track, and to sing the background vocal parts. Perry found Paul and Linda McCartney down the hall in the other studio working with producer George Martin. Harry Nilsson and Bonnie Bramlett were visiting their session and Perry brought everybody down to listen to the Carly Simon track and inveigled Nilsson to sing the background part with her. They had sung a few takes when she received a call on the studio phone from Mick Jagger.

She had met Jagger in June at Ahmet Ertegun's party for the Rolling Stones in Hollywood, and his interest had been piqued. He volunteered to come to the studio and sing. Nilsson excused himself shortly after Jagger arrived and the McCartney party disappeared back down the hallway, as Jagger and Carly locked eyes singing the "don't you . . . don't you . . . don't you" part on the same mike. When he left that evening, Jagger stopped by the control booth to tell Perry and Cable that he didn't think it had been his best work, and they should feel free to leave him off. Perry didn't give that a second thought. Jagger singing the vocal harmony was the cherry on top, what he needed to assure this would be the nice, fat, number one hit record he had imagined. And this time, the drums would be loud enough.

XV.
CALIFORNIA
GOLD

t was Jim's idea to get married. The day after returning from the road with Frank Zappa, he and Renee flew to Las Vegas and, on December 16, 1972, wed in a chapel on the Strip, returned home the next day, and went on with their life together without further celebration, honeymoon, or parties with friends. Acting on impulse, they were young and in love and, well, it seemed like a good idea at the time. Jim had been heartbroken when he heard Rita Coolidge and Kris Kristofferson got married, and he yearned for a lasting romantic partner, even if he wasn't geared for intimate relationships. He and Renee bonded through music, and she encouraged Jim's growing creativity.

Drums were still the center of Jim's world. In January 1973, Jim traveled to Vancouver, British Columbia, to make what would be as close to a real solo album as he would ever make, a record forgotten almost as soon as it was released but that would come back to an amazing afterlife ten years later. The Incredible Bongo Band was the creation of a music business hustler named Michael Viner, a one-time aide to Senator Robert F. Kennedy who fell into the movie business and needed to come up with music for a chase scene in the B-movie horror film *The Thing with Two Heads*. Viner hired studio musicians to re-create the 1959 Preston Epps hit, "Bongo Rock," which was released as a single.

The record bombed in the United States, but because Viner had added the emblem to the record label that indicated it was recorded in Canada—although it was not—the track benefited from Canadian content laws and hit the charts north of the border. Hollywood session stalwart saxophonist Steve Douglas had immigrated to Vancouver, and when Viner decided to take advantage of the Canadian opportunity by recording the subsequent album genuinely in Canada, Douglas wrangled a set of his old associates, including Jim on drums, for sessions at Vancouver's Can-Base Studios.

With his "Grazin' in the Grass" partner King Errisson on congas, the two percussionists led the team through an assortment of drum-laden instrumentals including the old Sandy Nelson number "Let There Be Drums" and the Jørgen Ingmann guitar hit "Apache." A Canadian drummer may have overdubbed some of the parts originally played by Jim after he left Canada, but Jim was also on hand when the tapes were brought into Original Sound Studios in Los Angeles that March for further post-production overdubs, so some of his playing may have been restored at those latter sessions.

The oddball record went almost entirely unnoticed for nearly ten years until it was discovered like buried treasure by DJ Kool Herc, an early hip-hop devotee who used the lengthy, ferocious drum break on "Apache" by Jim and Errisson to work up dancers and introduced the track to a new generation of crate diggers and deejays. A thousand samples later, "Apache" became a fountainhead of hip-hop, one of the most sampled tracks in history.

Jim was personally driving entire styles of pop music on drums. Producer John Florez, who watched Jim blow up the "Grazin' in the Grass" track on his first venture into the studio, brought Jim that spring when he found himself babysitting recording sessions by the Hues Corporation, a Las Vegas lounge act that landed some songs on the soundtrack to the black vampire movie *Blackula*. Florez was intent on the group covering "Freedom for the Stallion" by the great New Orleans songwriter and record producer Allen Toussaint, who had cut the song with Lee Dorsey as a one-off single after their landmark 1970 album, *Yes We Can*. The Hues Corporation version stalled halfway up the charts after it was released in September. The song "Rock the Boat" had been an afterthought cut, written by group founder Wally Holmes and originally recorded with another drummer. With two members of The Crusaders on the track with him, Jim introduced the trademark disco drum sound on the new version with thumping, offbeat accents on the toms that would soon echo on a thousand other records.

At this point, the sounds of disco were relegated to underground urban dance clubs largely frequented by blacks, gays, and Latinos. When "Rock the Boat" was initially released as a single in February 1974, radio roundly ignored the track, but when the label moved some fifty thousand copies in New York City with no significant radio play, only exposure at dance clubs, radio caught up seven months later as the Hues Corporation ascended to number one, one of the first popular breakthroughs by this emerging disco sound on the pop charts with Jim defining the beat. Hal Blaine liked to say that he invented disco drumming with his ticking the hi-hat on Johnny Rivers's "Poor Side of Town," but it was Jim's licks on

"Rock the Boat" that would be repeated ad nauseum before the disco era was through.

In late April 1973, Jim joined other members of the L.A. *Reggae* crew backing Johnny Rivers on a monthlong European tour that began at the Montreux Jazz Festival in Switzerland and wound up four weeks later at the Olympia Hall in Paris. Rivers was riding the success of "Rockin' Pneumonia and the Boogie Woogie Flu," his first hit record in five years, and gave exultant performances that mixed his old catalog with new tracks that he cut with his sensational studio band, many of whom joined him on this tour.

Jim and Renee continued to write and record together. "California Lady" was a song they wrote and released as a single after her album had come and gone. Jim asked Frank Zappa to put some guitar overdubs on one of Renee's tracks—the only time in his career anyone hired Zappa as a sideman—and offered the notoriously anti-drug Zappa some cocaine in the studio. As he watched Jim chop up the powder with a razor blade on the top of the organ, Zappa couldn't help but think about the bits of varnish he was picking up in the process. Zappa, who had never seen the drug administered before, was disgusted.

Renee tried but couldn't keep up with Jim on the drugs and alcohol. His metabolism absorbed massive quantities without much obvious effect. He could guzzle vodka out of the bottle all day and not lose a step, but living with Renee made it difficult for Jim to continually mask his inner distress. He never felt safe. His paranoia could flare up unexpectedly, and he would become rageful. They had some intense screaming matches. Renee insisted he see a psychiatrist who specialized in violence issues. Although Jim never attacked her, she was growing concerned about his ability to control himself. Jim saw someone at UCLA who prescribed tranquilizers, which he simply added to his daily intake.

Still, she never saw what happened coming. It was an ordinary day, and Renee was getting back home from an afternoon trip to the store. With bags of groceries in her arms, she walked up the front stairs and found Jim waiting in the hallway glowering at her. His narrowed eyes had a chilling intensity she'd never seen before. It was like he was on fire with fury and almost hot to the touch. His chest was heaving. He was clearly in the grip of some nightmare episode.

"I know what you're doing," he said.

She had no idea what Jim was talking about. She denied doing anything. He held out his hand, three objects on his palm—a scrap of paper, a pen, and a piece of string. "You're making the devil's triangle," he said.

Jim told Renee that she was trying to bring evil spirits into their home, and he wanted her to stop. Before she could move, he grabbed her throat and strangled her, then slammed into her with his fists and beat her savagely. Renee was beyond shocked; she was in mortal danger and knew it. Jim loomed over her like a giant and the rage gave him an almost superhuman strength. Renee was sure she was going to die. He broke a couple of her ribs and then, inexplicably, went to the kitchen for a drink of water. Renee was able to get free, crawl out the door, and escape to pianist Mike Melvoin's house.

She would not return. The marriage ended shy of the six-month mark. Despite his desire to be loved, Jim could not fully reveal himself to another human. He could not share the terrors hidden inside him, couldn't trust someone else to care about him and give him the understanding he needed. Nobody ever had. Jim remained alone with his black thoughts and demanding voices. He lived largely within himself. The last music he and Renee made together was the theme they wrote and produced for a TV movie starring Natalie Wood, *The Affair*. The song was called "I Can't See You Anymore."

This was Jim's psychotic break, the nightmare inside him forcing its way into the outside world, an eruption of his tortured inner turbulence. He couldn't understand what happened with Renee. His paranoid delusions were becoming his reality, and he was having trouble telling the difference. The massive amounts of drugs and alcohol only made his debilitating mental state worse, clouding judgment and impairing rational thinking. Jim tried over and over but couldn't connect to other humans on any empathetic, emotional level. He suffered alone and in secret, not daring to tell anyone about the raging war going on in his head. The drums, as always, remained his refuge.

With the Hollywood record business minting money in studios around town every day, there was as much work as Jim wanted. He could still escape his roiling mind by playing drums. Like the tape machines in the studio, Jim was there to make money. He was one of the essential components of the hit record machine that could unlock the mass market for poets, troubadours, and other dubious characters who had a way with a song. He expanded the role of the drums on every track he played, moving the instrument from the background into the fabric of the composition. To the casual listener, Jim's virtuosity might not be immediately obvious, only that the material had somehow been elevated to another level. He could single-handedly make a record into a hit. Everybody who worked with Jim knew that about him. His contributions were crucial.

The B. W. Stevenson hit "My Maria" was one of Jim's most masterful performances, transforming what could have been a relatively ordinary song and indifferent performance into a total gem and Top Ten hit. The grizzled regular from Austin's Armadillo World Headquarters, whose initials were short for his nickname "Buckwheat," was signed by producer David Kershenbaum from the Chicago office of RCA Victor, not exactly one of the hot spots of the recording world. For his second album, Kershenbaum took Stevenson to Los Angeles to work with the studio musicians where they cut the Daniel Moore song "Shambala."

Mad Dogs and Englishmen alumnus Moore wrote the song after receiving a letter in which a friend signed off by writing "Let your light shine over the halls of Shambala." After some study, Moore learned that Shambala was an underground city of Sanskrit myth thought to be behind the Himalaya Mountains under the Gobi Desert. Kershenbaum cut the song with Stevenson (and Jim on drums). One week after Stevenson's version was released, the Three Dog Night cover of the song barreled over Stevenson's record as it blasted its way to the top of the charts. Kershenbaum asked Moore if he had any more like that.

Moore did indeed have a song that he had started, built around the same guitar figure. He had the opening line, the basic melody, and the guitar licks on a cassette he brought to the studio. Stevenson took the cassette, excused himself, and returned fifteen minutes later with "My Maria."

In June, with Jim on drums, Joe Osborn on bass, and Larry Carlton on guitar, they tracked the song in a double session at RCA Studios along with five other numbers. On the record, Jim enters with a mysterious sound that came from a specialty percussion instrument of his own devising—a tin can filled with rice and welded shut. The little shower of shaken rice smears the beat as Jim opens the track on his kit, striking three notes to underline the opening lyric, "my Maria." As the song progresses, the drums pick up the arrangement, winding over and around the nagging little acoustic guitar riff, and motor the track to the chorus where Jim's big fill opens up the music to a rousing mini-climax. His bouncing breakdown under the bridge lifts the entire record into a swell of background vocals on the final chorus as Jim punches the track home with a clanging cymbal ride and skipping, rolling passes over the toms and snare—a thoroughly masterful performance that never calls attention to itself but gives the record everything it needs. Jim's brilliant work made the difference between something pedestrian and a big hit record.

Jim could light sparks under all kinds of different material. Take Maria Muldaur, recently separated from her husband, who was losing not simply a life partner but her musical collaborator. She had no idea what to do with herself and was thinking about getting a job working as a waitress in a coffee shop. She was headed to New York City from Woodstock, where she lived, to help sing on a friend's demo tape, and her soon-to-be-ex-husband, Geoff Muldaur, asked her to pick up a Brooks Brothers, button-down, oxford blue shirt for him while she was in town. Without really knowing how far she was going, she trudged off toward midtown on that steamy summer afternoon to the store, where she happened across the salesman helping an older gentleman. Maria recognized him—Mo Ostin, chairman and CEO of Warner/Reprise Records, where she and Geoff recorded as a duo.

When she informed Ostin of her pending divorce, he expressed his sympathy. "But what about you?" he said. "Have you thought about making an album?"

A meeting was arranged for later that afternoon, when she told Ostin how much she loved their albums by Randy Newman and Ry Cooder. He put producer Lenny Waronker on the phone, and before long, Maria was driving west in spring 1973 with her dog, Honey Pie, in her Toyota station wagon to make a record in Hollywood, staying with friends in Laurel Canyon.

With the album nearly done, Waronker felt the record was missing at least one medium tempo piece. "What about that weird song about the camel?" he asked.

"Midnight at the Oasis" was written by David Nichtern, a friend of Maria's whose "I Never Did Sing You a Love Song" she had already recorded for the album. Nichtern drove his VW from New York and slept on the floor to attend the sessions like a supportive little brother. Neither Maria nor Waronker thought much of the song, but it was the right tempo. They were standing around Amigo Studios having this discussion in the late morning and decided to cut the song that afternoon. They had been using Jim Keltner from the Ry Cooder albums on drums, but he couldn't make the date on such short notice. Jim Gordon could.

Throughout their long association, Waronker always turned Jim loose in the studio. He might make suggestions once he heard what Jim came up with, but he knew Jim to be the most musical of drummers. Giving Jim's creativity free rein was the way to get the most from his performance. At the studio that afternoon, with the quickly assembled group of Maria's old friends like bassist Freebo and guitarist Amos Garrett, Jim cooked up a nifty little modified bossa nova drive that perfectly framed the material. He instinctively knew where to put the backbone to the song and how to serve up the sultry vocal and lite-jazz accompaniment, resulting in a Top Five hit when the record was released in February 1974. Muldaur never had to take that job in the coffee shop.

In July, Jim went with bassist Joe Osborn and other session players to back Cass Elliot of The Mamas and The Papas for a live album to be recorded at the swank supper club Mister Kelly's in Chicago. Jim didn't know Cass well despite having played on her first solo album, back when she was junked out and Jim was straight. In Chicago, he was trying methadone as an alternative to heroin, but still drinking plenty. He found himself riding in the back of a limousine with Cass, who maintained her recreational interest in painkillers and other pharmaceuticals, and they fell into a lively conversation. They laughed and hit it off. Staying at the Playboy Club and working at Mister Kelly's for two weeks, they began an affair.

Elliott had unveiled her new show, *Don't Call Me Mama,* in February and played several cities before coming to Chicago to record. The show was designed by her new manager, Allan Carr, who handled actors like Tony Curtis, Peter Sellers, and Ann-Margret. He knew her days as a rock star were over and built the show around old-fashioned show business values and Tin Pan Alley chestnuts (along with some special material and a few specialty numbers specifically composed for the act).

Back in Los Angeles, Jim and Cass continued their relationship over dinners at her Laurel Canyon home or in restaurants. Jim went with her to play drums in Miami. They went all over town together—backgammon parlors, gay and lesbian bars. Jim was fascinated by the gays who surrounded Elliott; he knew little about their subculture. In truth, Jim was secretly a little starstruck to be seeing Mama Cass. They went sailing off Key Largo, Jim's first time out on the ocean. He was inexperienced enough that when the boat ran aground on a sand bar and one of the sailors hopped off to lighten the load, Jim tried to help him back into the boat. He played in the band for the television special based on her live show. They ran hot and heavy for a brief moment, and then Jim lost interest and drifted away.

In the wake of the second coming of "Layla" as a Top Ten hit, some efforts were made to sell the Dominos' rhythm section as a recording unit. In October, ex–Rolling Stones producer Andrew Loog Oldham used Jim, Radle, and Whitlock on sessions with Scottish folk singer Donovan at London's Morgan Studios for the album *Essence to Essence.* Oldham gladly took over the duties from Donovan's regular producer, Mickey Most, once he learned there was a $250,000 budget. He thought the lads had cleaned up for the sessions, but Whitlock still destroyed the studio piano nonetheless. He found Jim uniquely there / not there. Another Rolling Stones producer, Jimmy Miller, used them on his album with Los Angeles pop vocalist Joey Stec. Marin County rock band Ducks were unpleasantly surprised to discover that producer John Simon had replaced their playing on the key track from their album with the Dominos' rhythm section. However, the idea of the Dominos as a discrete rhythm section never jelled.

Lenny Waronker had long been working with studio drummers other than Jim, but there were still times when nobody else would do. Waronker and his coproducer, Russ Titelman, had tried Jim on the pungent new Randy Newman song "Rednecks," but Titelman decided Jim was too stiff and moved on without him. That didn't stop Waronker from bringing Jim with him to Toronto in November to work with Gordon Lightfoot.

Lightfoot was a veteran folkie who had been recording for more than ten years and was supported by a close group of experienced musicians who performed his concerts as well as his recording sessions. When he came to Warners in 1970, Lightfoot was better known as the songwriter of "Early Morning Rain" and others than as a performer. Waronker steered him to his first million-selling album with the hit "If You Could Read My Mind," but his subsequent albums had not fared so well.

Waronker knew Jim came back from England a changed man and that there were drug problems in the background, but he needed Jim's collaborative nature to break into the tight creative circle surrounding Lightfoot, who was a proud, hard-drinking, tough artist, very much in charge of his own vision. The first night at Toronto's Eastern Sound Studios was a typical mess. Waronker never expected anything else. The musicians needed to get accustomed to the setting, playing together, the sound they were seeking. He didn't have a problem until the phone rang in his hotel room at two in the morning. It was Lightfoot demanding he fire the drummer, not comfortable with the intrusion on his tightly proscribed inner circle.

Waronker didn't argue but pleaded for one more night in the studio with Jim. Lightfoot reluctantly agreed. The next night, the first song up was a new Lightfoot original titled "Sundown." The only instructions Waronker gave Jim were to leave space in the verses for Lightfoot's twelve-string rhythm guitar part. Jim heard the introduction and started playing, pulling back to halftime on the verse, hitting only the four, not the two and four. Into the space Jim opened, Lightfoot's guitar filled the room. Jim cast a rich atmospheric shadow over the dark song with what he *didn't* play. The song was finished in forty minutes, and everybody in the room knew it was going to be a hit record.

When Steely Dan was first signed to ABC Records, there was no band, only the two songwriters, Donald Fagen and Walter Becker, and their producer, Gary Katz. They added the requisite additional musicians and came up with the name in service of making the first album. By the time they approached recording their third album in October, Becker and Fagen could not get the kind of precise drumming they needed from group member Jimmy Hodder and summoned to the studio on short notice a nineteen-year-old phenomenon named Jeff Porcaro out of the Sonny and Cher road band. Porcaro, whose jazz drummer father played on sessions, went to Grant High School in Van Nuys and worshipped at the altar of Jim Gordon. It was Porcaro who suggested they bring in Jim.

For the new album, Steely Dan had decided to adopt a workshop approach to recording, using the best session musicians in town to augment their work in the studio. On one hand, the session players found it exciting to be called to make a record certain to go on the charts; they dealt more commonly with veterans who had already been there or aspiring acts hoping to be. On the other hand, Steely Dan sessions could be exacting, tedious, drawn-out affairs where the musicians weren't clear what the producers were seeking or when they found what they wanted. The playback in the control room was dry and flat, low volume, without any of the effects or excitement that would give the players some juice. Before long, they didn't even go to listen.

Jim covered most of the sessions for the *Pretzel Logic* album from October through the end of the year at Village Recorders, along with a crew that included Dean Parks on guitar, Michael Omartian on keyboards, and Chuck Rainey on bass. Jim was perfectly tuned for the endless takes and clinical work of Dan sessions. He and Porcaro played double drums on the Charlie Parker tribute, "Parker's Band," and Jim cooked up a scintillating Latin groove to "Rikki Don't Lose That Number" that not only underlined the track's relation to Horace Silver's "Song for My Father," but assured Dan the big fat hit record they sought. Ten years into his career, Jim was a hitmaking machine at the peak of his professional powers.

XVI.
SOUTHER,
HILLMAN, FURAY

The insects started coming out from under the floorboards in Jim's life. He grew consumed with fear and insecurities. Voices in his head that had been murmurs in the background were growing louder, moving to the foreground. He heard them when he was cold sober. He didn't understand where they came from, but he heard them. At first, they were helpful, advising him on how to take care of himself and his house. They would let him know when he was right and when he was wrong. He thought it strange, but he heard the voices all the time. They told him he was an important person in the universe, that his birth had been special and that he had responsibilities to God and country. They told him he must make sacrifices. It was a chorus of voices. The leader was an old man with a flowing white beard. There was a young blonde woman and a dark Greek. There was also his brother, his aunt, and, mostly, his mother. It was his mother who commanded him to cut his eating in half.

He ran five miles daily and practiced calisthenics at home, often exercising to the point of exhaustion. He cut down his drinking and limited his cigarette smoking. With all his boozing, Jim had put on a lot of extra weight. He played tennis now, and every weekend held down first base at a weekly softball game with other music industry types in Woodland Hills. He treated his drug problem with Lomotil, a prescription children's laxative with a touch of morphine recommended to him by Gram Parsons. Jim was frantic to regain control of his life.

His confidence had taken such a beating that when he heard about the formation of a would-be supergroup featuring Richie Furay of Buffalo Springfield, Chris Hillman of The Byrds and Flying Burrito Brothers, and songwriter J. D. Souther, he politely approached Hillman about auditioning for the group. He didn't need to try out. The job was his for the asking.

The group came together at the suggestion of mogul David Geffen, who thought he could fashion them into another Crosby, Stills and Nash. Jim knew Hillman from Byrds sessions and Souther from playing on the album by Longbranch Pennywhistle, Souther's group with Glenn Frey before he started the Eagles. But it wasn't the quiet, shy, genial Jim who showed up for the recording sessions at American Recording Company in Woodland Hills, where Steppenwolf and Three Dog Night producer Richie Podolor and engineer Bill Cooper supervised the group's album. Instead of the patient, compliant session player everybody remembered, instead of the man who had meekly asked to audition, Jim was quarrelsome and irritable. When the other band members needed to do extra takes to get their parts, Jim would openly show his frustration with them. He stayed remote, sitting alone in the corner when the group listened to playbacks, uncommunicative and cold. The mask was slipping.

He continued to work other sessions. He played on an album by an up-and-coming songwriter named Tom Waits. He substituted for regular drummer Hal Blaine at John Denver sessions and played on hits like "Annie's Song" and "Thank God I'm a Country Boy." He did an album with songwriter Mike McGinnis, who was living with Jim's ex-wife Jill and acting as stepfather to his daughter, Amy. Jim and McGinnis got along famously. Jim also supplied the proper drive and thunder to Mike Post's theme song for the TV show *The Rockford Files*, which wound up being a big hit record.

In June 1974, the Souther, Hillman, Furay outfit set out to tour all summer behind the release of their album. With Crosby, Stills, Nash and Young selling out football stadiums across the country that summer, the SHF band was lucky to draw half a house at smaller theaters where they were booked. Richie Furay was going through a painful marital split with his pregnant wife and converting to Christianity. Hillman could be difficult and arrogant. There was precious little genuine chemistry between the three songwriters. The musicians had been thrown together as a strategy, not any kind of an organic collaboration, and the seams were showing right from the start. Jim quickly became a problem.

On the road, Jim turned into a regular Jekyll and Hyde, depending on what he was ingesting. Nobody knew at any given time what that might be. If he was straight—or, at least, only drinking—he could be fine. But if he wasn't, all bets were off. He would snort, shoot, drop, or otherwise consume anything that was brought backstage and given to him. Furay was shocked to have an uncontrollable Jim take off like a freight train behind him on his song "Believe Me," leaning on the tom-tom with one arm and smacking the hell out of the snare with the other. At a Holiday Inn cocktail lounge, Jim threw a glass at Hillman, who was sitting with some of the fellows from the band. Jim, as was his custom on this tour, was seated by himself a few tables away when he hurled an empty glass across the room that shattered on the table in front of Hillman, who brushed off the shards, walked over to Jim, and slammed his open palm into Jim's nose, a maneuver he learned from his martial arts studies.

Early in the tour at Fort Wayne, Indiana, where they played with the Eagles, the band returned to the hotel too late for room service. Jim was furious. Clad only in a bathrobe, he crept along the walkway overlooking the parking lot on the second floor of the two-story hotel, foraging for leftovers on trays left outside doors. If he didn't find anything he liked, he tossed the plate over the railing to the parking lot below.

They were driving in a caravan of vans from Pennsylvania to Ohio on the busy Pennsylvania Turnpike when Jim asked the driver to pull over so he could relieve himself. When he didn't return to the car, his fellow passengers went out looking for him and found Jim bent over in a sprinter's stance, running imaginary races against semis that were blasting down the highway.

For the first time, his drinking and drugging affected his playing. Richie Furay was astonished to find Jim dragging time. Or not coming out from backstage promptly after the acoustic section of the show but walking onstage with the first full band song already underway. Furay grew so unhappy with Jim that he fired him onstage one night, although that didn't stick. Hillman and Souther remembered the shy, humble, loving Jim and wondered who this guy was. It was apparent all was not right with Jim. They went out for another round of dates in October and November, then fired him.

Jim bought a new home in the hills of Sherman Oaks on Valley Vista Boulevard, a ranch-style, midcentury, three-bedroom house with a swimming pool on a secluded lot. He purchased the house thinking it would make a great place to settle down with a romantic partner, but he spent endless nights alone, unable to sleep. He kept a full schedule of studio sessions—albums, TV shows, commercials, whatever double-scale work there was—and spent what leisure time he did have at his new home. He poured money into it. He installed a new heating and air-conditioning system. He redid the pool. He closely supervised teams of painters and house cleaners who were constantly coming and going. A San Fernando Valley pest control company made many visits to fumigate pests, real and imagined.

Jim also helped design the tall fence he had erected to shield himself from the blue-skinned, spear-wielding neighbors he imagined lived next door. Jim feared they meant him harm.

His daughter, Amy, spent weekends with her grandmother Osa, who controlled Jim's access to her. Osa was wary of Jim. She was convinced—perhaps not unreasonably—that her son had returned from England a messed-up drug addict criminal and was not a suitable, responsible parent (also possibly not unreasonable). She supervised his visits with Amy at her home and let Jim pick her up after ballet class or gymnastics. Jim was hurt. He nursed resentments over being *permitted* to see his daughter. He thought his mother and ex-wife were working to turn Amy against him. He also thought his mother had changed since his father died and had taken a harsh, controlling turn in their relationship, whether or not that was true.

In January 1975, Jim joined the all-star lineup assembled to back Joan Baez at A&M Studios along with keyboardist Joe Sample and bassist Wilton Felder from The Crusaders and guitarists Dean Parks and Larry Carlton. Long one of the most famous folk singers in the world, encouraged by her road manager and ex-lover Bernie Gelb, Baez had decided to join the twentieth-century record business. Under the production of David Kershenbaum, who had left RCA for a staff position at A&M Records, Baez was determined to make a commercial album for the first time in her career. She girded her loins for accommodations and compromises, looked around the room that first night at this collection of double-scale musical talent, unlike any accompanists she ever had before, and started the sessions with a new song she had written titled "Diamonds and Rust."

It was a song that had originated with a phone call from her old paramour and protégé Bob Dylan, who read her the lyrics to a new piece, "Lily, Rosemary and the Jack of Hearts," a lengthy, slightly surreal number that would appear on his next album, *Blood on the Tracks*. Baez's ruminations on their complicated relationship turned out to be the finest song she ever wrote. The second tune they recorded that first night was the Allman Brothers' "Blue Sky," picked from a list of candidates deemed "up"—never a Baez specialty—because it was the one she disliked the least. Carlton and Parks supplied the double guitar lead.

Deliberately avoiding overtly political material for the first time in her life, Baez steered her way through works by Jackson Browne, Stevie Wonder, John Prine, and Janis Ian. In the middle of the sessions, *Blood on the Tracks* came out, and Baez quickly learned "A Simple Twist of Fate," singing one verse in the Dylan impression she had honed to near-perfection over the years. The Hollywood session players carried her in the palms of their hands, all slightly amazed to be playing Joan Baez sessions, producing a supple, contemporary record that would become the best-selling album of her career. In his liner notes, executive producer Bernie Gelb cited "the M.V.P. of the sessions, Big Jim Gordon." They called him "Gordo the Magnificent."

While his mental condition may have been deteriorating, his playing didn't suffer. He cut albums with soul singer Minnie Riperton, French pop star Michel Polnareff, a solo album with James Griffin of Bread, a Hugo Montenegro album of Elton John tunes (with Montenegro's teenage son on synthesizer) alongside guitarist Larry Carlton and bassist James Jamerson, who played on all the original Motown hits in Detroit, where the Hollywood studio musicians laid waste to the Elton originals. He started working with The Carpenters, the hit pop duo who usually used Hal Blaine (if Karen Carpenter herself wasn't playing drums).

In April, Jim joined Larry Knechtel and Dean Parks backing David Gates of Bread on a solo tour of England (including *The Old Grey Whistle Test* television program). On the flight back across the Atlantic, Knechtel thought Jim, sitting behind him, had been kicking his seat all through the flight, only to learn that Jim had actually been repeatedly stabbing the seatback with a pocketknife.

After spending most of June in the studio with Hall and Oates while the blue-eyed soul duo made their first West Coast album with the Los Angeles session players, Jim went out on tour in July with Joan Baez in a band that included guitarist Dan Ferguson, ex-Motown bass great James Jamerson, and Nashville session veteran David Briggs on keyboards. Baez had never toured with a band this size or caliber before.

Jim's condition was iffy. He could be charming and upbeat, or remote and churlish, even volatile. Checking the band into a hotel, road manager Gelb stepped inside the office while the bus unloaded. When he turned back around, Jim had pushed record producer David Kershenbaum up against a wall, his face glowing crimson, snorting through his nostrils. Gelb had no idea what Kershenbaum had said to evoke this violent response, it had happened so quickly, but he stepped in between the two men and the tension broke. Kershenbaum was scared out of his mind.

Gelb introduced an ex-girlfriend to Jim on the New England swing, and they spent a few nights together. She traveled on the bus with the band, but the next morning she was gone. Something happened, and she left in the middle of the night. Baez herself was not immune to Jim's appeal and came on to him, which flustered Jim. He was too intimidated to follow through on her advances.

Jim's relations with women continued to be fraught. Despite his deep desire to be loved, he could no longer contain his rage. With paranoia feeding his brain, his mind was overcrowded with noise. He really couldn't connect with people on an emotional basis. The dam was breaking, and the turmoil of his inner life was spilling over into his daily existence.

For some time, he lived at Valley Vista with Stacey Bailey, who first met Jim when she worked as a secretary for the soft-rock group Bread. She found him attractive, nearly irresistible. He brought her breakfast in bed and read to her from the Bible. He arranged for tickets to the Joan Baez concert at Hollywood Bowl and she sat next to Bob Dylan. He took care of her dog and her puppies when she went to visit her parents.

Jim told her the secret of the voices. She was the first girlfriend to whom he confessed this information. He also complained extensively about his mother wanting to control his life, like all women did, he said. She never put the two things together and did not see the real import of what Jim was telling her. Consequently, she never saw what was coming.

That relationship came to a sudden end when Bailey woke one night, unable to breathe, with Jim's hand wrapped around her throat choking her. She reached the point that she was about to pass out and Jim released his grip, letting her gasp for air. She tried to remain calm and talk to Jim while he repeated the cycle of choking her and letting go. Finally, he fell back on the bed laughing, as if it had all been a joke. Bailey sprinted to the neighbors'. Jim cried. "I just wanted to see if you really cared for me," he said, but the relationship was over.

Samantha Marr was a tall, thin, beautiful, and young kindergarten teacher who lived in a house she built in the New England countryside. She met Jim in Connecticut on the Baez tour. They had a promising fling on the road, and Jim flew her out to California. They went to the beach and Disneyland. They drove up to San Francisco and checked into the Hyatt Regency, where they started fighting, yelling at each other, and having a miserable time. Jim drove her back to Los Angeles and put her on a plane to Massachusetts.

Even as his efforts to find a romantic relationship failed, his professional life was shining brightly. The same fire burning in his brain was also like an engine driving his creative abilities. He was playing on a level of expertise he had never reached before. His skills had been honed to a razor's edge, but it was more than that; he was capable of practically superhuman, heroic feats on the drums.

Tom Petty was a young, unknown rock musician from Florida whose band Mudcrutch had broken up after one failed single. His producer, Denny Cordell, also a producer for Joe Cocker and Leon Russell, wanted to hold some experimental sessions for a prospective Petty solo album. Petty brought Mudcrutch guitarist Mike Campbell with him to the session at Wally Heider Studios in August where Cordell had assembled a top-drawer studio band that included Al Kooper on organ and Emory Gordy Jr. from the Gram Parsons' *Grievous Angel* band on bass. These guys had played with Dylan and Elvis. Jim was paid triple scale and, with a half-hour overtime, earned $400 for the session, while the other four players were happy to make $100 apiece. Petty and Campbell were thunderstruck to be in session with the drummer from "Layla." Dwight Twilley and Phil Seymour of the Dwight Twilley Band were present to sing background vocals. They cut the track to Petty's "Strangered in the Night" and went into the control room to listen.

"Do you have a couple of spare tracks?" Jim asked the engineer. "Because I could double my drums."

Petty and Campbell exchanged looks. Double the drums? They had never heard of such a thing. It sounded impossible. That would mean Jim would have to duplicate every stroke, precisely match the volume, the value, the rhythm of every cymbal crash, paradiddle, kick drumbeat. The slightest variation would leave echoes and smears on the track. Jim went back to the studio and did it in one take.

XVII.
OSA

When Osa first started dating, Jim was upset. He thought of his sixty-five-year-old mother as an old lady and was shocked that she would display an interest in sex. He felt it was still too soon after his father's death for any kind of relationship. She went off to a church convention with a gentleman she met through her Religious Science worship, a postal carrier who happened to be African American, which further inflamed Jim's disapproval. In fact, Jim's anger may have helped sink the relationship, although he was not much happier with her subsequent partner, a Jewish fellow she met through Alcoholics Anonymous named Morey with about twenty-five years sobriety. He had known Jim's dad.

Jim's relationship with his mother had always been complex. Growing up with an absent, alcoholic father, Jim lived in a house run surreptitiously by his mother. As is often the case with wives of alcoholics, Osa developed practiced skills at manipulating her husband and the boys. She had been the true head of the family. When her husband got sober, she had already established herself as the primary parental figure in the household, no matter how tyrannical and authoritarian his father acted.

A nurse by profession who had grown up in the small-town Midwest, Osa controlled the men in her life through attention. She hovered over the details of her sons' lives and quietly kept her husband in order. She could be warm and giving, work to make the people around her comfortable, but she always kept her hand on the steering wheel. She worried about Jim's drug and alcohol use and stayed close to his ex-wife, Jill. She spent a lot of time with her granddaughter, Amy, and closely monitored Jim's visits with his daughter at Osa's home. Jim talked with his mother on the phone frequently and still lived in the neighborhood. Her nurturing nature made her want to take care of Jim, to enfold this troubled child in her love and protection.

He called her one afternoon in the grip of a terrifying hallucination. He told her he found himself in a room covered in slime, and he was being attacked by some strange creatures from outer space. He was aware that it was a hallucination and yet it was all too real to him. He wanted his mother to talk him down. She tried her best to speak quietly and rationally with him and, by the end of the call, he had calmed down, but the episode left Osa bewildered and frightened.

Jim's head buzzed with voices now. He began to experience the dreaded command hallucinations, one of the most severe symptoms in all mental illness. If Jim did not obey the instructions from the voices, he would feel a searing pain encircle his head. Other victims have described it as an electric hatband. Jim called it "white hot cruelty pain." If he didn't do as he was told, his mother's voice would threaten to "fit" him—inflicting crippling pain that would leave him squirming on the floor, making him have a fit.

It was his mother's voice that controlled his eating. Ever since he was a young boy, Jim felt shame over his tendency to put on weight, but now he could hear his mother's voice telling him if he ate one more bite, he would die. He would put down a forkful of food mid-bite and leave the table. When he grew desperately hungry, he would sometimes pick up a box of fried chicken, check into the Sportsmen's Lodge at Coldwater Canyon and Ventura Boulevard in Studio City, and wolf down as much as he could before the voices caught up with him and forced him to regurgitate. He went hungry routinely.

Whatever calories he lost, he more than compensated with his alcohol intake. Drinking, he learned, could quiet the voices. The only other thing that could silence them was the drums. Predictably, the voices spoke out against both drums and booze. Jim was lost. Between the cacophony in his head and drinking himself senseless, there was little room left for him to lead a life.

His mother, of course, was convinced that Jim's problems were solely the result of drugs and alcohol. She encouraged him to attend AA meetings with her and her boyfriend, Morey, which Jim did although he was still uncomfortable with his mother's affection for her new partner. She was a regular at the Radford Hall in North Hollywood, the center of her social life. Jim was conflicted; he knew he was drinking like an alcoholic, but without the liquor, the voices were blaring nonstop.

Jim was losing his customarily conscientious control over his life. Usually obsessively meticulous with his finances, the son of an accountant and all that, Jim was distressed to find himself $100,000 in debt to the Internal Revenue Service. He began scrupulously noting his expenses down to every dime for the newspaper. His mother eventually convinced Jim to see a psychiatrist named Donna Aguilar she knew through AA. He spent a few sessions complaining about depression over the breakup of his marriage and anxiety over his finances without ever discussing the thunderstorm of auditory hallucinations inside his head. He tried another therapist and then another. He saw a half dozen different doctors over the course of the year without admitting his most drastic symptoms to a single one. They all wrote off his flat, dulled sensibilities to depression and didn't see Jim as a harm to himself or others. The various tranquilizers, antidepressants, and sleeping pills they prescribed did little but add to the confusion.

For the first time, the carefully maintained, discreet boundaries between his private life and professional world began to leak. Session work was still plentiful, but now Jim did the unthinkable and occasionally failed to show for sessions he booked. His reputation suffered; producer Jimmy Bowen, who first started working with Jim ten years before at Warner Brothers, wouldn't use Jim two days in a row on the sessions for vocalist Tracy Nelson because he didn't think Jim was consistent anymore. When he did play, however, he still delivered monumental performances. In March 1976, Jackson Browne and his producer, Jon Landau, brought him in to cut "Here Come the Tears Again" for *The Pretender* album, and Jim was his magnificent self. Jackson, who first met Jim hanging out with the Mad Dogs & Englishmen crew, had used him a couple months earlier on sessions with songwriter Warren Zevon that Browne was producing, but this was the first time he heard somebody say that something was not right with Jim. That didn't mean anything to Browne; as far as he was concerned, Jim made that track happen.

Later the same week, however, Jim was locked down with Hall & Oates cutting their next album, *Bigger Than Both of Us,* at Larrabee Sound in North Hollywood. Jim played on "Camellia" and the other songs on the sessions, but there was a perplexing incident when Jim started having an animated conversation with invisible parties from behind the kit. Although the musicians couldn't hear the other side of the discussion, it was clearly an argument. The voices they couldn't hear were obviously badgering Jim and, as the volume and intensity in Jim's end of the dialogue grew, they retreated to the control room, watching while Jim stayed behind shouting at unseen figures and unheard voices. The musicians had no idea what was going on. These fellows had been around plenty of drug casualties, but this was not like anything they had seen before. Every so often, the engineer would pot up the microphone in the studio, they would hear Jim still yelling, and he would pot back down. Then, as suddenly as it began, it was over, and Jim was wondering where everyone went and what were they waiting for.

His paranoia flared up unexpectedly. Guitarist Thom Rotella, a second-tier session player, found himself in the studio with Jim on drums and other big dogs on a Peter Allen session with producer Brooks Arthur. He knew Jim well from getting beaten every week by Jim on the tennis courts in Studio City. Producer Arthur was chasing some elusive sound only he could hear on the song "I Go to Rio" with the Australian pop singer. Somewhere around take eighty-four, Rotella spoke up to the producer. "I don't really know what you're looking for there," he said. "If Jim Gordon doesn't know, how the hell am I supposed to?"

That night, the phone rang, and Jim was on the line, stern and upset with him. They needed to talk, Jim told him, and they met for lunch the next day. Despite the years of playing tennis together, this was the first time Rotella had sat down for a meal with Jim. He was concerned about having hurt Jim's feelings, because he was new to playing sessions and Jim had been particularly encouraging. The Jim sitting across the table was not the person he knew. He leveled black beady eyes at him with a searing stare. He thought Rotella had been making fun of him, and it wasn't easy for Rotella to dissuade Jim that that wasn't the case.

Even Mike Post was not exempt. When Jim showed up ninety minutes late for a session Post booked, his onetime best friend took him out in the hallway to express his displeasure. Jim responded with attitude, acting tough. He called Post a square. "I don't know if you have any touch with albums," Jim said. "You're not FM." Pissed off and disgusted with Jim, Post canceled the session and sent everybody home. He wrote off Jim's behavior to drugs.

Even with all of this, Jim was still greatly in demand. He cut an album with "Brand New Key" singer-songwriter Melanie under the supervision of Atlantic Records founder Ahmet Ertegun. He did the follow-up to the *Diamonds and Rust* album with Joan Baez. He played on Cher sessions for producer Jimmy Webb. For producer Richard Perry, he took over the drum chair at sessions in May for the first solo album by Burton Cummings, former lead vocalist for Canadian rock institution Guess Who. He was beginning to worry enough about his reputation that when he ran into producer John Boylan doing a minor session for a television show, he told Boylan he was only there because he needed to buy some furniture.

Jim knew. He could tell something had gone drastically wrong. He had descended into yet another level of hell. His golden life had turned into a waking nightmare. The voices were taking over. His head overflowed with the noise. Not only was this frightening, but Jim was unable to admit to anyone else what was happening to him. In an effort to keep the secret of his voices under wraps, he isolated himself from the rest of the world, living alone in a vivid, real-life hellscape his mind created for him. He would phone his mother and complain about things that he had imagined she said to him, and she would have no idea what he was talking about.

Diana Whitman was one of a few women Jim had been seeing. Originally from Boston, she met Jim when she was a nineteen-year-old singer in San Francisco and Jim helped her get established on the Hollywood club scene. She was quite taken with the successful, handsome drummer and fell for him, even though he hardly responded in kind. His mood swings and sullen periods confused her, but she hung in there even if the relationship did not make her happy. In August, Jim went to Toronto to record with Alice Cooper, and she looked forward to hearing from him on his return. When Jim didn't call, she dropped by his house after a gig in the middle of the night, snuck in, and sat down to write him a letter:

Dear James,

Good morning. I hope that you are well. I came by this morning after work because I thought maybe you would be up even though you don't like to be surprised. And the hour is late. I guess it's about 2:00 a.m. In a way I'm glad that you weren't awake. Sometimes it's easier to say certain things in a letter. And I have so many things I would like to say to you. There is so much I don't understand about what went down between us. You have me totally confused and I wish you would help me straighten it out. I haven't stopped thinking about you at all since I saw you last and I wanted to see you so badly since you got back from Toronto. I couldn't believe how I missed you and you didn't give me the chance to say it or show it. I don't understand why. Maybe I'm not supposed to but I'd sure like to talk about it with you. I mean listen to this, the first time I talk to you after your trip you tell me good-bye, no explanation except that you couldn't find me and that was that. Then the next time I talked with you, and believe me I was very frightened about calling, you say to "keep in touch." Lightly? I don't know and yet I leave a message on your service last week and you didn't call. So here I am writing a letter to you in the moonlight. I'm very lost in this matter. You are in my heart. I want you to stay there. And you will no matter what is said and done. Maybe I was getting too heavy for you. Or something I didn't say? But tell me, please. Have a good day. I'll be hoping to hear from you.

All my love,
Diana

Before she could slip out of Jim's house unnoticed, he awoke in the grip of some horrendous hallucination. Jim was terrified by the intrusion and not able to speak rationally. His sudden raging appearance frightened the poor girl as he forcefully, angrily escorted her out the front door and gate. She was so scared she went back to Boston and never spoke to him again.

Though he had never been a social animal, Jim kept more and more to himself. He never stopped for beers with the guys after work. He didn't go out to dinner at restaurants or other people's homes. The people he worked with in the studios knew him from sessions as a fellow laborer but had little relations with him beyond that. Jim did not make human connections with any ease. Ironically, the only person he could turn to for help was his mother, whose voice was screaming at him all day and night in his mind. His bad news was beginning to spread around town, and the prestige bookings started to slack off. Life was getting tricky. Jim decided to take himself out of the way.

Moving day: fresh from England, Jim inveigled help moving from his friend Mike Post, January 1972. *Courtesy of Amy Gordon.*

Record company publicity photo for *The Rain Book,* the album by Renee Armand, Jim's second wife. *Courtesy of A&M Records.*

With Frank Zappa in rehearsals for the "Grand Wazoo" tour, August 1972. *Anthony Loew & Sam Emerson/Warner Records.*

Jim playing as a member of The Marketts with other studio musicians at a surf music revival concert, August 23, 1973, at the Hollywood Palladium. *Photo by Sherry Rayn Barnett.*

Cover of the second album by the Incredible Bongo Band with producer Michael Viner dressed as the villain, conga player King Errisson holding the rifle, arranger Perry Botkin Jr. in back, Jim on the horse, 1974. *Alamy Stock Photo.*

With Mama Cass on her CBS-TV special *Don't Call Me Mama*, September 1973. *ABC Photo Archive.*

ABOVE: Souther, Hillman, Furay left to right: Al Perkins, Jim Gordon, JD Souther, Chris Hillman, Richie Furay, and Paul Harris.

LEFT: In concert at Casino Arena, Asbury Park, New Jersey, July 1974. *Photos by Henry Diltz.*

Jim at Souther, Hillman, Furay sessions at American Studios, March 1974. *Photo by William Cooper.*

Jim at Record Plant, Hollywood, 1975. *Courtesy of Amy Gordon.*

The Diamonds and Rust band on the Joan Baez tour, left to right: guitarist Danny Ferguson, road manager Bernie Gelb, keyboardist David Briggs, Jim Gordon, and bassist James Jamerson, August 1975. *Courtesy of Bernie Gelb.*

With Johnny Rivers at the Montreux Jazz Festival, April 1973. *Photo by Georges Braunsweig/GMPress.*

With Jackson Browne at Mountain Aire Festival, Angels Camp, California, June 1978. *Photo by Larry Hulst.*

Jim posed for photos in his garage to accompany his interview with *Modern Drummer* magazine, January 1982. Photographer Eric Keltner, eighteen-year-old son of drummer Jim Keltner, had to assemble the drum kit. *Courtesy of* Modern Drummer.

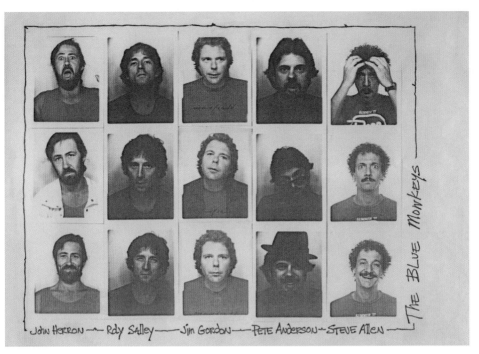

Blue Monkeys, 1983. *Courtesy of Steve Allen.*

With guitarist Gene Sarazen at Automatt Studios, San Francisco, August 1981. *Photo by Michael Reif.*

At Van Nuys Superior Court, the day he was found guilty of second-degree murder, March 1984. *Photo by Con Keyes*/Los Angeles Times *Photographic Archive, Library Special Collections, Charles E. Young Research Library, UCLA.*

Burton Cummings never imagined going on the road with Jim. From May through September, Jim attended the sessions for his album at Richard Perry's new headquarters, Studio 55, on Melrose Avenue next to the KHJ studios where Bing Crosby had cut "White Christmas" when it was Decca Records' studio. Cummings had brought down a drummer from Canada with the rest of his band, but Cummings's man couldn't meet the exacting standards of producer Perry. Jim breathed new life into Cummings's band in the studio. Of course, his reputation preceded him—"Layla," Mad Dogs, and so on—but Jim had taken Cummings to the promised land, and he instructed his management to see just how much it would cost to have Jim go on the road.

As luck would have it, a road trip suited Jim fine. He might be able to leave the voices behind. He certainly could get out of the way of some of his problems. There was nobody who would miss him, nothing keeping him. It seemed like the right idea at the right time. In late October, Jim handled a few last-minute sessions, got his hair cut, closed his house, had a farewell dinner with Amy and Osa, and boarded a plane for chilly Winnipeg to begin rehearsals.

XVIII.
BURTON

I n the United States, Burton Cummings barely registered with rock fans, but in Canada he qualified as a major star. For ten years during the band's golden run on the charts, Cummings belonged to Guess Who, the leading Canadian rock band of their time. With collaborator Randy Bachman, Cummings was cowriter and singer of indelible hits like "American Woman," "Laughing," "Undun," and "No Time." He was a burly, curly-headed, amiable oaf whom Jim nevertheless towered over. Twenty-nine-year-old Cummings was born and raised in Winnipeg, the capital city on the eastern edge of the Canadian prairie, the so-called Gateway to the West where temperatures stay below zero degrees Fahrenheit for a quarter of the year, unimaginable to a California kid like Jim.

But Canada was a perfect hiding place. Jim could stay insulated in the tiny world that is a rock band on tour, far from the pressures of Hollywood and home life. He brought an extraordinary level of musicianship to Cummings's homegrown Canadian band, and the other, younger, less experienced musicians in the group were overjoyed with the association. Jim worked himself into the fabric of the group during the album sessions. Though the other members may have found him to be something of an odd fish, cool, diffident, and taciturn, they thoroughly appreciated his abilities.

Jim kept his distance. The voices could still cause problems. His self-control could slip. He was determined to keep his balance. Playing with the less experienced musicians lowered the pressure on him to perform at his peak, and putting distance between him and his mother eased that stress, as did not having to go through the efforts of maintaining a relationship with his daughter in what he saw as a hostile environment created by Osa. Just getting away and devoting his life to playing drums was appealing. The drums kept the voices at bay.

Road manager Jimbo Martin, a veteran of ten years with Guess Who, went to the Winnipeg airport to pick up Jim in late October 1976. Martin already knew Jim from the album sessions, where Jim would hang back against the wall by himself while the other musicians crowded around the board to listen to playbacks. He sensed their superstar drummer might be slightly unstable and wanted everything to go smoothly on his arrival. Jim carried his equipment through Immigration and Customs and, because there was no paperwork done in advance, there were predictable hassles and obstacles to clearing customs. While Martin went back and forth with customs officials, Jim stayed calm. Martin was concerned, but he could never have imagined how difficult the ordeal really was for Jim.

The band was waiting at the rehearsal hall, wondering what was keeping Jim and Martin. When they finally pulled into rehearsal and set up Jim's gear, Jim sat down behind the kit, and they started playing. Everything was instantly all right. Straight off the plane into rehearsal, the drums made Jim feel like himself again. They bunked up at the Northstar Inn and after a few days of driving the band back and forth from rehearsal, Martin felt like he had come to know Jim well enough to engage in conversation. Jim was sitting on a couch at rehearsal and Martin walked up. "I want to shake your hand," he told Jim.

"Why?" said Jim.

"'Layla,' man, 'Layla,'" Martin said. "I'm finally getting to thank the guy who cowrote the tune and did the piano solo."

Jim stared back at Martin like he didn't know what he was saying. Martin thought maybe he didn't hear him. Jim looked at him blankly as an awkward silence filled the air. It was an embarrassing moment for Martin, who further resolved to take special care of Jim.

Jim still minded his manners. He watched the presidential debate between Jimmy Carter and Gerald Ford in his hotel room and realized that he had not arranged for an absentee ballot. He sat down and wrote to ask for a ballot, making sure to apologize for his late request.

But Jim was never far from the edge. During the run-through before the tour's opening concert at Winnipeg's Centennial Concert Hall, a lighting technician dropped a gel while hanging lights behind the band, and it crashed to the stage near Jim. He freaked and exploded in anger. He had to be restrained from pounding the poor guy. Martin took note and realized he was going to have to pay even closer attention to Jim.

Off they went on a November swing through the frigid north. "Stand Tall," the first single from Cummings's solo album, had launched and was well on its way to becoming a big hit. There was a great festive air to the opening of this chapter of Cummings's career and splurging on having Jim in the band was part of it. In Vancouver, Cummings opened the show with a medley of Guess

Who hits that he usually saved for the finale, dedicating it to "a very special person in the audience." He had not spoken to former bandmate Randy Bachman in seven years since Bachman left the group and embraced the Mormon religion. He'd had five kids since then and made hit records with his new group, Bachman-Turner Overdrive, which Cummings saluted on his album with a big band swing version of the BTO hit "You Ain't Seen Nothing Yet."

At the after-party CBS Records hosted at a local disco, Cummings and Bachman happily posed for photographs. "Man, I had tears in my eyes during that medley," Bachman told *Rolling Stone*. "It was beautiful."

In Canada, this reunion was greeted on the order of John and Paul getting back together; simply shaking hands at a concert after-party was big news, Bachman anointing his ex-bandmate's solo excursion. Bachman joined the band as a special guest on a Canadian Broadcasting Company network television Burton Cummings special a week later.

Temperatures hovered near freezing as Cummings and company continued to make their way across Canada. They opened for the Bee Gees at Forum de Montréal. The Gibb brothers knew who was drumming with Cummings and all watched from the wings. Powered by their inspiring drummer, the Cummings band put on a tidy, ripping show, sprinkling Guess Who favorites among the songs from his solo album, an old rock and roll number for Burton to do his Jerry Lee Lewis thing on his white grand piano, and a new original he had yet to record, "My Own Way to Rock." After the Canadian dates, the band flew to Los Angeles for their US debut on December 12 in a showcase performance hosted by the label at the Roxy nightclub on Sunset Strip.

Although tired and disoriented from the road (and not eating), Jim went right back to playing sessions because he thought he needed the money. He spent his off-hours supervising work on his Valley Vista place and Christmas shopping. He went for a tense holiday dinner at Osa's house with Amy and his aunt Thelma. Osa was worried because Jim had lost so much weight and seemed to have no appetite, even for the turkey dinner.

Unable to sleep, Jim haunted local clubs, stayed until closing, and then spent endless hours strumming his guitar on his living room couch, trying to ignore the hunger pangs and constant chatter in his head. He kept several appointments with one psychiatrist and scheduled visits with another recommended by his mother, but he told neither of them that he was hearing voices.

Jim spent New Year's Day at home paying bills, carefully noting each check in his diary. He spent the first two weeks of January 1977 in the studio with Manhattan Transfer and producer Richard Perry and did some Merle Haggard sessions. The next week he was back in the psychiatrist's office complaining of depression, anxiety, and fatigue, without mentioning that the voices in his head were depriving him of food. At the end of the month, the Burton Cummings band was back in town to begin sessions for the next album with producer Perry and appear on the afternoon TV talk show hosted by Dinah Shore, along with guests George Carlin and Ray Charles. Cummings was thrilled to sing the Ray Charles song he did on his solo album, "That's Enough," with Ray Charles himself supplying the Raelettes background vocal part. But for Jim, it was simply another day at the office, watching out for potential threats.

He took more appointments with both psychiatrists, spent an afternoon watching Amy at her ice-skating lessons, and then packed for the second leg of the Burton Cummings tour, including the antidepressants and tranquilizers his doctors prescribed. In the car traveling from the first date in Minneapolis to the next in Kansas City, "Stand Tall" came on the radio; hardly surprising considering it was currently one of the top hit records in the country. Jim stunned everyone in the car into silence. "Burton," he asked, "who's playing drums on that?"

He was dead serious. He didn't know. Cummings told him. "Jim, that's you drumming on that," he said.

A slight smile twitched across Jim's lips. "I'll be darned," he said.

Jim made detailed notes in his diary of his observations on his condition, which he had determined came in three-part cycles. He titled them with Roman numerals. Stage I is the most manageable; things start brewing. At stage II, they reach a boiling point. At stage III, they overcome Jim and he finds himself immersed. The cycles varied in length from twenty-four to forty-eight hours. By the time he reached the third cycle, his delusional system would be working overtime. He would have difficulty simply leaving his hotel room. He would walk past strangers on the street and hear them say distressing and discouraging things to him. *It's all over. What's the use of doing anything anymore? This is the end of the line.*

Through the Midwest, as the band opened concerts for the soft-rock act America, Jim repeatedly wrote in his diary an enigmatic phrase—*the way of the land is a desert, hot, cold.* In Toledo, Ohio, he noted fifty cents spent playing pinball, then scrawled *stay up.* In Detroit, he wrote *Detroit is black, all dark and black. No nap, no bath.* He found the crowd there *a little off* and again reminded himself, *stay up.* On February 17, he found himself experiencing cycles II and III simultaneously. He wrote there would be *a test in the desert, hot and cold, a maze.* With some dates canceled due to sluggish sales, the band returned to Los Angeles for an unscheduled break—*under fire,* Jim wrote.

Back home, believing what was happening to him might also be happening to other people, he scoured the newspapers and television news for clues, but found none—*in hot water and having hunger attacks,* he wrote. He took himself to the movies to see *The Sailor Who Fell from Grace with the Sea* and could enjoy watching Rita Coolidge's husband, Kris Kristofferson, die in his on-screen role, but the next day he was trapped in his third cycle. *Missed Amy skating. Very hard to get anything done. New high. Everything is affected and in my way.* Not eating left him weak and light-headed, yet he felt powerful—*unlimited energy. It was a euphoria kind of thing.*

When he went to Amy's next skating lesson, his ex- Jill, was there. Completely thrown, Jim excused himself. He drove straight to Kentucky Fried Chicken and gorged himself until the meat hit his shrunken stomach and he vomited. His mother's voice screamed in his head. *I told you not to eat that.*

The voices did not want him to drum anymore. They made him turn down a Barbra Streisand date, and Jim threw himself into a flurry of activity around his Valley Vista place. Even though the pool had been redone recently, he found small pieces of maintenance that needed tending. He studied the Polaris leaf sweeper system so that he could repair it himself if necessary. Although he hired a gardener to visit twice a week, Jim was receiving command hallucinations from Osa about weeding the big sloping hill behind his house. It was an especially dry, hot March in Southern California, and Jim would rise at dawn to take out the weed killer and start weeding. The clay earth was like a clenched fist. Anything that wanted to live there had to dig in. Jim battled every slender stalk out of the ground. He hated doing it. He didn't want to do it. But he had to do it.

The tour started back April 1 in Seattle in time for Jim to join his brother for his birthday. After visiting the bank where John worked as an executive, Jim went with him to see his wife, Martha, and her two daughters. Jim toured the improvements on their home, and the brothers amiably discussed whether—when their mother retired—she would move to Seattle or Lake Tahoe, where she had been spending time with her boyfriend, Morey. Delicate subjects such as Jim's condition were avoided.

On the road, Jim kept largely to himself. He often ate dinner alone while the other band members dined together across the room. If he did stop by the party suite after a concert, he didn't stay long. Jim wasn't doing much drinking. He would join the guys for a beer at the hotel after the show, then worry about some stranger across the room staring at him and leave. His paranoia was raging. The medications his psychiatrists prescribed kept him in a zone of his own. While the other, younger band members stayed up all night howling at the moon, Jim tended toward early bedtimes, often drifting off on the light-headed feelings of euphoria that could be a side effect of starving himself.

Traveling through Florida, Jim would rent cars and drive for hours by himself after the shows. In Gainesville, he had to have his stage clothes altered again to accommodate his weight loss. Still, he was feeling well enough to play poker with some of the guys. In Atlanta, he was able to visit with an old girlfriend. In Norfolk, Virginia, Jim wrote in his diary, *Burton up all night banging on walls.* Cummings and one of the other band members had taken to rolling empty beer bottles down the hall, trying to hit each other's door. Jim emerged from his room annoyed, wearing pajamas covered with pictures of Popeye. After that, the road manager made sure to book Jim's rooms on a different floor.

After a few days of feeling well, the cycle changed, and the voices took over again. Now the voices of the other band members had joined the crowd in his head, and Jim could hear them saying things to him they didn't actually say. He grew increasingly suspicious of his fellow musicians. He strongly suspected they did not have his best interests at heart, and he knew he would have to keep his eye on them. At a tour meeting in a hotel room waiting for road manager Martin to lay out some schedule details, the band sat around in silence, tired from the plane ride. Jim tapped bassist Ian Gardiner on the shoulder.

"Ian, did you say something to me?" he asked.

Of course, he hadn't and told Jim that. A couple minutes later, Jim spoke up again. "Hey, Ian, did you say something to me?" he asked.

They went back and forth, Gardiner denying he said anything, and Jim grew agitated. "Listen, if you've got something to say to me, let's go out in the hall and you can tell me."

When road manager Martin walked into the room, he assumed Ian had been picking on Jim and told him to lay off, which caused the other guys to break out laughing. Martin saw how uncomfortable this made Jim and quickly told them to shut up. He turned to Jim and told him to relax. "Let's go back to your room," he said and led him away.

The tour with America closed in Providence, Rhode Island, and the band went to Toronto to shoot the next CBC Burton Cummings TV special. Jim enjoyed his stay in Toronto. He was able to sleep, caught some movies, took the subway to get a haircut, shopped for antiques. He went with Burton when he dropped by a local club and sang. They shot the special before returning to Los Angeles after one last, giant, open-air concert at Charles River Esplanade's Hatch Shell in downtown Boston with Orleans and Heart. Back home, still riding on the good feelings of Toronto, Jim saw a few friends, even took in a Dodgers game, and had Mother's Day dinner with Osa and Morey. That night he wrote in his diary, *watching water intake.*

When Amy broke her leg and Jim visited her in the hospital, the voices bombarded him with messages of guilt and anxiety, telling him his efforts to soothe her were inadequate, that he was a terrible father. He struggled through uncomfortable dinners with Osa and Amy after she got out of the hospital, trying to find something to say. Dinners with Osa were a special hell. Osa would be wondering aloud why Jim didn't eat more while her screaming voice filled his head, telling him not to touch a bite. His mother urged him to visit his father's grave at the Los Angeles National Cemetery near the Veteran's Administration in West Los Angeles (*V.A. is quiet and seems solid,* he wrote in his diary). After having spent a month at home, with the pressures of a daughter with a broken leg, his mother, and her boyfriend, Jim was ready to go back on the road, even though some of the band members had been "sending" him bad thoughts.

In May at the Worlds of Fun Amphitheater in Kansas City, Jim joined the rest of the band in an amusement park ride, grabbing the common steering wheel in the capsule they shared and spinning the thing as fast as it could go, laughing maniacally while the other band members held on for their lives seventy feet above the ground. In Chicago, Jim visited another old girlfriend at her family home outside the city. The band shot the WTTV live music showcase *Soundstage* with Randy Bachman joining the party for a few Guess Who numbers.

But mostly, Jim stayed wary and remote from the other band members on this tour. In Nashville, he visited Music Row and took a boat ride. He walked along the river in Charleston and ate dinner at Long John Silver's, a meal he recorded in his diary as *not bad.* On a week's break, he returned home to celebrate Amy's eighth birthday at Osa's home. The night before leaving to rejoin the band in New York, he wrote in his diary, *Watch out! Keep on your toes!*

In New York, Jim went with the rest of the band to Madison Square Garden to see Led Zeppelin, one of his favorite rock groups. When John Bonham started his drum solo, Jim disappeared and never returned (the same thing had happened when the band took Jim to see *Star Wars;* he left after the alien creatures scared him— *Went to see Star Wars. I couldn't stay,* he noted).

While his cycles had eased up during the first part of the tour, by the middle of June, they had returned. He felt his body was changing. He grew self-conscious about his appearance. In his diary he wrote *hermaphrodite,* and under that, *seems very high,* and under that, *sat all day.* Back in Los Angeles on another break, he discovered he'd left the cat locked in his studio and tried again to go see Led Zeppelin at the Forum but the voices wouldn't let him. He had to stay home and get up early to finish clearing the hill in his backyard, they said. After spending the whole week weeding in the torturous summer sun, Jim could note in his diary, *all areas back of the house are fairly clean.* After the Fourth of July, Jim was back with the band on tour with Hall & Oates. His dinner tabs for the next eight days averaged $1.09, he noted.

By the last date in Salt Lake City, Jim had concluded he could not continue. He was depleted, mentally, physically, emotionally, and the voices were going crazy in his head. He told road manager Martin he wanted his equipment sent home. Martin resisted, telling Jim there were only two days before they had to be back on the road. Nevertheless, Jim insisted. The next day, Martin's wife got a call from Jim. He told her to tell her husband that he wouldn't be going back on tour and not to call him. Martin called anyway. Jim told him he had a lot of work to do around the house and didn't want to go out on the road anymore. Martin hung up and hurriedly turned to finding a new drummer—the next show was five days away.

XIX.
SNAKE PIT

Getting off the road didn't mean Jim could get his life under control. He had only been home one day before producers began calling for sessions. He booked a Record Plant date with producer Brooks Arthur and Keith Carradine, the actor who had scored a hit off the *Nashville* soundtrack with "I'm Easy." Jim was happy to be back on the scene; actress Laraine Newman was visiting the rehearsal. But Jim had not been eating and didn't feel well. Consumed with hunger, Jim thought not eating was making him glow white like some radiant ghost. It was a bad day. He quit the project and went home.

He did manage to do a commercial two days later on his birthday, July 14, but when he went to his mother's house for a birthday dinner, he couldn't bring himself to stay. He fled. That weekend, he continued to work on the hill behind his house, swam in the pool, drove around town, winding up that night at the Troubadour in West Hollywood. A letter his mother wrote the morning after his birthday arrived for him:

Dear Jim,

I was very concerned about you last night. I'm sorry you didn't feel like eating your dinner but I know if you don't feel well you would rather be home.

I called Donna Aguilar about 9:30 p.m. to see if she could suggest anything I could do. I told her you felt like you would probably not go back to her. She feels like you need help, Jim, whether from her or someone else. She said you might feel more comfortable with a man. I probably should have thought about this before I talked to her. I was told she was very good and had helped a lot of people. She thought if you would continue you could probably notice much improvement and would not need more than six visits possibly.

She said the medication would help the anxiety and the medication is not habit forming. I hope you will take it.

Jim if you are awake by 6:45 a.m. I think you would find it worthwhile to turn on radio station KIEV 870 on the dial and listen to Dr. Richeleau from 6:45 a.m. to 7:00 a.m. and Dr. Hainaday from 7:00 a.m. to 7:15 a.m. They are Science of the Mind ministers and they give some good points on this business of living. I know they help me a lot as they help many people.

I hope you will stop by for your presents and some cake and a little visit.

Ben Barrett called here for you about 9:30 a.m. I gave him your home phone. I hope that was okay. I don't have the number of your exchange.

Jim, I love you and would do anything I could for you, if I just knew what to do.

Mom

He spent the next several days in hectic activity around the house. The voices were clamoring. *You didn't get all those weeds on the hill. You did a lousy job. You can't do anything right.* He heard his aunt Thelma's voice. *Dirty, dirty, dirty, this house is filthy, just like you,* she told him. Despite having cleaning crews working twice a week, Jim went to work buffing every window in the place. After several days of this, the voices building to a screeching crescendo, Jim burst out of his home and ran straight to the Sportsmen's Lodge.

The next morning, he phoned Dr. Daniel Auerbach, a psychiatrist whose name Jim had been given. Sensing a crisis, Dr. Auerbach told Jim to come in at three thirty that afternoon, Thursday, July 21.

Dr. Auerbach was a tall, handsome gentleman with a soft but authoritative manner. At age thirty-four, he was two years older than Jim. He listened as Jim outlined his depression and anxiety. He confessed to thinking about suicide. He was full of remorse over ending his marriage, guilt over using drugs, and frustrated with his inability to properly express his love to Amy. Auerbach recognized the tortured, sad, and defeated man in his office, but also understood that Jim was a fully functioning professional at the top of his field. He certainly did not appear psychotic, although he was clearly depressed. Auerbach was touched by the sweet, gentle man who loved his daughter. They set another appointment.

Encouraged by the doctor's visit, Jim checked out of the Sportsmen's Lodge in Studio City and shifted camps to the Carriage House in Encino, hoping the voices wouldn't follow him. He bought a box of chicken and tried to eat, but the voices found him and made him stop. They made him check out of the hotel. Driven out of his house and two hotels, he found a pay phone on the street and, distraught and disoriented, he called Dr. Auerbach.

"I can't handle it out in the world," Jim told him. "You gotta put me in some place where I can at least get something to eat."

200 DRUMS AND DEMONS

What happened next broke the seal. Over the phone, for the first time to another human being, Jim started to pour out the elaborate details of his highly evolved delusional system. He told him about his mother persecuting him in his head. He spilled out enough of his secret world that Auerbach took immediate action. He checked Jim directly into Van Nuys Psychiatric Hospital.

Jim was embarrassed, frustrated, discouraged with himself. Despite all his intelligence, he couldn't figure any way out of this situation. He had spent so many years trying to manage the disturbing feelings by himself, but now he could barely get past more than even a taste of food at meals. He would go to a restaurant, order from the menu, take one bite and leave, still hungry. He could no longer run away from the voices. They found him wherever he went. He wasn't drinking. He stopped taking drugs. He was told that he needed to quit for the good of the country. He was certain the telepathic messages were genuine and not something he was making up because why would he do this to himself? He wanted to eat. He wanted to sleep. He was living in a turbulent, frightening world over which he had no control. He checked into the hospital and the phrase "hospital admission" was never more appropriate. He was finally admitting he needed help.

The first thing Jim saw as he walked into the hospital was a naked woman running down the hall. The place looked like a real snake pit to Jim, but he didn't care. He hoped he could get some help. He wanted to win this battle. He was weary of starving himself. He wanted to rid his life of this constant adversity.

Hospital staff had to help encourage Jim bite by bite. But he had been drilled for so long by the voices—*don't eat this bite, you can't eat that bite, no, don't eat that*—that he couldn't make himself eat. He developed all the symptoms of anorexia.

Jim was treated with the powerful antipsychotic medicines Elavil and Haldol, but they had no evident effect. Jim's ability to consume massive amounts of drugs extended to pharmaceuticals. Dr. Auerbach prescribed fifteen milligrams of Haldol three times a day, for a total of forty-five milligrams, but Jim was instead mistakenly given forty-five milligrams three times a day, enough to turn a lumberjack into a zombie. Auerbach discovered the error after several days of Jim taking the massive doses and was, first, relieved that Jim suffered no untoward consequences and, then, astonished that there had also been no therapeutic effect.

Dr. Auerbach thought Jim was suffering from some form of manic depression. His mood cycles were more common to that condition. He diagnosed Jim with psychotic depression—severe depression with suicidal ideation. He knew Jim operated on a high level in society and understood that the patient had engaged in extensive drug use in the past. His detailed delusional hierarchy could be symptomatic of a severe depression or an atypical manic-depressive condition.

Jim told Dr. Auerbach that, for the previous two and a half years, his life had grown increasingly under the control of this family who were free to inspect every aspect of his daily life. He had no privacy from them—because the voices were in his mind, they knew his every thought, everything that had ever happened to him. Their instructions to him could be communicated through spoken commands and other nonverbal signs coming from television, people's motions, facial expressions—classic paranoid delusions. Chief among his tormentors was his mother's voice, harsh, critical, dismissive, and discouraging. He also told Auerbach that Osa was his only friend. She did come and visit Jim at the hospital. The doctors were encouraged enough, even considering his ambivalent feelings toward her, to allow Jim to spend weekends with his mother at her home.

After weeks of treatment at Van Nuys Psychiatric with little or no progress, Jim now added the failure of his hospitalization to the list of reasons to be depressed. Nothing worked. Even the professionals couldn't help. The hospital admission failed to yield results. He felt caught in a world he hated without any recourse. He was doomed to be tortured for the rest of his life. At last, exasperated, disappointed, and against medical advice, Jim checked out and returned to his home, although he continued to see Dr. Auerbach as an outpatient.

On September 3, after Jim missed a scheduled appointment, Dr. Auerbach called his mother. She went to check on Jim at his home and found him slumped on the floor, unconscious from an overdose of sleeping pills prescribed by his psychiatrist. He was readmitted to Van Nuys Psychiatric and, at his first meeting with Dr. Auerbach, he apologized for attempting suicide, but told Auerbach that the voices didn't care whether he lived or died.

Whether it was the antipsychotic drugs finally taking effect, the shock of a suicide attempt, or simply a long overdue victory of his rational mind, Jim started to experience recovery. Auerbach had admitted Jim the second time with a diagnosis of "psychosis ideology unclear," but soon after Jim began to show improvement, he signed him out with "psychotic depression." He had explained to Auerbach that he understood that the voices inhabiting his head were his own invention, although still expressing considerable anger toward his mother. He was living with Osa and, while he was grateful for her help, he resented what he saw as her control of his life, keeping him dependent.

Dr. Auerbach referred Jim to the UCLA Adult Development program, and he dutifully drove to Westwood daily to attend group

therapy sessions, lectures, and take instruction in independent living. He was taking his medications and giving the UCLA program
his full attention. He finally felt like he might be getting somewhere.
He took a weekend trip in October with his mother and aunt that
went well. In November, Osa joined Jim for a session with Dr.
Auerbach, and Jim aired his anger toward her, something he had
previously been unable to confront her about. He found an apartment he liked in Brentwood and went back to work in the studios.

With things looking up, Jim even found a girlfriend, a short,
adorable gal named Wendy Benner whom he met when they both
witnessed a car crash on Wilshire Boulevard. They went dancing,
took daily trips to the beach. For a while, she brought some fun
back to Jim's life, but of course nothing was easy.

He took whatever sessions he could—commercials, TV shows,
soundtracks—record dates were few and far between. Despite the
progress he was making at UCLA, Jim was hanging on by his fin-
gertips. Voices were still flying around his head. He struggled to
maintain a game face. The antipsychotic medications he was taking
came with unpleasant side effects. His frustration could be unbear-
able, bursting into the open at unpredictable moments like the end
of a Johnny Rivers session at Western Studio for his album *Outside
Help.* The band was preparing to track one final song before the
session ended, when Jim started shouting across the room at guitarist Dean Parks.

"Stop that," he yelled. "I know what you're doing."

Parks had no idea what Jim was upset about. They had spent
hundreds of hours in recording studios making music together
without ever really coming to know each other as people. Parks, like
everyone else, knew Jim's extraordinary abilities, but had never
grabbed more than a few desultory pieces of conversation with Jim
between takes.

"What are you talking about, Jim?" Parks said. "I'm not doing anything."

"You're moving my hands," Jim said. "You're messing with my time. You're making me miss the whole note on beat one of every bar."

As everybody in the room went silent with astonishment, Johnny Rivers, both the artist and producer on the sessions, broke the ice.

"He can't do that from over there, Jim," Rivers said. "Now count it off and let's go . . . 1 . . . 2 . . . 3 . . . 4."

Jim nodded and came right in at the top like he was supposed to do, as if nothing had happened. Of course, the incident supplied irresistible fodder for gossip, and the story was quickly whispered around Hollywood. Given the blind eye the music scene trained on mental illness, Jim was in danger of being written off as another superstar drug casualty. Even Richard Perry was working with other drummers. Sometime later, Jim admitted privately to Parks that he heard voices and had himself committed, but at the time, it simply went down as some strange, unexplained episode.

In February 1978, Jim graduated from the UCLA program with a certificate. Dr. Auerbach considered Jim in remission. He had seen Jim stabilize his dramatic mood swings—from grandiose elation to deep depression—into a more manageable middle ground. He had responded to his medication and was compliant about taking the drugs. Even though Jim still harbored doubts about his mother, Auerbach stopped seeing him as a regular patient.

It still wasn't always simple for Jim. That same month, he found himself in an increasingly rare record date for the debut solo album of vocalist Steve Harley of British rock group Cockney Rebel. Jim was sitting behind the drums directly across the narrow Sunset Sound room from bassist Bob Glaub, who had played with Jim on a few occasions, including "Here Come Those Tears Again" with

Jackson Browne. Glaub was a younger session player who had looked up to Jim since he'd heard Mad Dogs & Englishmen. He had seen Derek and the Dominos play when he was a teenager. Glaub knew Jim to be a quiet, serious musician who didn't joke around a lot and was stunned when Jim threw his sticks at the drums, let them bounce to the floor, rose up behind his kit, and glowered at Glaub.

"Did you call me dumb?" he said.

"What?" said a shocked Glaub. "I don't know what the fuck you're talking about. I didn't say anything."

The small, crowded space filled with tension. Large as he was, Jim could cast an intimidating physical presence. He muttered as he sat down and picked up his sticks. "I could have sworn I heard you call me dumb," he said.

"I'm waiting for you to count off the song," Glaub said. "Sit down, count off, and let's play."

Jim did just that, counted off the track and started playing. Like nothing ever happened.

Glaub found the incident disquieting, but a month later, he was talking to Jackson Browne about finding a drummer for his upcoming tour and brought up Jim. "He's kind of nuts," Glaub said, "but nobody's better than Jim Gordon. I don't think he's doing that much."

Jackson Browne had tired of the cyclical routine of writing new songs, recording the album, and then going out on the road to promote the album and play the new songs, which only got better as the tour progressed and the band grew more comfortable with the material. Something about that process struck Browne as backwards, and he had toured the previous year playing the new songs and recording the album on the road, as the band got better playing them. *Runnin' on Empty* had been a joyful, whimsical, and altogether successful experiment, but now the album had been released, and he would be going on the road again, this time to promote the album recorded on the last tour.

His regular rhythm section of bassist Lee Sklar and drummer Russ Kunkel had already been reserved for the next year by their other main client, James Taylor, so Browne needed to recruit a new rhythm section to go with him, bassist Glaub, guitarist David Lindley, and keyboardist Craig Doerge. Jim Gordon struck Browne as a great idea. He had heard vague rumors about Jim having problems and going through rehab, but assumed it was drug- and alcohol-related issues, which were endemic to the industry. He didn't give the matter a second thought.

Jim showed up later that week at The Alley Studios in North Hollywood, a well-worn, homey complex where Little Feat and Bonnie Raitt liked to rehearse, and he rocked everything he played. Guitarist Lindley was especially enthusiastic. The first outing was a quick nine-concert, two-and-a-half-week run through the Midwest, to be followed by a long weekend of festival dates in June and an East Coast swing in August. Osa took eleven-year-old Amy to see her father play at the first show with Browne at the Terrace Theater in Long Beach.

On the road, Jim kept to himself, maybe just snickered at a joke or mumbled some inconsequential remark. But he played racquetball and ran daily with Browne. He was in fine shape and feeling good about himself. He knew this was a chance for a comeback and the circumstances could hardly have been more encouraging. Still, it was a struggle. His meds kept him zeroed out, on the edge of sullen. The fire was missing. His eyes no longer twinkled; the easy smile was more like a sick grin. He also started drinking again and before long there was a red plastic cup with vodka sitting by his kit every night.

Back home, he was living again with his mother, an uncomfortable situation. Her voice in his head had insisted he leave the apartment in Brentwood that he liked. He could, however, enjoy checking into the Sportsmen's Lodge with a bottle of wine to watch TV and spend the night. The voices allowed him to do that, even though the wine dulled their command over Jim. They were still making it hard for him to eat. His mother would fuss over him and worry aloud about his eating—or rather, *not* eating—at the dinner table, while in Jim's head he heard her voice—*don't touch another bite.* The voices took over again. By November, he was back in the hospital.

Session work grew slender for Jim, even as the record industry entered the multi-platinum era. Album sales continued to grow like there was no end and recording studios throughout Los Angeles were pumping out product. There was still plenty of opportunity, but drummers like Jim Keltner, Jeff Porcaro, Ed Greene, Rick Shlosser, and others were getting jobs that would have been Jim's two years before. He did an album with TV star Cheryl Ladd of *Charlie's Angels*, albums with the Japanese pop singer Mariya Takeuchi, French pop star Michel Berger, and Christian music guitarist Phil Keaggy. He backed the puppeteers/vocalists on the soundtrack of *The Muppet Movie.* For the Danny O'Keefe album *The Global Blues,* he was brought in to lay down a drum track alongside an already-recorded part by jazz great Tony Williams from the Miles Davis group, which had some tempo problems that Jim's overdubs sought to mitigate.

In March 1979, singer-songwriter Terence Boylan hired Jim to work on his next solo album. Jim had played brilliantly on the 1977 Asylum Records debut album by record producer John Boylan's younger brother. Terence Boylan had been roommates with Walter Becker at Bard College and watched as Becker and classmate Don Fagen began a collaboration that would eventually become Steely

Dan. They backed the younger Boylan on his 1969 solo debut. When he moved to Los Angeles, he roomed with an up-and-coming Glenn Frey, affording Boylan a similar inside view on the beginnings of the Eagles, members of which had sung and played on his previous Asylum album.

Terence Boylan had been blown away by Jim on sessions for the first 1977 Asylum album with Jim's telepathic abilities to know what other musicians were going to do before they did it. It was Boylan's custom to teach the studio musicians the song in a run-through that he also recorded. While most drummers would spend the first time only listening, maybe hitting the four with a kick drum, Jim jumped in at the beginning and played along from the start. Boylan was beyond amazed when they ran down the song "Trains" and Jim perfectly forecast what keyboardist David Paich was going to play on the bridge, opened up the space, and danced around the keyboard part before he ever heard it. The run-through ended up as the master take.

Two years later at Westlake Audio, recording the second Asylum album by Terence Boylan, a different Jim Gordon came to play. He was edgy and frail. Unlike the gentle giant Boylan remembered from the previous album, this Jim could be ornery and irritable. He got upset with himself if he did something he deemed unworthy. Listening to playbacks, he tucked himself behind the tape deck in the control room, standing apart, in the shadows, arms folded, unsmiling. He was so concerned about leaving the three-hour session on time that Boylan figured he either had another session booked or wanted to go do drugs.

The voices were still running the show. In September, Bob Dylan called to ask Jim to join his band for his "Slow Train Coming" gospel tour. Dylan had long admired Jim through his association with Clapton and contacted Jim about doing sessions several years before. Jim had even auditioned at Rundown Studios in Santa Monica for the drum chair on Dylan's 1978 world tour. This time, the job was his for the taking. Jim desperately wanted to work with Dylan, but the voices didn't like the idea at all. Led by his mother's voice, they made him turn down Dylan's offer and hang up the phone.

Jim was deeply hurt that he couldn't play with Dylan. Nearly frantic to find some way back into the mainstream of the music business, Jim accepted an offer to play an engagement with Paul Anka at Caesars Palace in Las Vegas. He knew Anka from doing a soundtrack with Burt Bacharach where Anka supplied some lyrics and vocals; Jim had worked a few Bacharach sessions, in fact, including the *Butch Cassidy and the Sundance Kid* soundtrack. He offered his services to Anka, who sent Jim his music book and flew him out to Vegas to try out for the job.

Though he was in bad shape—despite the eating problems and because of his drinking, he tipped the scales at 250 pounds—he joined the band in rehearsal at the Circus Maximus, the hotel sports arena where they presented prizefights when they weren't doing concerts. Jim watched as the conductor jerked and twitched with a baton in his hand. He struck a few beats and then stopped. His mother's voice reverberated through his head. He was not to play another note. Panicked, he told the musical director he couldn't do it. The MD got Anka on the phone and Jim told him he was suffering psychological problems and had to go home. He got on a plane and flew back to Los Angeles. It was effectively the end of his professional music career.

XX.
THE COMEBACK

T he Paul Anka episode left Jim so depressed that he checked back into Van Nuys Psychiatric in November. It was a nightmare hospital stay. In his highly agitated state, Jim complained about pain in his back, and when a nurse suggested it was psychological, Jim became enraged, threatening the nurse and breaking a potted plant, running down the stairs screaming, "Let me go . . . let me go." As he had done in the past, he checked out against medical advice and went home to medicate himself with booze and cocaine.

He had become convinced that Osa wanted him in hospitals because, as a nurse, she knew the systems and could control his life more effectively. She would command him to check into the psych ward and, when her voice died down in his head, Jim would check back out. At Pathways Alcoholic Treatment Center at Valley Presbyterian Hospital in Van Nuys, medical director Dr. Paul Rosenberg, who had been seeing Jim off and on for several years, at least knew that Jim's primary problems were psychological, and that drug and alcohol issues were secondary.

The recovery community at the time had little understanding of what came to be known as dual diagnosis—organic mental illness entwined with addiction. Despite all his hospitalizations and her own medical education, his mother still believed all Jim's problems had to do with drugs and alcohol. The available psychological treatments also proved to be little help. With the age of medical psychiatry only dawning, doctors used heavy-handed antipsychotics and tranquilizers on Jim such as Thorazine, Stelazine, Prolixin, and Haldol—not that any of the medications proved effective with him.

Jim found self-medicating more efficient. Alcohol dulled the voices, and cocaine could normalize his dopamine levels. He had tried going without and the voices would take over, bleating and screeching repeatedly in his head. He had spent nearly two years clean and sober, and it had done nothing to help. His brother, John, who was admitting to his own problems with drinking, took Jim to a couple AA meetings (although John himself did not belong), and now John's voice joined the chorus in Jim's head, hectoring him about drinking and using. His daughter, Amy, had also recently joined the choir, insisting on being called Queen Amy. It was getting noisier and noisier in Jim's head.

The voices didn't like him living in any one place too long. He parked himself for a while at the Oakwood, the temporary residential complex on the hillside above Warner Brothers Studios in Burbank, before he moved to another apartment building in Van Nuys and then across the street from that. He drank himself to sleep every night. He was drinking more than he ever had. When he checked into the hospital again in June 1980, he had already consumed two-thirds of a bottle of cognac and a half-gallon of wine that afternoon.

Larry Rolando was a guitarist who knew Jim from playing sessions together. He had long before noted Jim's decline into sullen introspection by simply being around him at studios. In early 1980, Rolando ran into an outgoing, upbeat Jim at a downtown Los Angeles new wave/punk rock club. Jim looked dashing in a long, black overcoat with a good-looking female accomplice. He gave Rolando his number and urged him to call. Over lunch at Hamburger Hamlet in Van Nuys, he told Rolando he was resigned to the end of his professional music career, but that he needed to play. Like the shaman, Jim knew the drums were a beacon to guide him home. He wanted to do a band.

By 1980, the Los Angeles record scene had turned a page. On the cusp of the MTV age of rock, record companies suddenly focused on rock groups. In a Hollywood minute, singer-songwriters and solo artists were yesterday's news, and groups of musicians with moussed hair and skinny ties were the order of the day. Session musicians down the food chain like Rolando were hard pressed to find work. Bassist Jerry Scheff knew a songwriter named Randy Hanley who had a publishing deal and management. With Jim and keyboardist Mark T. Jordan, who had played with Van Morrison, Dave Mason, and others, they assembled at Leeds Instrument Rentals in Hollywood and liked how they sounded.

After several weeks of rehearsals, the band was ready to make some demos when Jim called Rolando at seven in the morning and told him he couldn't do it. "I hear this voice and it tells me what to do and what not to do," he told Rolando, who sensed some vulnerability he couldn't quite understand but was sympathetic. "My jaw, my shoulder, you don't know the pain. If I picked up my drumsticks, it would kill me," Jim said.

They replaced Jim with a drummer Jordan knew from the Dave Mason band and started playing gigs at local clubs like Madame

Wong's. After a meeting with management during which they complained about how much money they had invested without return, the musicians realized they would never make any money even if they landed a record deal, and so they decided to go their separate ways, leaving Hanley with his publishing deal and management firm.

Rolando was out of the band business, but he stayed in touch with Jim. They had become friends and spoke on the phone regularly. Rolando liked Jim's sly sense of humor and his self-deprecating manner; he didn't hold himself above other musicians who had not achieved the peaks he had and, in fact, rarely mentioned his past. Jim met Rolando for lunch to talk over his situation.

Over the meal, he explained in detail to Rolando about the voices. He told him how they regulated everything in his life, not just what music he played, but what he ate, how much he ate, when he could sleep.

Rolando asked if he had been diagnosed and wasn't there anything that could help. Jim explained how he would go into hospitals when the booze stopped working, dry out, start a new regime of medication, check out, and start the cycle over again.

As difficult as it was for Jim to explain himself to another person, he needed Rolando to help him. He apologized for dropping out of the last band and told Rolando he wanted to try again. "I've got to play," he said.

As it happened, Jerry Scheff had heard about a songwriter named Steve Moos from a fellow session player whose brother wrote for the *Los Angeles Times* and was sponsoring the writer. Jim, Scheff, and Rolando went to the reporter's Los Feliz home to hear him. Moos played them a half dozen songs and the three of them walked out wondering how they'd gotten so lucky to find this guy.

Jim located a rehearsal space in a garage owned by a nurse from Van Nuys Psychiatric whom Jim had befriended. Her husband was deceased, and for her teenage son, Andy, who played drums in a band, she had converted the garage into a rehearsal room. It was a perfect, low-maintenance setup. They could bring a couple amplifiers and have at it. Andy's drums were already set up. Danny Timms from the Kris Kristofferson band joined them on keyboards. After almost two dozen rehearsals, they made arrangements to cadge some free time on the weekend at Westlake Audio to record a demo.

Quincy Jones had the big room locked down, so they went into the smaller studio B. Jim was in a great mood, kidding around, offering suggestions. He joked that if he had brought his tablas, he could have made the track sound like Derek and the Dominos' "Bell Bottom Blues." The next day, a rainy Sunday, Jim and Rolando were walking down the hall to go to the bathroom when the back door opened and in walked guitarist Steve Lukather.

"Look at these assholes," the rowdy Lukather greeted them.

Quincy Jones came into the hall and Lukather made introductions with the veteran producer. Jones was handling the new Michael Jackson album. The guitar solo Eddie Van Halen laid into the song "Beat It" needed some repairs, and Lukather was there to fix it. Jeff Porcaro, an acknowledged Jim Gordon disciple, had played drums on the track.

The four songs Jim's new band recorded turned out great, and Tom Bradshaw, a high school friend who worked as Jim's accountant, had an office in the same building as Shep Gordon's Alive Enterprises, managers of Alice Cooper, Burton Cummings, and others. They found some interest there, but the four songs were all in the folksy vein of The Band or Van Morrison, and the management firm wanted them to go back in the studio and cut a couple, more rock-oriented songs.

Again, Jim phoned Rolando and told him he couldn't do it. Rolando was discouraged, not wanting to go through the process of finding another drummer a second time. So, he stalled getting back to their manager about the new songs. Jim was having problems again, but after almost eight weeks, he called back, ready to go.

The band—called I-5 after the Interstate Highway 5 that runs through the middle of California—started doing weekly dates at The Central on Sunset Boulevard in Hollywood and began attracting interest. Joan Baez producer David Kershenbaum came by. Other music business types were sniffing around. Rita Coolidge stopped at the club one night and chatted amiably with her old boyfriend. But the manager dropped them, and with record deal dreams shattered, Jerry Scheff took a job touring with John Denver. The band fell apart.

Before he left, Scheff had contracted a session in San Francisco for a cocaine dealer who wanted to bankroll some recording for a friend he thought was talented, an unknown Texas blueslinger named Gene Sarazen. Scheff tabbed bassist Larry Russell to replace him, and with Scheff's former bandmates from the Bob Dylan tour, guitarist Billy Cross and keyboardist Alan Pasqua, they headed north for two weeks of sessions that August 1981 at San Francisco's Automatt Studios. Cross, whom Sarazen knew from Denmark where he had lived, was set to produce. Somehow Jim made the trip. He was paid $15,000 in cash.

Jim stayed in a motel in San Francisco's Marina District, across town from the studio, while the rest of the band went over the Golden Gate Bridge to Marin County, where the impresario rented a rehearsal space for the project. Michael Rief ran his illicit business out of his Sausalito jewelry store and moved enough product to finance the sessions. As the band packed it up after the first day at the San Rafael rehearsal hall, Jim slid behind the keyboard at the piano bench and started playing his piano part from "Layla," almost as if he wanted to remind everyone who he was. It was not lost on anyone.

After a week in San Rafael, the session moved to the Automatt. Jim had been there before, playing an Albert Hammond session for Simon and Garfunkel producer Roy Halee, who ran the place when it was CBS Studios. They took over the big room where Halee had recorded the first solo albums by both members of the duo. Jim was pasty-faced, overweight, quiet, almost noncommunicative. At his feet, he kept his ever-present beige gym bag, containing towels, extra drumsticks, and a surreptitious bottle of vodka. He would wipe sweat off his face and take a furtive slug out of the bottle and stash them back in the bag, as if nobody noticed.

Producer Billy Cross laid down the firm rule—no drugs until the work was done. Over the next two weeks, the crew tackled a half dozen songs with Jim's specialty of playing deep grooves on slow tracks coming in especially handy. The band did a first-class job at trying to pump life into Sarazen's unremarkable songs and lackluster vocal performances. For Sarazen, it was an incalculable opportunity; these guys were definitely above his pay grade.

After the sessions, before everybody flew home the next day, Rief threw a bon voyage party at his Novato home in Marin County. He drove down to pick up Jim at his hotel and brought a glittering half gram rock of pure Peruvian flake as a party favor. Jim chose shooting over snorting, so Rief dissolved the entire half-gram and filled a new diabetic syringe. Jim asked Rief to do the honors and Rief stuck the needle in Jim's arm. He told Jim to let him know when he had enough, as he started to depress the plunger. Somewhere past halfway through, Jim nodded and Rief finished off the shot in his own arm. Jim grabbed the gym bag and off they went. "I love art deco," said Jim as they cruised through the majestic arches of the Golden Gate.

With cocaine candor, Jim admitted to Rief on the ride that he was not doing well. He told Rief he had lost interest in session work, that it was "no fun" anymore. He sounded so lost and despairing that Rief took off the eight-carat emerald ring he wore but never cared for particularly and suggested Jim try it on his pinky. The ring fit beautifully and Rief told Jim to keep the ring for good luck. When his luck came back down the road, he could return the ring. Jim was pleased with the gift.

At Rief's house in the summer sun, band members sat around the hot tub, drinking Danish beer, smoking pot, and snorting blow. Pasqua brought a blonde bombshell girlfriend, Miss July 1979, Dorothy Mays, certified Playboy Playmate. Cross, coming from sun-deprived Copenhagen, basked in the California sun on the red-wood deck. As the afternoon wore on, Rief cooked up a batch of freebase and the party revolved around the pipe. When he returned from taking Jim back to San Francisco in the late afternoon, all the musicians and revelers were gone, except Dorothy Mays, who had stayed behind with Sarazen and the pipe.

It was a dying flare from a sinking ship. Jim went back to his new condo at 6540 Hayvenhurst Avenue in Van Nuys and stayed there. In that two-bedroom, two-story townhouse, Jim carefully arranged his gold records over the wall of his study and kept his drums in the garage. He ate what could be delivered—pizza, fried shrimp from a local restaurant. Simply going out to the neighborhood liquor store was a big production. When he did go out in public, unkempt, disoriented, bloated, a lumbering giant with a frozen face, he could look scary. He was spending two or three hundred dollars a day on cocaine. Larry Rolando, sick and disgusted with the end of I-5 and the Hollywood scene, had moved to Nashville, leaving Jim largely friendless and alone. Their last night out together was the first time Jim sat in with the Blue Monkeys. He would go days without bathing or changing his clothes and then brush himself off, dress up, and go to church.

Jim Keltner knew his old pal was going through tough times, and he thought it might give Jim a needed boost to have a feature article about his work in *Modern Drummer*. He asked editor Scott K. Fish if he would be interested. When he readily agreed, Keltner said he didn't know if Jim would go for it, but he would ask. Weeks passed without hearing until one night in January 1982 when the phone rang in Fish's New Jersey home and Jim Gordon was on the line.

Fish was unprepared, but he sensed an opportunity he couldn't afford to let pass. No telling when he could get Jim Gordon on the phone again. He had not reviewed Jim's career or listened to any records. He only had one unused cassette and one other he could record over, but he stuck the suction cup on his phone, pressed record on his Radio Shack special, and initiated dialogue.

For more than an hour, Jim was at his lucid best, getting under the hood about drums and drumming, warming up as he went along. He was in his element talking drums. Fish asked what technique served him best.

"The paradiddle is probably the most important one to me," Jim said. "I always tried to subdivide everything. I always tried to make a logical pattern out of anything I did and tried to make it logical and equal, so it didn't ramble. And I'd try to divide the tune into sections and make phrases out of it so it would all be even."

Jim was happy to detail his equipment, talk about the mechanics of recording sessions, the responsibilities of touring, but he made no comments about the character of any of his associates; their personalities and interactions with Jim were entirely absent from his account. Yet he clearly loved the opportunity to discuss his work. He described his approach to playing his drum solo at Derek and the Dominos concerts.

"The band would stop and I'd go into my solo," Jim said. "I try to play phrases and more or less play the tune, then kind of go off on some kind of tangent. It wasn't always prepared. I liked to do it spontaneously. I had a few things that were prepared, but then there'd be a portion of it where I'd try to divide the beat or do some kind of syncopated, polyrhythmical thing around what I'd laid down as the basic flow of the solo. Then I'd try to get into some kind of technical thing; some type of snare drum, rudimental, dexterity thing. Then lead back into the time and back into the tune."

The closest Jim came to revealing anything personal was replying to a question about his spirituality. "I believe in God and Jesus very much and try and stay aboveboard on all that. It's not easy. The Bible is definitely something to help you. I find that every time I study something from the Bible, or even hearing some of these people on television who talk about it—Bible studies or something like that—it's real uplifting. I really feel that."

"Has the spiritual part of your personality always been with you," asked Fish, "or is that something that developed later on?"

"Well, lately . . . I don't know," Jim said. "I always went back and forth. I've always believed in God, but I questioned myself a few years ago, because there were a lot of my friends questioning themselves. I thought, 'Maybe I should ask a few questions again, and see where I'm at.' So, I bought a Bible and started getting into it again a little bit and found it real helpful. I go to church from time to time and enjoy that very much. But I've always tried to be with God. I don't think I've ever been away from spiritualism in one way or another. It would be kind of tough not to have something to believe in."

Jim managed the interview like a pro, but the ensuing photo shoot threw him. Keltner arranged for his eighteen-year-old son, Eric, to photograph the profile. When he arrived at Jim's condo, Jim had pulled a drum set out in the garage and had the pieces spread out on the floor. He just couldn't figure out how to put them together. Shocked that the greatest drummer his father knew couldn't even remember how to assemble his kit, young Keltner, a drummer's son, put the set together and photographed Jim behind the kit. Jim did not even appear to know what to do with the drums once they were assembled and he was sitting behind them. He couldn't really engage in conversation. He kept asking young Keltner the same question repeatedly. "How's your dad?" he would say.

XXI.
DUMPSTER
DAYS

ohnny Carson used to make cracks about the fellows in *The
Tonight Show* band making trips to Chadney's, the steak-
house and watering hole across the street from NBC Studios
in Burbank, where band members would often go to catch a little
taste between sets. At lunch, it was not uncommon to see stars like
Bob Hope or Milton Berle dining. At night, the cocktail lounge
throbbed with a jazz combo led by Harry Middlebrooks, a good
old fellow from Atlanta, coauthor of the hit song "Spooky."
Danny Timms started playing there after the breakup of I-5.
Before long, he had a four-piece band holding down four nights a
week at the spot.

Chadney's became a session musician hangout. Players like
James Burton, Albert Lee, or John Hobbs would come by for a few
drinks and a couple numbers. Timms's band—all session veterans
like bassist David Jackson—played as jazzy as they could for a
bunch of guys who were essentially rhythm and blues musicians.

Jim lived nearby in the neighborhood and, when he could handle it, he would stop by, have a drink or two, maybe play, maybe not. He knew people in the bar. Sometimes he hung out with Mike McGinnis, who was living with Jim's ex-wife and daughter. When he was capable, Jim could relax at Chadney's, but those occasions were growing increasingly rare.

When he checked into the hospital again in October 1982, his fourteenth admission to Pathways since April 1979, he told doctors he was dying of hate, and the world was falling apart. He could barely handle life in the real world, although he continued to promptly pay his child support payments and all his bills, careful to not owe anybody. In spring 1983, he was working Blue Mondays at O'Mahony's with the Blue Monkeys, but he was done playing sessions. Chadney's became a convenient clubroom for him to frequent. Jim even substituted for the group's regular drummer on occasion.

The few rare hours at Chadney's—or with the Blue Monkeys—were carved out of a living hell Jim was now walking through night and day. The voices constantly flooded his head. Living by himself, Jim sunk deeper and deeper into a dark world of fear and paranoia. He rented a storage space and filled it with freeze-dried food and other survival supplies. He disconnected his telephone and stopped returning the messages that collected on his answering machine. His contact with the outside world was largely limited to phone conferences with his accountant about an ongoing lawsuit against Eric Clapton over royalties.

Osa was back—although her voice had never left Jim's mind. His mother had been living in Lake Tahoe for the previous couple years and had been almost entirely out of contact with Jim. She had bought property there many years before and built a place where she lived with her boyfriend, Morey. She had retired as a nurse, although she still worked part-time as a physical therapist. After Morey died and she was named executor of his estate, she moved back to San Fernando Valley. Having his mother back in proximity did nothing to salve Jim's troubled state.

The voices raised a cacophony in his brain. He heard his ex-wife Jill and his old buddy Mike Post. He had an entire Greek chorus of raucous, critical voices chattering in his brain, an argumentative executive committee vying for control over the smallest details of his life. Every day was a struggle. Chief among his tormentors, as always, was the voice of his mother, Osa. He believed her to be so insidiously powerful as to infect other people with negative feelings toward Jim—doctors who treated him, people who waited on him in stores, strangers passing on the street. He began to believe that his mother was a truly evil person who had a hand in the deaths of Karen Carpenter and Paul Lynde.

The voices were clamping down on Jim. They hated his music. They refused to allow him to play his guitar or piano any longer or even let him listen to music. He would sit in his study and stare at his gold records on the wall and remember his grand career that had seemed like it would never end. They did not allow Jim to read newspapers and magazines or watch TV news. With reruns of *Charlie's Angels* or old movies playing in the background, he would spend his afternoons lolling around, drinking, trying to staunch the flow of nightmare images. He had no visitors other than people making deliveries. No girlfriends. No friends of any kind. He was a lonely guy living alone with a madman.

He continued to take the psychiatric medicines he was prescribed, along with copious amounts of alcohol and illegal drugs. His metabolism continued to devour these substances at some superhuman rate. He slept as much as he could, gorged on fast food, and drank as much as he could. He was gaining weight and doctors warned him he was ruining his liver, but Jim didn't trust doctors. What did they know? They hadn't been any help. He only went into the hospitals to play his mother's little game and try to hide from the voices.

The commands seemed to grow more demanding, more outrageous, more cruel. The punishments they meted out also became increasingly torturous. To Jim, it could feel like he was having his skin peeled off . . . slowly. Or the sharp, stabbing pains in his chest and arms like broken bones rubbing together, becoming more intense and lasting longer. Or a pain would radiate from his jaw to encompass his whole skull, filling his head with blinding, white-hot molten fire. Sometimes the overwhelming pain would knock him to the floor and cause him to wet himself.

Lying on the floor in urine-stained pants alone in his North Hollywood condo was a long way from walking through London with Beatles or doing a Streisand session, let alone the long-ago, innocent days of the Beach Boys and the Everly Brothers. Where had this gone wrong? Jim believed he had done everything he was supposed to do to have a wonderful life. He had faithfully followed his path, but how did it lead here? Jim could not understand what had happened to him or why. He only knew that it had happened and there was no refuge.

He lived in a hallucinatory universe, no longer able to distinguish his illusions from reality; his illusions were his reality. Even if there were glimpses of life as it used to be for Jim, he couldn't find his way back. He was lost in a world he didn't know, screaming voices resounding endlessly in his head. He lived in fear and doubt. Without his drums, he was adrift in a hostile, dark, storm-tossed sea.

Somehow, Jim was pulling it off with the Blue Monkeys. The other band members suspected nothing. He made every gig, every rehearsal. He did the demos in the studio. He acted like another band member, maybe a little on the quiet side, somewhat with-drawn. They had no idea how difficult it was for Jim simply to be there. But that is how much it meant to him.

Jim Gordon lived to play drums. As mental illness slowly stripped him to the core, the drums loomed large as a sanctuary. While the rest of the world made no sense, in the world of rhythm Jim could restore order to his life. He could command time, divide it, and reallocate it. He was the master of the realm. He was freed from earthly bounds. Where he went, the voices were left behind.

Every Monday, Jim packed up his drums and drove down the 405 freeway to slightly seedy downtown Santa Monica to play with the Blue Monkeys. The music was not demanding, a kind of bar band R&B along the lines of, say, the Fabulous Thunderbirds; Jim was renowned for his scientific shuffle. The other guys were easy enough to get along with, and Jim loved playing with rock-solid bassist Roly Salley. Three sets a night left him exhausted and drained, the tide of the voices at low ebb after a night of silencing them with the drums.

The quiet never lasted long. With Osa back in town, Jim couldn't bring himself to visit her, but was resentful that she had returned to control his life even more. He knew her tricks and games. Osa, on the other hand, was bewildered by Jim, refusing to understand that his problems went beyond drugs and alcohol. One of Jim's psychi-atrists had advised her sometime before to cut off contact with Jim, but she couldn't bring herself to do that. It was against her nurtur-ing nature. She would always want to help her wounded child, if she could only figure out what he was talking about and what she could do about it. Still, she had grown to fear Jim and was contemplating a move to Seattle, where Jim's brother, John, and his wife, Martha, had prepared an in-law unit for her.

With his family's background in Alcoholics Anonymous, Jim also tended to see himself that way. He checked in and out many times at Pathways Alcoholic Treatment Center at Valley Presbyterian. He trusted the center's medical director, Dr. Paul Rosenberg, whom Jim considered immune to Osa's influence, unlike all his other doctors. He was convinced that she had taken over all the other medical professionals, who conspired with her to keep Jim under her control. But even kindly Dr. Rosenberg couldn't stop the voices in Jim's head.

When the voices first commanded Jim to throw away his gold records, he was shocked. Why would they want him to do that? They had robbed him of so much already—his daughter, his beautiful homes, his cars—why must they take his trophies? These relics of his glory days meant a great deal to Jim. They reminded him of the heights his life had reached, the extraordinary accomplishments in the studio and on the road, all of which had disappeared from his life—leaving the gold records as their only trace. They hung neatly on the walls of his study, carefully arrayed next to one another. He saw no reason to part with them.

When the pain first struck him, it was so intense that Jim nearly fainted. He felt himself glow white with hurt. The sheer viciousness astonished him. Why would his mother do this to him? What had he ever done to deserve such pain? He was left with no other choice. Meekly, he took his gold records down from the wall one by one and carried them outside, where he carefully stacked them beside the condominium dumpster outside the garage. He went back to his condo and guzzled a fifth of scotch and, when the voices calmed down, he went back outside and retrieved his gold records, carefully hanging them back up, making sure the frames were even and in their right places.

The next night, the voices started yammering again about his gold records. He knew resistance was futile and, once again, he took down all his framed awards and carried them to the dumpster, went back to his apartment and drank until the voices died down before he could take them back. The voices caught on and made him take the gold records down again and repeat the whole process. This went on daily, sometimes as many as ten times a day, for weeks—taking down the gold records, moving them to the dumpster, drinking the voices into the background, and returning for the records. He refused to give in.

He kept his two sets of Camco drums in the garage and still tended to them conscientiously, keeping them clean, keeping the heads maintained. He was tuning the drums one afternoon when his mother's voice shrieked through his head. *THROW OUT THOSE DAMN DRUMS.* He couldn't believe what he had heard. Not his drums. Nothing in his life meant more to him. They were the foundation of his existence. He knew what was coming, and he steeled himself for the pain. They would not make him give up his drums. His drums were life.

No matter how much he drank or snorted, his mother's voice would not go away. *The drums have to go.* His brother's voice picked up the chant. *Throw away those drums.* Jim tried fooling the voices by moving the drums around in the garage, but that didn't work. The more he resisted, the more they hurt him. They refused to let him sleep. Finally, exhausted and defeated, Jim hauled his drums out of the garage and stacked them neatly next to one another beside the dumpster. He returned to the apartment and started drinking. When he was finally drunk enough to quiet the voices but still able to walk, he went back to the dumpster and returned his beloved drums.

Dragging the gold records and drums out to the dumpster continued as a daily routine. Night after night, Jim would trudge around the back of his apartment building carrying his precious load and return after he had managed to subdue the voices. After one session, he was snorting a line of cocaine when his brother's voice bloomed in his brain. *Stop that—clean up your act.* Jim felt his brother reach through dimensions with such fearsome intensity, Jim thought he would die if he didn't obey.

He hadn't played with the Blue Monkeys since he'd heard his mother's voice insist that he quit. *If you hit that drum one more time, you will die,* she told him. His brother was demanding that he stop drinking and using, which were the only tools Jim had to fight the voices. He was alone and confused, caught in a crossfire of conflicting commands. There was nothing left but surrender. In May, after months of nightly trips back and forth from his condominium dumpster, despondent and depleted, once again, he checked into rehab and entered the Crossroads Alcoholic Recovery Unit.

XXII.
CROSSROADS

G oing into treatment at Crossroads this time was a disaster. Without drugs and alcohol, the voices rampaged through Jim's mind. He didn't sleep. He ate next to nothing. He craved his liquor and cocaine—they worked better than the medicine doctors prescribed—and without that buffer from the voices, his life was sheer hell. The recovery community at the time was ill-equipped to deal with dual diagnosis cases like Jim; treatment focused exclusively on the AA twelve-step program. Jim stayed at Crossroads for as long as he could stand it before checking out.

He was still so distressed that he headed straight to Pathways Alcoholic Treatment Center at Valley Presbyterian and Dr. Rosenberg, where he was admitted on May 21, 1983. He was seeking sanctuary. He wanted to eat. He needed to sleep. Unfortunately, Dr. Rosenberg was not working for the next two days. Another doctor gave Jim a Valium and told him to try to get some sleep.

The voices went crazy over Jim checking into the hospital. And Jim was furious that he was being ignored by the staff. With none of the attending physicians familiar with Jim's delusional hierarchy, they couldn't understand what he was talking about when he told one of the doctors that there were people trying to make him commit a crime. After two nights in the hospital, Jim checked out and went back to Hayvenhurst and the cacophony.

Meanwhile, Osa was making plans to move to Seattle. She loved her younger son but had finally come to the conclusion that she could do nothing to help him. With Morey gone, there was nothing keeping her in the Valley. On May 23, the same day Jim checked out of Crossroads, she wrote him a letter:

Dear Jim,

I wanted to let you know I am moving. I am going to move to Issaquah, Washington.

When Martha and John built their house they did not finish the lower level. It was partitioned off and rough plumbing and rough electricity were installed.

The State of Washington as have a lot of states, passed a law whereby a "mother-in-law" apartment could be built on a lot zoned R-1. We are finishing this apartment (I say we because I am paying for it) for me to live in. I feel it will cost about as much as a nice mobile home but I will not have to be making a monthly rental fee. Most mobile home parks charge a minimum of $250.00 a month.

I am sorry I sold my house in Truckee. Had I been sixty years old instead of seventy years old I would have stayed there. It seems that sometimes things begin to happen to people seventy years old and older.

This way I will be near John and Martha but not living with them. I will have two bedrooms, a bathroom, my own kitchen, dining and living room. I will have my own garage and private entrance and I think it will be real nice. I am excited about moving but sure don't like packing.

Jim, I have those two nice patio lounge chairs and I thought you might like to have them, they are yours and they are stored in a garage nearby where you could get to them easily. Most of my furniture has been in storage at North American there on Kester near Osmond. I have some of my things here and some in a garage nearby that belongs to a friend. I will be happy to get all my things together.

About a week ago I went to Foresters Haven (remember that place?) and was taken on a tour through it. It's beautiful out there and if I stay well I hope to try to get in there in about 6 to 8 years. You have to be physically well to get in there, but once you are there, they will take care of you as long as you live.

Martha and John are coming down to go to Jayne's graduation from San Diego State College on June 19th. We will drive back to Seattle in my car, leaving here on June 22nd. I sure wish we could get to see you before I leave. I think of you so often and wonder how things are going for you. I love you Jim more than you know. Just remember I am as close to you as your phone.

Love as always,
Mom

Jim never opened the letter. He distrusted his mother's motives in writing to him, but he received another letter the same day from his brother that he did open and read. The letter detailed his mother's plans to move to Seattle. Jim was pleased with the news, happy that she would be farther away and less able to interfere with his life. As he was reading his brother's letter, however, his mother's voice thundered unbidden in his head, repeating the same astonishing thought. *You're going to have to kill me.* At first, Jim was shocked and didn't believe what he was hearing, but the command played in an endless loop in his head, accompanied by the white hot cruelty pain.

He had been trying—without success—to stay off drugs and alcohol, and he heard his brother ridiculing his failure, before joining the demands coming from their mother. *You're going to have to kill her.* Jim drank himself into a stupor and lapsed into an alcohol-induced sleep. But as soon as he woke, the voices started clamoring again. The volume of the din inside his head grew, squeezing out all other thoughts. Jim was thrown into deep anguish. The voices wouldn't stop.

For days, Jim had battled the incessant chatter in his head. He was in such pain that he was crawling on his floor or lying on his living room couch in agony shouting at the voices. "I can't stand it anymore—I've thrown away everything; I've done everything you said. Leave me alone." In the dizzying cloud of noise and voices in his head, his mother's voice rang out clearly above the grainy distortion. *Why don't you kill me? Why don't you just go ahead and do it?*

Jim jumped up from the couch and crossed the room to his bookcase. His ex-wife Jill appeared in his head. *You're going to have to do it, you know. You have to kill her. Go on. Just do it.*

Osa spoke out again. *Kill me. Kill me. You have to kill me. You're going to have to do it.*

A cool, calming breath of relief settled in Jim's distorted brain. Jim had frequently considered suicide, but never murder. This brilliant suggestion suddenly loomed as a way out of the hell in which he lived. The torture did not have to go on forever.

No other thought could enter his mind. He was being bombarded with the message all day and into the night. He finally decided he needed to take action or else he would have to follow the commands. He called Osa on the phone. Something about his tone of voice scared Osa. She had never heard Jim like this before. With her nurse's training, she wrote down a record of their talk in a notebook:

Wednesday, June 1, 1983

About 9:30 p.m. the telephone rang. The voice said "is this Osa Gordon." I said "yes." The voice said "this is Jim Gordon." I said "well how are you Jim." He said "not very good." He said "you are bugging me again You want me to get rid of my guitars, my drums, my gold records and if you don't leave me alone I'm going to kill you. I am warning you." I said, "was it because I had written you the letter telling you I was going to move up to John's." He said "I didn't get any letter." I said "did you get a letter from John." He said he had been in North Hollywood Medical Center Hospital. I asked him how long he had been there and he said one day. He said again "you better leave me alone." I said "I sure will, Jim, I promise I'll leave you alone." He hung up.

Osa called the Medical Center of North Hollywood and was referred to the recovery unit, where she spoke with a nurse named Wynn. She told Osa that Jim had checked in around ten that morning but left by four in the afternoon. He was supposed to see a Dr. Rogers but left before he did. Osa described their phone conversation and the nurse told Osa that if Jim was hallucinating, he needed medication. She also suggested Osa call the police.

The North Hollywood Police gave her an emergency number and told her to call it if Jim showed and they would send a patrol car over right away. She called the police a second time and spoke with the radio room to get a second emergency number, in case the first number was busy when she tried it. This time, she was told not to count on a police car being immediately available. The policeman advised Osa to keep her lights turned on and wished her luck. Osa made another entry in her notebook:

> *I have been trying to get John and Martha since Jim called. They are not home. I know they were going to Susan's today. I wanted to tell them about the new will I had made. It is in the bank box. My key to the bank box is in a little plastic box in the 2nd drawer of the chest in the service porch. I made out the checks for the income tax, they are also in the same drawer but I need to get money from the credit union and deposit in the bank before I mail the checks. Wynn suggested I call the PET Team and they will go give psychiatric treatment. I have been calling them but get no answer.*

As the clock neared midnight, Jim called again. Osa had not been able to sleep. She answered the phone, spoke with Jim, and took notes on the conversation:

> *11:40 p.m. Jim called. He said "Mom leave me alone, quit bugging me, you want me to get rid of my drums, my guitars and my gold records. What am I to do?" I said "Jim where are you." He said "it is none of your business. Just quit bugging me." I said "Jim are you alone." Again he said "leave me alone." I said "Jim you better get to a doctor or a*

*hospital and get some help." He hung up. 10:20 p.m. I didn't
try any more after 11 p.m. to get John. I thought it would
just upset them and there isn't much they can do. I mainly
wanted to tell them about the will.*

Jim spent Thursday, June 2, struggling with the voices. He was
consumed by his illusions. The voices barked and squawked. His
entire being was awash in delusion. That night, when he brought his
gold records back from the dumpster and hung them on the wall,
he stepped back and realized they were all crooked, not in their
right places, and an overwhelming sadness enveloped him.

Meanwhile, Osa recorded her thoughts again in her notebook:

*Thursday, June 2, 1983. Last nite when I was talking to
Wynn at the hospital I asked her if Jim had been drinking
and taking drugs. She said he had been drinking. I called the
PET Team and talked to Ben. He said I should go to the City
Attorney and have a restraining order put on him. He said it
would cost $55.00. He said there is nothing they can do until
Jim does try to do something. I don't know what to do about
the restraining order. I am going to think about it for a while.*

Jim awoke Friday morning, June 3, and the battle was over. The
voices had won. He was surrounded by his mother, his brother, his
ex-wife, and others haranguing him, and he had surrendered. He
was entirely under their power. He clicked into autopilot. It wasn't
his idea. It was not his plan. The voices were firmly in charge. He
knew he didn't want to kill his mother, but the voices reassured
him. *You'll go to prison for twenty years, but you'll be all right.*
Everything was being taken care of for him. All he had to do was go
along with the plan. He felt some relief. He'd just have to do it.

Jim looked up his mother's address and picked up an eight-inch kitchen knife from a set he and Renee had bought in San Francisco. He received a suggestion to bring a hammer because if he knocked her out with a hammer blow, she wouldn't feel the knife. As much as she had done to torture him, Jim still loved his mother and had no desire to hurt her. He grabbed a large claw hammer from his toolbox and dropped it and the knife into a leather carrying case.

Around two in the afternoon, Jim pulled up outside Osa's apartment and went to the door. A neighbor watering his lawn would later remember seeing "a great big fellow" walk up her steps, but he returned to his watering and did not see him leave. Osa was not home, and Jim went back to his condo to have a few drinks of vodka while he waited. He felt peaceful, out of pain. He was floating on a river that the voices in his head were navigating. All he had to do was go along.

Around 5:30 p.m., Osa knocked on the door of the next-door apartment and introduced herself to Rochelle Shonley, private duty nurse for eighty-seven-year-old Anita Ryan. Osa told Shonley that she was a registered nurse and to feel free to ask her for help. Shortly thereafter, dressed in a lavender blouse, pants, and light-colored shoes, carrying a white purse, Osa picked up a friend to have dinner at Marie Callender's on Riverside Drive and attend the eight o'clock AA meeting of the Camarillo/Lankershim group, where Osa maintained many acquaintances. Over dinner, she told her friend about Jim's threatening phone call, but did not seem overly concerned to her friend.

She returned home after dropping off her friend and changed into a nightgown, robe, and slippers. She prepared a snack and sat down in her living room chair to watch television. Jim arrived at 10:50 p.m.

He knocked at the door and heard his mother say to come in. The door was open. He saw his mother sitting in her chair with a tray on her lap and Jim thought she glowed all white. He was glad to see her, and somewhere in the back of his mind he struggled to break free of this trance. He wanted her to talk him out of it. To do something, yell, scream for help, anything to jar him out of this waking dream. But the voices were in control. They spoke as one through Jim's mouth. "I'm going to kill you," he said.

Osa put down the tray and stood behind the chair. Jim took the hammer and struck his mother on the head four times. Although she did not lose consciousness, she crumpled to the floor. Jim grabbed the knife and averted his face as he viciously stabbed her straight in the heart three times. He was swathed in noise and voices, drowning in delusion. Osa died instantly as the knife pierced her aorta. The third blow was so savage the blade stuck in the floor beneath her. He left the knife protruding from her chest and walked, but didn't run, to his car.

Next door, Nurse Shonley had been waiting for her shift to end when she heard a knocking at Osa's apartment. A few minutes later, she heard a scream and a cry for help. She dialed the police. Her relief nurse was walking up to start her shift and she, too, heard the screams. She turned toward Osa's apartment and saw a man leaving whom she would later describe as "male, Mexican, six-foot to six-foot, one-inch tall, 250 to 275 pounds, thirty to forty years old with dark, wavy hair and wearing dark clothing."

Jim drove to a nearby gas station and washed the blood from his hands and face in the bathroom. He went to a Mexican restaurant and ordered a couple margaritas. He wanted to get drunk, and the margaritas were not doing the trick. He drove to Chadney's feeling stone cold sober and glugged down a couple Long Island iced teas before switching to Pernod. He joined some friends. They would later say Jim seemed friendly but quiet. He sat listening to the band until closing time and left the bar alone. Some people noticed the cuffs on his khakis were splattered with what looked like mud but wasn't. He went home and drained a fifth of vodka.

North Hollywood police officers Art Castro and Russell Lyons arrived at 11023½ Hartsook Street at 10:59 p.m., responding to a code two call—female screaming for help. Officers Castro and Lyons approached the front door and saw blood stains. The door was open a crack. When Lyons pushed on the door, he encountered resistance and had to shove the door open. Behind the door, lying in a pool of blood, was Osa Marie Gordon, wearing a pale green nightgown and pink robe, a knife sticking out of her chest. A bloody hammer lay by her side. Backup police were called, and North Hollywood rescue was alerted. She was pronounced dead at 11:14 p.m. The officers secured the premises and waited for the homicide squad.

After the three homicide inspectors made their initial examination, they allowed the coroner to remove the body. Osa was zipped into a body bag, her glasses still perched on her nose. After finding Osa's diaries with detailed entries from as recently as that morning—plus a subsequent phone call with her oldest son, John Jr.—evidence quickly pointed to her other son, Jim Gordon.

Officers William Welch and Kevin Harley, along with backup, arrived at Jim's Hayvenhurst Street condo at 5:30 a.m. and knocked on the door, identifying themselves as police. No response. They continued knocking until they heard a low voice moan, "Just a minute." The cops forced open the door.

Jim was lying in a fetal position on the floor, wedged between his living room sofa and the coffee table. Two empty vodka bottles sat on the table. The detectives approached, and he broke into racking sobs.

"I did it. I did it," he said. "I killed my mother. She's been tormenting me for fifteen years. I did it. I'm sorry."

XXIII.
CRIME &
PUNISHMENT

The black and white police car with Jim handcuffed in the back seat delivered the prisoner to North Hollywood Field Services Division of LAPD on Tiara Street, a nondescript beige building in a neighborhood of strip malls, donut shops, and pizza parlors. Jim was clearly intoxicated and, in fact, registered .33 on the sobriety test. He had been sobbing and shaking all through the ride, asking repeatedly if Osa was dead. "I'm sorry," he said. "I'm sorry, but she tormented me."

After waiving his rights, Jim gave a full statement to Detectives Welch and Harley, veteran homicide inspectors. Something about this huge, pathetic creature touched the two seen-it-all cops. They treated him gently and carefully. Jim was booked for the murder of Osa Gordon. He was stripped and searched; his bloodstained clothes impounded as evidence. He was given a jail uniform and paper slippers, fingerprinted and photographed, and then the still-sobbing prisoner was led to a large front cell to wait his turn at the single telephone available to prisoners. He phoned his ex-wife Jill.

His brother, John, had called her the night before to give her the news and tell her that Jim was still at large and that she could be in danger. In grief and panic, Jill called Mike Post, who came over to make certain nothing happened to Jill or Amy. He answered the phone when Jim called.

"Is Jill there?" Jim asked.

"It's not a good time for Jill to speak with anybody," Post said.

"Who is this?" Jim asked.

"Mike Postil," Post said, using his real name.

"Hi, Mike," Jim said. "I guess you heard what happened."

"Yeah, I did," said Post.

The two longtime friends had not spoken to each other in many months. Jim was shaken and upset and so was Post. He asked Jim if he had a lawyer, and Jim said no. Post wanted to know if there was anything he could do for him, and Jim said no, he was going to spend the rest of his life in jail. Post told Jim he didn't understand and couldn't believe it. Jim told Post that his mother had been tormenting him for fifteen years, that she was always there.

Post had no idea what he was talking about. "But, Jim, you haven't seen Osa in two or three years," he said.

"Well, with voices," Jim explained.

"Jim, that's all in your head," said Post.

"That's easy for you to say," he said.

Jim said he wanted to offer his condolences to Jill and Amy, who was a high school student, and then switched gears. "I'm real happy everything is going great with your career," he told Post.

"Jim, what does all that matter in these kind of circumstances?" Post said.

"Yeah, I guess you're right," Jim said.

"Is there anything I can do for you?" Post asked again.

"No," said Jim.

"God bless you," said Post and hung up the phone.

Jim stayed in North Hollywood in isolation for the weekend. When he woke on Sunday morning, he saw his cell ablaze in flames. The fire burned only in his imagination, but he couldn't tell. He tried to find a door and kept reaching for the towel rack. He was filled with terror and self-loathing. The relief he had experienced had vanished. It had lasted only a short time before the crime, after which he tumbled through time and space in a blinding daze. On Monday morning, he was loaded in a sheriff's bus and driven to Van Nuys Superior Court where he was arraigned on murder charges and transferred to Los Angeles County Jail in Chino, a forty-five-minute drive away. By the time Jim arrived, he was so thoroughly disoriented and confused, he had no idea where he was.

The Los Angeles jail system was an overcrowded, Dickensian boondoggle. Prisoners being processed moved slowly through endless lines in an admission process that could take up to eight hours. Jim was florid with hallucinations and barely able to register a rational thought. At one point, he was taken out of line and slammed against a wall for staring back blankly at someone screaming instructions in his face.

On Tuesday, Jim contacted his longtime friend and business manager, Tom Bradshaw, who was shocked and dismayed by the events. He was quite aware of his client's personal problems and would not have been surprised if Jim had killed himself, but killing his mother had been unimaginable. When Bradshaw arrived at the jail, he found Jim scared, crying uncontrollably, shaking like a caged animal who had been beaten.

Bradshaw contacted the law firm of Howard Weitzman, best known for his successful defense of car manufacturer John DeLorean. Weitzman assigned one of their brightest young attorneys, Scott Furstman. The attorney took Bradshaw and Bradshaw's wife with him for his first meeting with his client, so that Jim would know there were people who cared about him on his case.

Jim was so disoriented that he thought he had been taken to Minnesota. "Tell me again where Chino is," he asked Furstman.

Voices still filled his head. His mother's was gone, but his brother, John, had moved into a central role. At first, Jim was enthusiastic about being fed three meals a day, but quickly his brother's voice ordered him to eat only half his meals. *You need to get in shape.* He started losing weight. The voices began to issue orders in his cell to lie down and sit up in his bunk. All day long, he would be sitting up, lying down, and sitting back up. He offered no explanation to his cellmates, who undoubtedly thought he was crazy. But what did they know? One of his cellmates spent his time praying. Jim was off all his medications, dressed in a blue jail suit with no shoes, and the voices were having a field day. They would no longer allow him to smoke, although occasionally he would sneak a Camel.

Attorney Furstman read Jim the letter that Osa sent him. Jim was unimpressed. "That's just like her," he said. "That patio furniture wouldn't work anyway. She'd give it to me so I'd have it and want to sit in it and then her voice would come, and she'd say Jim you can't sit in that furniture—get out of that chair. You can't enjoy that chair. That's just what she'd do. It was all part of her game. What else could I do? I had to do it."

His family of voices expanded. Now they included his aunt Lena from Colorado, his father's sister, among others. She demanded retribution from Jim and eventually pushed him to attempt suicide.

He cut deeply into his wrist but the wound did not bleed sufficiently, and he finally had to call the guard and tell him. He was taken upstairs to the hospital unit and placed in a straitjacket for seventy-two hours.

Jim had a preliminary hearing on July 23. Then, on August 11, Jim entered a plea of not guilty by reason of insanity before Judge James A. Albracht at the Van Nuys Superior Court. He went to trial in May 1984, after nearly a year in county jail, rejecting a jury trial in favor of a ruling from the bench. There were no TV cameras or front-page newspaper stories. Of all the people Jim worked with and came to know over the years, only one person turned up to show support for Jim—Jay Osmond, the drummer of the Osmond Brothers who first met Jim when they were playing the Andy Williams show together in Las Vegas almost fifteen years before. Jim looked like hell, wild-eyed and unshaven. He was a hulking shell of himself, unable to make eye contact with the judge or witnesses, staring down at the table most of the time. He appeared disoriented, vacant, detached from the proceedings. He was only partly there.

Five psychiatrists testified that Jim was insane. Dr. Rosenberg from Pathways told the court that he had treated Jim from April 1979 to June 1982 over the course of thirteen admissions to the hospital. He said he had diagnosed Jim with acute paranoid schizophrenia and chronic alcoholism, which he said was a result of self-medicating with alcohol. He explained that although Jim was capable at times of living in the real world, he also inhabited a delusional world where he did not know the difference between right and wrong, nor could he understand the nature of his acts.

Dr. Auerbach also testified that he had treated Jim and that he suffered from an acute schizophrenic-type disorder. Three additional doctors—Dr. John Mead, Dr. William Vicary, and Dr. Michael

Coburn—all examined Jim after his arrest, studied his medical records, and came to the identical conclusion. Jim's business manager Tom Bradshaw, told the court that although Jim could operate in his professional life, his severe mood swings could sometimes make him scary to be around. Jim did not testify.

Deputy District Attorney Burton J. Schneirow put on the stand Jim's ex-wife Jill and his old pal Mike Post to describe Jim as manipulative and thoroughly capable of premeditating the shocking crime he committed. Both Jill and Post were devastated by Osa's killing, terrified of Jim, and sought the most extreme punishment. His brother, John, who called for Jim to be executed, testified that their parents did not deprive Jim, that growing up when he got a present, so did Jim. The facts of the case were not in dispute. The question revolved around Jim's mental illness.

Under the new provisions added to the state constitution by Proposition 8, a Reagan-era law and order initiative that passed on the ballot in June 1982, the so-called Victims' Rights and Restitution Act outlawed the diminished capacity defense and strictly defined the qualifications for insanity defense. Essentially the new law held that a person would have to not know what they were doing when they committed the act to qualify as insane. While Judge Albracht allowed that Jim clearly suffered from mental illness as the experts testified, he did not meet the standards for insanity as laid out by Proposition 8. The judge did rule that Jim was incapable of the premeditation required for first-degree murder and found Jim guilty of second-degree murder, which came with a sentence of fifteen years to life.

"This is not a murder case," defense attorney Furstman told the *Los Angeles Times*. "This case is a tragedy."

■ ■ ■

At the thirty-fifth annual Grammy Awards on February 24, 1993, at the Shrine Auditorium in Los Angeles, women turned out in aggressive haute couture, and the men in their tuxedos all looked like maître d's at a French restaurant. Michael Jackson would be celebrated with a special Legend Award, and it appeared that it would be a big night for Eric Clapton, who was experiencing a surprising late-career renaissance with his album *Unplugged*, already past the four million mark in sales, driven by the treacly ballad "Tears in Heaven." Clapton wrote the song with songwriter Will Jennings in memory of his four-year-old son who fell to his death from a fifty-fourth-floor Manhattan apartment. Going into the show, he led the field with nine nominations.

"For those of you who just tuned in, Eric Clapton is two-for-two, just as Dionne Warwick predicted on the Psychic Network," quipped host Gary Shandling after Clapton accepted the award for Best Song. Halfway through the three-hour program, two more Grammy wins by Clapton later, Shandling took note. "I'm going to go out on a limb here," he said. "If you're up against Eric Clapton in any other categories, I'd go home now."

By the end of the evening, Clapton took six awards, sweeping the three majors, Record of the Year, Song of the Year, and Best Album. His sole previous Grammy was for his participation in George Harrison's *The Concert for Bangladesh* in 1972.

In a smartly tailored tux, clear plastic-framed eyeglasses, a carefully manicured beard, his brush-cut hair swept up off his forehead, Clapton looked more like a diplomat than a rock star. He made humble acceptance speeches, graciously demurring the honors ("I thought there were better songs"). He closed the show, both with a performance of "Tears in Heaven," and an emotional acceptance for Record of the Year. "I want to thank a lot of people," he said, "but the one person I want to thank is my son for the love he gave me and the song he gave me."

With host Shandling making jokes about how Mick Jagger was older than the president of the United States, rock music was clearly no longer the wild and unruly problem child of pop but had clearly grown up and entered the elite streams of American show business. Clapton looked like a proper gentleman, well groomed and well dressed, far from the decadent, disheveled hippie drug addict of Derek and the Dominos days. Being the bereaved father of a young son lent him a becoming tragic aura. His triumphant night at the Grammys was a public celebration of his miraculous renewal.

Buried among the pile of Grammys he took home was an award for Best Rock Song, given to the acoustic version of "Layla" that appeared on *Unplugged* (selected over the landmark Nirvana record "Smells Like Teen Spirit," no less). When the original version had been released in 1970, there were no Grammy nominations. It took nearly two years for the public to even discover the record, which over the course of time went on to become one of the single defining tracks of the classic rock era. This subsequent award was presented before the telecast and only announced on the TV show, but it was widely viewed as a typical, clueless, sentimental Grammy nod to correcting oversights of the past, like giving Jethro Tull the first Grammy in the heavy metal category.

It was a stellar, glamorous evening. James Brown and Gloria Estefan gave Clapton his first award of the evening, Male Vocal Performance. Bonnie Raitt and Lyle Lovett presented him Song of the Year, and Tina Turner and Shandling gave him the Record of the Year award. In between performances by Celine Dion and Peabo Bryson, Tony Bennett and Natalie Cole, Red Hot Chili Peppers with George Clinton and P-Funk, the stream of awards won by

Clapton made the show seem like a ceremonial tribute to him, viewed by a television audience of more than thirty million.

Two hundred miles north in San Luis Obispo County, another couple dozen khaki-clad viewers gathered around the set in the day room of the ward at the Atascadero State Hospital where Jim Gordon was an inmate. Jim had been parked at Atascadero since shortly after he was sentenced nine years before. He was long gone from his artistic life as a musician. He was already lost and forgotten by the music world of which he was once such an important part.

His home in Atascadero was a one-thousand-bed, maximum security hospital on a seven-hundred-acre site, the small town's number one employer. Opened in 1954 as a prison for sex offenders, the place went through its medieval stages and was called "Dachau for Queers" because of the experimental medical procedures they used on inmates trying to rid them of their perversions. By the time Jim came aboard, ASH had cleaned up its act and served as a repository of convicted criminals found not guilty for reasons of insanity or declared incompetent to stand trial—a rich stew of child molesters, killers, and lunatics of all stripes.

The twenty-eight wards were each staffed with five or six psych techs in three shifts around the clock. There were no prison guards, only security, and they didn't carry weapons outside of the receiving and releases areas. Psych techs once needed a college diploma, but by the time Jim arrived, all they had to do to qualify was pass a test. Psych techs were also often the source of black market drugs in the maximum security hospital.

Jim received no visitors. His daughter, Amy, never answered his weekly letters; he stopped writing so frequently, but she still wouldn't reply. He bought her a car, paid for her education, sent her red roses on her birthday, but he hadn't laid eyes on her since she was ten years old, although he thought that she may have been the young girl with strawberry blonde hair he saw in the courtroom during his trial. She was a student at Providence Christian College in Pasadena, although Jim had no idea where she lived.

Jim's world had been reduced to a six-by-nine-foot cell with bed, dresser, toilet, and sink—a long way from the vast, empty rooms at Clapton's country estate, Hurtwood Edge. The ward consisted of a corridor, a courtyard, and a day room. The hospital store sold cigarettes and sundries, and the canteen served breakfast and lunch. Jim liked the food and put some weight back on.

Jim quickly adapted to the routine; up at seven in the morning, breakfast at a quarter to eight, back to his cell for medication. On his admission to the hospital, Jim had signed a document agreeing to take medicine, and he was dosed daily with the antipsychotic Navane and another powerful drug for mood disorders, Tegretol. He took an antidepressant as a sleeping pill at night, but rarely went under, instead finding himself suspended in a dreamlike state that only resembled sleep. Jim felt that the meds were helpful. He didn't have a prison job—he didn't need the money; his royalties made him one of the wealthiest prisoners in the California state penal system. He attended group therapy three or four times a week and otherwise kept to himself as much as was possible.

As relaxed as the discipline could be, the hospital staff would move quickly if an inmate refused his medication, strapping him down bodily and giving him the drugs. After getting into a beef with a fellow prisoner and punching him, Jim found himself strapped to a bed in the day room. They kept him bound in leather straps until lights out and moved him to his cell, where they kept him tied down until midmorning the next day. The prisoners were routinely subjected to random searches of their cells. It was, after all, a prison.

Jim still harbored resentments toward his mother. The way he saw it, she'd ruined his life, turned his daughter against him, both starved him and made him fat. She persecuted him, controlled him, took over the doctors who were treating him. He did not consider himself a murderer, although he knew everybody else did. His lucidity waxed and waned like a distant radio signal, and voices still chattered in his head.

Opinion was divided among his fellow prisoners. While some of the inmates thought it was cool to have a rock star drummer with them, a sizable number looked down on Jim for having wasted his advantages and privileges. These men had lived hard lives in bad circumstances and had never known the world Jim did. Jim didn't care. He could be friendly, but they weren't his friends. Still, the Grammycast was quite the occasion on the ward; it was a rare event for one of their fellow inmates to be acknowledged in the outside world.

Jim joined the crew as the show began. He watched Clapton accept his first award, although he barely recognized the buffed and scrubbed English rock star. In his heart, he still longed to play with Clapton—some of his best days in music had come with him in Delaney and Bonnie, the George Harrison sessions, or Derek and the Dominos. That was a different world. His three drum sets were locked in a storage unit in San Fernando Valley, along with his clothes, his diaries, his record collection, all his earthly possessions, and Jim had saved everything. They belonged to a life to which he would never return. He soon lost interest in the TV program.

That life was dead to Jim. He could hear his drumming turn up on an old record on the radio occasionally. He could remember the hectic sessions, the intense performances, and the glory of a finished take. Driving a band through a concert was a distant memory, the applause long vanished. His golden road out of San Fernando

Valley had led to his own private hell. It was best not to dwell on thoughts of the past. He wasn't going back there. In his past life, Jim had attended the Grammys, dressed up like a groom off the wedding cake, but that was then, and this was now. Where he was now, he was going to stay, and what he had now was all he could look forward to. His days in the sun were done and regrets were useless.

He was out of the room when the award for the Best Rock Song was announced. It was only a slide with a voice-over explaining that the award had been given already at an earlier ceremony, but the ward burst into cheers when the announcer said the song had been written by Eric Clapton and Jim Gordon. Some of the inmates went to find Jim and give him the news. He was down the hall, smoking a cigarette.

A sly smile creased his lips. "I'll be darned," he said.

ACKNOWLEDGMENTS

Any book like this, of necessity, depends on the kindness of strangers. So many people helped piece together this story, almost shred by shred. Jim was difficult to know. Many people didn't want to talk at all. The research was full of challenges, which makes my appreciation for the help that I did receive all the more profound.

This was a richly emotional topic for many people. Soulful Jim Keltner wept recalling his drum brother. Former Warner Brothers president Lenny Waronker spent an entire afternoon in his home discussing the most musical drummer he ever knew. Van Dyke Parks saluted Jim as "the esprit de corps." His ex-wife Renee Armand made a special trip to California to talk.

Hail to Adam Minkoff, who operates the internet's top Jim Gordon discography (jimgordondiscography.blogspot.com). Minkoff, a top-rated drummer himself, shared around one thousand union contracts, extensive additional information, encouragement, deep knowledge, and support. He is the unindicted coconspirator on this project, and it wouldn't have been the same without him. Thanks to filmmaker Jesse Lauter (*Learning to Live Together*) for introducing us.

Special thanks to Patti Cappelletti and the estate of Nyna Cravens for permission to use research collected by her aunt Nyna Cravens and associates for a proposed book in 1988.

Deep appreciation goes to Amy Gordon, Jill Gordon, and Mike Post, who reversed an initial decision to not participate in the project. Their endorsement was meaningful far beyond the wealth of details from their interviews and cornucopia of photographs. None of them had ever publicly discussed their relations with Jim, and the trust they placed in me is humbling. "I wish to remember him," his daughter, Amy, wrote in an email, "as the father who loved me and fought as hard as he could so that I might feel *this* above all the rest."

Dr. Patrick O'Reilly of Napa State Hospital patiently introduced me to the world of schizophrenia in several meetings and many phone conversations. Thanks to *Chronicle* colleague Kevin Fagan for the introduction.

And thanks to all the folks who generously agreed to share their time and recollections: Andy Newmark, Boston Woodard, Jim Keltner, Don Peake, Van Dyke Parks, Rowland Salley, Tom Scott, Steve Allen, Denise Leighton, Pete Anderson, Larry Rolando, Barry Melton, Bruce Barthol, Sal Valentino, Ron Meagher, Ron Elliott, Cubby O'Brien, Bill Bentley, Bernie Gelb, Danny O'Keefe, John Simon, Mickey Hart, Linda Ronstadt, Jeremy Clyde, Joan Baez, David Jackson, Tracy Nelson, Lenny Waronker, Joey Paige, Maria Muldaur, Andrew Loog Oldham, Bruce Brymer, Bruce Botnik, John Florez, Fred Tackett, Dave Kemper, John Hobbs, Rita Coolidge, Don Randi, Bobby Torres, Laura Choate, John Boylan, Terence Boylan, Russ Titelman, Daniel Moore, Bonnie Bramlett, Dean Parks, Matthew Moore, Pamela Polland, Bobby Whitlock, Mike Campbell, Ron Nevison, John McEuen, Benmont Tench, Chris Blackwell, Tony Horowitz, Richie Furay, Anna Capaldi, Chris

O'Dell, King Errisson, Larry Russell, Michael Rief, Gary Puckett, Claudia Lennear, Jackson Browne, Booker T. Jones, Billy Cross, James Lee Stanley, Bob Glaub, Bill Cooper, Thom Rotella, Dave Mason, Lee Sklar, Toxey French, Danny Timms, Renee Armand, Scott K. Fish, Dr. Daniel Auerbach, Dr. Michael Goldstein, Scott Furstman, Buffy Ford Stewart, Dick Waterman, and Steve Moos.

Investigator Jayson Wechter provided his customary invaluable research assistance. Many people helped find contact information, but it was a special pleasure to hook back up with old pal Brian Blevins and have him once again, forty years later, arrange an interview with Island Records' Chris Blackwell. Thanks also to Denny Tedesco, Jake Feinberg, Harvey Kubernik, Tom Arnold, Michael Jensen, Dennis McNally, Domenic Priore, Peter Asher, Canada's own Larry LeBlanc, Rob Roth, and everybody else who gave me an email address or phone number.

Thanks to publisher Scott Waxman and editor in chief Keith Wallman at Diversion Books, marketing and publicity manager Shannon Donnelly, marketing and publicity assistant Alex Sprague, publishing coordinator Evan Phail, cover designer Jonathan Sainsbury, and editorial assistant Clara Linhoff.

Partner-in-crime Frank Weimann of Folio Literary Agency has gone through nearly two dozen books with me, and you have to wonder—how much can he take? Expert technical assistance and digital supervision provided by Miles Roa of Light Source in San Francisco. Also, thanks to Bob Merlis of Merlis for Hire for his customary peerless representation.

Charlie Winton, who guided me through *Here Comes the Night* and *Hollywood Eden*, provided strength, hope, and experience, as well as editorial consultation through the process. Judith Lovejoy, who used to be Michael Crichton's editorial assistant, worked below her pay grade reading this manuscript. My fabulous, close associate Pamela Turley made important contributions. As always, shout-out to darling daughter Carla.

One incidental note: The immensely talented group of Hollywood studio musicians in this account have come to be called over the years the Wrecking Crew. This was not contemporaneous nomenclature, but popularized by drummer Hal Blaine around the time he published his autobiography. It is also the title of the excellent film documentary about these musicians by Denny Tedesco. I purposefully eschewed the terminology as inaccurate and trivializing, but in case you were wondering, those are the same people we are talking about.

DRUMS BY JIM GORDON

PLAYLIST

Everly Brothers
Love Is Strange

Dino, Desi and Billy
I'm a Fool

Stone Poneys
Different Drum

Lee Hazelwood
Friday's Child

Mel Tormé
Comin' Home Baby

Merle Haggard
The Bottle Let Me Down

Beach Boys
God Only Knows

Beach Boys
I'm Waiting for the Day

Ike & Tina Turner
River Deep—
Mountain High

Chad & Jeremy
Distant Shores

The Ronettes
I Wish I Never Saw
the Sunshine

The Monkees
Mary, Mary

Paul Revere & the Raiders
The Great Airplane Strike

Beau Brummels
Are You Happy?

Merle Haggard
I'm a Lonesome Fugitive

Bobby Darin
Reason to Believe

Nilsson
Everybody's Talkin'

Sonny & Cher
The Beat Goes On

Harpers Bizarre
Feelin' Groovy

Buffalo Springfield
Expecting to Fly

Glen Campbell
Gentle on My Mind

Mason Williams
Classical Gas

Gary Puckett
and the Union Gap
Woman, Woman

Tiny Tim
Tiptoe Thru the Tulips

Glen Campbell
Wichita Lineman

Lou Rawls
Love Is a Hurtin' Thing

The Byrds
Goin' Back

Beach Boys
Heroes and Villains

Mama Cass
California Earthquake

Judy Collins
Who Knows Where the
Times Goes?

The City
Now That Everything's
Been Said

Crosby, Stills and Nash
Marrakesh Express

Friends of Distinction
Grazing in the Grass

Arlo Guthrie
Coming into Los Angeles

Delaney & Bonnie
(w/ Eric Clapton)
I Don't Want to Discuss It

King Curtis
(w/ Eric Clapton)
Teasin'

Delaney & Bonnie
(w/ Eric Clapton)
Only You Know and I Know

Randy Newman
Have You Seen My Baby

Joe Cocker
The Letter

Dave Mason
Only You Know and I Know

Leon Russell
Pisces Apple Lady

Eric Clapton
After Midnight

George Harrison
What Is Life?

Derek and the Dominos
Layla

John Lennon
Power to the People

Traffic
The Low Spark of the
High-Heeled Boys

Buddy Guy & Junior Wells
Man of Many Words

Nilsson
Jump into the Fire

Nilsson
Coconut

B.B. King
Caldonia

Helen Reddy
I Am Woman

Johnny Rivers
Rockin' Pneumonia and
the Boogie Woogie Flu

Carly Simon
You're So Vain

Frank Zappa
Apostrophe'

Incredible Bongo Band
Apache

Seals & Crofts
Summer Breeze

Albert Hammond
It Never Rains in
Southern California

B.W. Stevenson
My Maria

Disco-Tex and the Sex-O-Lettes
Get Dancin'

Donovan
Operating Manual to
Spaceship Earth

Maria Muldaur
Midnight at the Oasis

Steely Dan
Rikki Don't Lose
That Number

Gordon Lightfoot
Sundown

Hues Corporation
Rock the Boat

John Denver
Thank God I'm a
Country Boy

Minnie Riperton
Adventures in Paradise

Hugo Montenegro
Blastoff

Tom Waits
Looking for the Heart of
Saturday Night

Mike Post
The Rockford Files

Souther, Hillman, Furay
Border Town

Righteous Brothers
Rock and Roll Heaven

Sammy Johns
Chevy Van

Joan Baez
Diamonds and Rust

Hall & Oates
Camellia

Jackson Browne
Here Come Those
Tears Again

Burton Cummings
Stand Tall

Tom Petty and the
Heartbreakers
Strangered in the Night

The Carpenters
There's a Kind of Hush

Neil Diamond
Jungletime

The Muppets
Rainbow Connection

BIBLIOGRAPHY

Baez, Joan. *And a Voice to Sing With*, Summit Books, 1987.

Bergreen, Laurence. *Louis Armstrong: An Extravagant Life*, Broadway Books, 1997.

Blades, James: *Percussion Instruments and Their History*, Faber and Faber, 1984.

Blaine, Hal, and Goggin, David. *Hal Blaine and the Wrecking Crew: The Story of the World's Most Recorded Musician*, MixBooks, 1990.

Bleiel, Jeff. *That's All: Bobby Darin on Record, Stage & Screen*, Popular Culture Ink, 1993.

Bowen, Jimmy, and Jerome, Jim. *Rough Mix: An Unapologetic Look at the Music Business and How It Got That Way, A Lifetime in the World of Rock, Pop and Country as Told by One of the Industry's Most Powerful Players*, Simon & Schuster, 1997.

Boyd, Pattie, with Junior, Penny. *Wonderful Tonight: George Harrison, Eric Clapton, and Me*, Harmony Books, 2007.

Bronson, Fred. *The Billboard Book of Number One Hits*, Billboard Books, 1997.

Campbell, Glen, and Carter, Tom. *Rhinestone Cowboy: An Autobiography*, Villard Books, 1994.

Cantwell, David. *Merle Haggard: The Running Kind*, University of Texas Press, 2013.

Carlin, Peter Ames. *Sonic Boom: The Impossible Rise of Warner Brothers Records from Hendrix to Fleetwood Mac to Madonna to Prince*, Henry Holt and Company, 2021.

Clapton, Eric. *Clapton: The Autobiography*, Broadway Books, 2007.

Coleman, Ray. *Clapton!: An Authorized Biography*, Warner Books, 1985.

Collier, James Lincoln. *Louis Armstrong: An American Genius*, Oxford University Press, 1983.

Collins, Judy. *Sweet Judy Blue Eyes: My Life in Music*, Crown Archetype, 2011.

Collins, Judy. *Trust Your Heart: An Autobiography*, Houghton Mifflin Company, 1987.

Condon, Eddie, and Sugrue, Thomas (narration). *We Called It Music: A Generation of Jazz*, Henry Holt and Company, 1947.

Coolidge, Rita, with Walker, Michael. *Delta Lady: A Memoir*, Harper, 2017.

Cornyn, Stan, and Scanlon, Paul. *Exploding: The Highs, Hits, Hype, Heroes, and Hustlers of the Warner Music Group*, HarperEntertainment, 2002.

Crowther, Bruce. *Gene Krupa: His Life and Times*, Universe Books, 1987.

Dodge, Consuelo. *The Everly Brothers: Ladies Love Outlaws*, CIN-DAV Inc., 1991.

Einarson, John, and Furay. Richie. *For What It's Worth: The Story of Buffalo Springfield*, Rogan House, 1997.

Fiegel, Eddi. *Dream a Little Dream of Me: The Life of Cass Elliott*, Chicago Review Press, 2005.

Furay, Richie, with Roberts, Michael. *Pickin' Up the Pieces*, Waterbrook Press, 2006.

Gilbey, Anna Capaldi. *Many a Mile to Freedom: A Journey Through the Sixties and Beyond*, 2018.

Giuliano, Geoffrey. *Dark Horse: The Private Life of George Harrison*, Dutton, 1990.

Glass, Daniel, ed. *The Roots of Rock Drumming: Interviews with the Drummers Who Shaped Rock 'n' Roll Music*, Hudson Music, 2013.

Gooch, Brad. *Hall & Oates*, Ballantine Books, 1984.

Granata, Charles L. *Wouldn't It Be Nice: Brian Wilson and the Making of the Beach Boys' Pet Sounds*, Chicago Review Press, 2003.

Hart, Mickey, with Lieberman, Frederic. *Planet Drum: A Celebration of Percussion and Rhythm*, Harper San Francisco, 1991.

Hart, Mickey, with Stevens, Jay. *Drumming at the Edge of Magic: A Journey Into the Spirit of Percussion*, Harper San Francisco, 1993.

Henderson, Richard. *Song Cycle, 33 1/3*, Continuum, 2010.

Heylin, Clinton. *Bob Dylan: Behind the Shades, Take Two*, Viking, 2000.

Heylin, Clinton. *Bob Dylan: A Life in Stolen Moments Day By Day—1941–1995*, Schirmer Books, 1995.

Hillman, Chris. *Time Between: My Life as a Byrd, Burrito Brother, and Beyond*, BMG, 2020.

Hjort, Christopher. *So You Want to Be a Rock 'n' Roll Star: The Byrds Day-by-Day 1965–1973*, Jawbone, 2008.

Hjort, Christopher. *Strange Brew: Eric Clapton & the British Blues Boom 1965–1970*, Jawbone Books, 2007.

Holzman, Jac, and Daws, Gavan. *Follow the Music: The Life and High Tomes of Elektra Records in the Great Years of American Pop Culture*, First Media, 1998.

Hoskyns, Barny. *Waiting for the Sun: Strange Days, Weird Scenes and the Sound of Los Angeles*, St. Martin's Press, 1991.

Janowitz, Bill. *Leon Russell: Master of Time and Space's Journey Through Rock and Roll History*, Hachette Books, 2023.

Jasinski, Laurie E., editor. *The Handbook of Texas Music*, Second Edition, Texas State Historical Association, 2012.

Jennings, Nicholas. *Lightfoot*, Penguin, 2017.

Jensen, Joli. *The Nashville Sound: Authenticity, Commercialization, and Country Music*, Country Music Foundation Press and Vanderbilt University Press, 1998.

Jones, Alan, and Kantonen, Jussi. *Saturday Night Forever: The Story of Disco*, A Cappella Books, 1999.

Karpp, Phyllis. *Ike's Boys: The Story of the Everly Brothers*, Pierian Press, 1988.

Kelly, Michael "Doc Rock," *Liberty Records: A History of the Recording Company and Its Stars 1955–1971*, Volumes 1 & 2, MacFarlane and Co., 1993.

Kenney, William Howland. *Chicago Jazz: A Cultural History, 1904–1930*, Oxford University Press, 1993.

Keys, Bobby, and Ditenhafer, Bill. *Every Night's a Saturday Night: The Rock 'N' Roll Life of Legendary Sax Man Bobby Keys*, Counterpoint Press, 2012.

Korall, Burt. *Drummin' Men: The Heartbeat of Jazz—The Swing Years*, Schirmer Books, 1990.

Kosser, Michael. *How Nashville Became Music City U.S.A.: 50 Years of Music Row*, Hal Leonard, 2006.

Koster, Rick. *Texas Music*, St. Martin's Press, 1998.

Kramer, Freda. *The Glen Campbell Story*, Pyramid Books, 1970.

Kubernik, Harvey. *Turn Up the Radio!: Rock, Pop, and Roll in Los Angeles 1956–1972*, Santa Monica Press, 2014.

Lawrence, Tim. *Love Saves the Day: A History of American Dance Music Culture, 1970–1979*, Duke University Press, 2005.

Lennon, Nigey. *Being Frank: My Time with Frank Zappa*, California Classics Books, 1995.

McDonough, Jimmy. *Shakey: Neil Young's Biography*, Random House, 2002.

Mezzrow, Mezz, and Wolfe, Bernard. *Really the Blues*, Random House, 1946.

Miles, Barry. *Zappa: A Biography*, Grove Press, 2004.

Nichols, Geoff. *The Drum Book: A History of the Rock Drum Kit*, Balafon Books, 1997.

O'Dell, Chris, and Ketcham, Katherine. *Miss O'Dell: Hard Days and Long Nights with The Beatles, The Stones, Bob Dylan, and Eric Clapton*, Touchstone, 2009.

Priore, Domenic. *Riot on Sunset Strip: Rock 'n' Roll's Last Stand in Hollywood*, Jawbone Books, 2007.

Reddy, Helen. *The Woman I Am: A Memoir*, Jeremy P. Tarcher/Penguin, 2006.

Reid, Jan. *Layla and Other Assorted Love Songs by Derek and the Dominos*; Rodale, 2006.

Rice, Tim, and Jo with Gambaccini, Paul, and Mead, Mike. *The Guinness Book of British Hit Singles 1952–1977*, Guinness Superlatives, 1977.

Richards, Keith, with Fox, James. *Life*, Little, Brown and Company, 2010.

Roberty, Marc. *Eric Clapton: The Complete Recording Sessions 1963–1992*, Blandford Press, 1993.

Roberty, Marc. *Eric Clapton, Day by Day: The Early Years 1963–1982*, Backbeat Books, 2013.

Rogan, Johnny. *The Byrds: Timeless Flight Revisited—The Sequel*, Rogan House, 1997.

Rogan, Johnny. *Lennon: The Albums*, Calidore Books, 2006.

Rogan, Johnny. *Neil Young: Zero to Sixty—A Critical Biography*, Calidore Books, 2000.

Rubini, Michel. *Life In the Key of Rubini: A Hollywood Child Prodigy and His Wild Adventures in Crime, Music, Sex, Sinatra and Wonder Woman*, BookBaby, 2018.

Ruppili, Michael. *Atlantic Records: A Discography—Volumes 1 & 2*, Greenwood Press, 1979.

Russell, Leon, edited and annotated by Todoroff, Steve, and Wooley, John. *Leon Russell: In His Own Words*, Stevetodorffarchives, 2019.

Sadie, Stanley, ed. *The New Grove Dictionary of Music & Musicians*, Grove Press, 1980.

Scherman, Tony. *Backbeat: Earl Palmer's Story*; Smithsonian Institution Press, 1999.

Schumacher, Michael. *Crossroads: The Life and Music of Eric Clapton*, Hyperion, 1995.

Selvin, Joel. *Hollywood Eden: Electric Guitars, Fast Cars, and the Myth of the California Paradise*, House of Anansi, 2020.

Selvin Joel. *Ricky Nelson: Idol for a Generation*, Contemporary Books, 1990.

Shapiro, Peter. *Turn the Beat Around: The Secret History of Disco*, Faber and Faber, 2005.

Sidran, Ben. *The Ballad of Tommy LiPuma*; Nardis Books, 2020.

Simmons, Sylvie. *Neil Young: Reflections in a Broken Glass*, Mojo Books, 2001.

Starr, Michael Seth. *Bobby Darin: A Life*, Taylor Trade Publishing, 2004.

Sweet, Brian. *Steely Dan: Reelin' in the Years*, Omnibus Press, 1994.

Teachout, Terry. *Pops: A Life of Louis Armstrong*, Houghton Mifflin Harcourt, 2009.

Templeman, Ted, with Renoff, Greg. *A Platinum Producer's Life in Music*, ECW Press, 2020.

Thomson, Elizabeth. *Joan Baez: The Last Leaf*, Palazzo Editions, 2020.

Turner, Steve. *Conversations with Eric Clapton*, Abacus, 1976.

Wallis, Ian. *American Rock 'n' Roll: The UK Tours 1956–72*, Music Mentor Books, 2003.

Watson, Ben. *Frank Zappa: The Negative Dialectics of Poodle Play*, St. Martin's Press, 1993.

Weinberg, Max, with Santelli, Robert. *The Big Beat: Conversations with Rock's Great Drummer*, Billboard Books, 1984.

Welch, Chris. *Steve Winwood: Roll With It*, Perigee Books, 1990.

Whitburn, Joel. *Top Country Singles 1944–1993*, Record Research, 1994.

Whitburn, Joel. *Top Pop Singles 1955–1993*, Record Research, 1994.

Whitlock, Bobby, with Roberty, Marc. *Bobby Whitlock: A Rock 'n' Roll Autobiography*, MacFarland and Company, 2011.

Wiener, Jon. *Come Together: John Lennon in His Time*, Random House, 1984.

Wiseman, Rich. *Jackson Browne: The Story of a Hold Out*, Dolphin Books, 1982.

Wolf, Linda. *Tribute: Cocker Power*, Insight Editions, 2020.

Womack, Kenneth, and Kruppa, Jason. *All Things Must Pass Away: Harrison, Clapton, and Other Assorted Love Songs*, Chicago Review Press, 2021.

Wyman, Bill, and Coleman, Ray. *Stone Alone: The Story of a Rock 'N' Roll Band*, Viking, 1990.

Zanes, Warren. *Revolutions in Sound: Warner Brothers Records—The First Fifty Years*, Chronicle Books, 2008.

Zanes, Warren, ed. *Tom Petty and the Heartbreakers: Runnin' Down a Dream*, Chronicle Books, 2007.

Zollo, Paul. *Conversations with Tom Petty*, Omnibus Press, 2006.

NOTES ON
ADDITIONAL SOURCES

The two major journalistic accounts of the Jim Gordon story are "When the Voices Took Over" by Barry Rehfeld in *Rolling Stone* on June 6, 1985, and "Bang the Drum Slowly" by Martin Booe for *Washington Post* on July 3, 1994. There is also the remarkable interview by Scott L. Fish for *Modern Drummer* magazine in January 1983 (the author posted the audio recording of the interview on the internet). Interview transcripts provided by the estate of Nyna Cravens included Jim Gordon, Mary Shields Tucker, Dr. Daniel Auerbach, Richard Perry, Frank Zappa, Burton Cummings, and others. Public documents surrounding Jim Gordon's arrest and trial were consulted. Many stops were made on the information superhighway, chief among them www.discogs.com, www.rocksbackpages.com, and, of course, www.wikipedia.com.

INDEX

ABOUT THE AUTHOR

JOEL SELVIN, *San Francisco Chronicle* pop music critic for thirty-six years, is author of more than twenty books about pop music, including the definitive account of the Rolling Stones free concert at Altamont and the biography of songwriter Bert Berns that paved his way into the Rock and Roll Hall of Fame, as well as the number one *New York Times* bestseller *Red: My Uncensored Life in Rock* with Sammy Hagar.